Urban Planning and the Pursuit of Happiness

EUROPEAN VARIATIONS ON A UNIVERSAL THEME (18TH—21ST CENTURIES)

JOVIS
diskurs

Urban Planning and the Pursuit of Happiness

ARNOLD BARTETZKY/
MARC SCHALENBERG (EDS.)
WITH THE ASSISTANCE OF LOUISE BROMBY AND CHRISTIAN DIETZ

EUROPEAN VARIATIONS ON A UNIVERSAL THEME (18TH—21ST CENTURIES)

SHAPES OF HAPPINESS

Planning Concepts and
their Manifestations
in Urban Form

Arnold Bartetzky
Marc Schalenberg

The pursuit of happiness can be considered a universal concern, taking on a wide variety of forms. It has meant different things in different places and at different times. In this way, it possesses a cultural and intellectual history. In the Western tradition, the belief that we can attain happiness through our own efforts can be traced back at least to ancient Greek times.[1] However, for the larger part of its history this belief was restricted to a small elite number of individuals, e.g. the wise philosophers in Greek and Roman times, powerful sovereigns or the saints and sages of Christianity. According to this view, happiness was exclusive and at the same time metaphysical; the prerequisite for attaining happiness was thought to be a special connection with a reality beyond this world. Eudaemonism has been addressed throughout the history of philosophy, particularly in early modern political theory. However, as Darrin McMahon points out in his book on the intellectual history of happiness conceptions, the idea that *all* human beings could achieve happiness, did not strike roots until the Enlightenment. From then on, felicity was established as something to which everyone could aspire, not only in the afterlife, but also during life on earth.[2]

Just one step further leads on to the idea that people not only *can* be happy, but that they *should* be happy—that they are destined for happiness in this life and thereby have a natural right to it. Thus, in the second half of the eighteenth century, the issue of happiness and its fulfilment as a human right became central to philosophical and political reflections all over Europe.[3] In the United States of America, it even gained entry into the 1776 Declaration of Independence.

If happiness on earth is considered to be the natural destiny of mankind, an obvious conclusion would be that it is not primarily personal misfortunes and incapacities that cause people to fail in their pursuit(s) of happiness, but the inadequacy of their living conditions. Let us change the living conditions—is the logical consequence of this assumption—and people will invariably be happy.

Architecture and urban planning have played a prominent role in concepts aiming to achieve happiness by means of changing living conditions. Do cities not shape the everyday environment of the majority of the population? Their architecture forms a space that clearly has a bearing on the way people feel on a daily basis. As Wolfgang Pehnt puts it, life welcomes us in an architectural setting and bids us farewell in an architectural setting.[4] Furthermore, over the last few centuries, the impact of cities on the pursuit of happiness has grown at the same immense rate as the urbanisation of Western societies has progressed. Hence, cityscapes reflect ideas of public happiness[5]—as opposed to private happiness in the intimacy of one's own home, which was recently the subject of a witty essay by Alain de Botton.[6] Urban projects have often been conceived and staged as model islands, in anticipation of a bright(er) future for a city, a country, or even the whole of humanity.

This volume explores the ideas, discourses and images attached to the city as a space for the creation of public happiness. It does not aim to provide an "archaeology of happiness," nor a proper conceptual history of the term—although the essays collected here do pay tribute to the rhetorical strategies surrounding urban planning. Rather, its aim is to analyse how happiness was a manifest issue in projects and reflections associated with the built environment, or indeed in the promotional campaigns surrounding new urban developments.

The phenomenon in question, in our view, required neither professionalised urban planning nor the explicit vocabulary of "happiness," This is implied just as much by terms such as "ideal city," "well-policed space," "public sphere," "new homes," et cetera. Besides, both top-down and bottom-up activities are to be considered equally as attempts at pursuing and promising happiness: as prescriptive notions, defined by the authorities for urban planning, and as appropriations of urban space, possibly running contrary to the original intentions. Rather than focussing on a narrow time scale or geographical area, and with no "handbook" pretensions, we have opted for a wide spectrum of thorough case studies in both the conception and reality of town planning. Although some reference to the Americas is made, the geographical scope of the volume is deliberately centred on Europe, breaking some of the common academic communication boundaries: Eastern Europe meets Western Europe, the Baltic Sea meets the Mediterranean, and the remodelling and extension of existing cities is juxtaposed with the creation of new ones, all with regard to what can be—or indeed has been—described as a "pursuit of happiness." This brings a wide range of disciplines and research agendas together, notably architectural and political history, sociology and geography, literature and anthropology. While the articles are arranged in a chronological sequence, they also invite comparisons to be made over longer periods of time. On a morphological level, one might find striking analogies between the early modern predilections for radial grids of long, wide, linear streets and the similar patterns found in socialist towns of the Stalin era. The geometrical furore applied to the creation of urban space, wide open squares and a strategic positioning of politically central *points de vue* pervade Baroque and totalitarian aesthetics in a similar fashion, as do the pathetic effects of the stone materials employed. But conversely, are curved streets and detached houses made of glass necessarily an indicator of a democratic regime? Obviously not. Urban form and building substances are important aspects for the interpretation of planning; however historical contextualisation is called for if all too easy conclusions are to be avoided.

The starting point of this volume is the age of Enlightenment. Just as the idea of public happiness on earth originated in the Enlightenment, the idea that rationally planned urban space should pave the way towards this goal emerged at the same time. It is true that, since antiquity, there had been various conceptions of the ideal city on earth, linked with attempts to create the perfect space for urban living.[7] The Italian Renaissance in particular showed a predilection for the *città ideale* designed on the basis of rationalisation and the aesthetic unification of urban space. The importance of controlling and defending a city was accentuated by the sixteenth-, seventeenth-, and early eighteenth-century fortress towns such as Palmanova, Neuf-Brisach, or Mannheim, which strictly adhered to geometrical patterns.

A special mention within the context of this volume should be given to the Northern German fortress town of Glückstadt (literally: happiness city, or city of fortune), founded by the Danish king Christian IV in 1617 on the Elbe estuary as a hugely supported counterweight to nearby Hamburg. In its political function as well as in its layout, promising prosperous living conditions to its citizens, who were religious refugees of various creeds, this fortress city represents a princely-planned social and urban model, in a way that was paradigmatic for early modern European ambitions[8]. Still, pre-Enlightenment conceptions of ideal cities were not based on the idea of general happiness for the residents in a modern sense, but on visions of a hierarchic order with the divine or worldly power in a dominant position. Even in the case of Glückstadt, the optimistic name seems to have referred more to the personal fortune of the founder and the hope of success for the project than to the future prospects of the inhabitants. "This shall succeed, this must succeed. Therefore the city shall be named Glückstadt!" ("Dat schall glücken un dat mutt glücken, un denn schall se ok Glückstadt heten!"), as the Danish king is said to have uttered upon undertaking the hazardous business of building the city in wild open countryside.

Even in the eighteenth century, the scheme of order decreed from above remains central to the conception of a city. However, from this time onwards it becomes more and more intrinsically linked with the purpose of common well-being. Like other contemporary thinkers and officials adhering to cameralism, the German Enlightenment author Johann Peter Willebrand considered the state of order, regulation and systematisation achieved by a well-organised, authoritarian government and obedient subjects to be a vital precondition for the common *Glückseligkeit* of an urban society. As Mascha Bisping points out in her contribution to this volume, Willebrand's term *Glückseligkeit*, sometimes not quite appropriately translated as "felicity," is fundamentally different from the Anglo-Saxon notion of the "pursuit of happiness," if not opposed to it, as the latter places far more emphasis on the individual fulfilment of personal needs as a precondition for common well-being.

Notions of happiness vary from one country to another, or even within the social order of a single city. Mohsen Aboutorabi and Andreas Wesener analyse how the particular perceptions of happiness of various social classes influenced the development of the urban form of Birmingham in the Georgian era, a period characterised by the rapid expansion of industry with all its corollaries for the city's spatial and social structure.

The early industrialisation of English cities anticipated the developments in Continental Europe in the nineteenth century. A massive influx of industrial workers led to a population explosion. Cities were bursting at the seams, and more or less uncontrolled building activities resulted in structures that were full of functional deficiencies. More and more, urban space was experienced by contemporaries as chaotic. A logical reaction to this, in hindsight, was the emergence of modern urban planning at the end of the nineteenth century, constituting a truly European communication network with increasingly specialised members.[9] Institutionalised besides as an academic discipline, urban planning has usually been regarded as constituting a counterbalance to market forces, and thereby as somewhat incompatible with liberal ideology. However, according to Christa Kamleithner's interpretation of the writings of three significant liberal representatives of German planning theory around 1870, modern urban planning did not arise in opposition to liberal thinking, but rather on the basis of it. They are united in a rejection of the inflexible forms of urban organisation imposed from outside, as favoured in the era of an all-embracing absolutist state (such as that propagated by Willebrand). Instead, new flexible forms of order are advocated, which are able to adapt to the pursuit of individual interests and preferences.

Only a little later, in his famous *Städtebau nach seinen künstlerischen Grundsätzen* (1889), Camillo Sitte would call for a proper historical and aesthetic quality to be established in cities, city centres in particular. The city molochs emerging in the course of industrialisation did not only produce urban chaos and aesthetic dissatisfaction, but also profound social problems. In working class areas, squalid quarters had grown up where the living conditions were diametrically opposed to any conceivable pursuit of happiness on the part of the inhabitants. These were the breeding grounds of discontent and revolutionary ideas. But the middle classes also complained of a deterioration in the quality of life and a loss of identity, resulting from the rapid modernisation which went hand in hand with the destruction of buildings and the fragmentation of urban communities. As a reaction to this, various urbanist and cultural reform initiatives arose, with the aim of restoring a sense of harmony to city life. A good example for this is the *Heimatschutz* (homeland protection) movement, concerned with various issues ranging from natural conservation to the revival of local architectural traditions and the promotion of culture. In his essay, Sándor Békési examines the programme of the Heimatschutz movement in Vienna around 1900 as an attempt to preserve and reshape the city whilst catering for emotional needs, focussing on the notion of *Heimat*. This liberal-conservative movement, which has long been described as reactionary romantic aestheticism, is interpreted here as a moderate version of modernity. It was aimed at bridging the gap between the old and the new, tradition and change, aesthetics and economy, thus promising the possibility of a sense of belonging and a happier life in the (big) city.

Other contemporary responses to increasingly industrialised and congested cities include the semi-rural Garden City, both in Great Britain and on the Continent, and other reform-minded ideas aspiring to create spacious urban settlements full of light and greenery, with the emphasis on a harmonious relationship between the city and the landscape. Allotment gardens—known as *Schrebergärten* in Germany and rapidly increasing in popularity in the *Kaiserreich*—played an important role as a possible remedy at the height of European urbanisation around the turn of the century. Often derided as petty bourgeois escapism, but highly recommended by social reformers at the time, they were heralded as a solution in that they provided a considerable proportion of the population with a leisure area set apart from working and living quarters.

Such approaches were taken up and radicalised after World War One; with their classic modernist visions of fundamentally new structures Bruno Taut, Walter Gropius, Ludwig Hilberseimer, Le Corbusier, Hans Scharoun, and other avant-garde architects left profound marks on the design and conception of the city as a potential setting for happiness. This period saw a momentous turn towards a functionally separate city, as defined in the Athens Charter of the *Congrès International d'Architecture Moderne* (CIAM) in 1933. This charter can be seen as a culmination point in the modernist aspirations of inter-war urban planning, and—though to a varying extent, and not always explicitly—as the predominant rationale behind urban projects after World War Two. The results of these projects were countless disintegrated cities, dismal and monotonous, which appear almost inhuman today. The CIAM modernists, however, all laid claim to promoting the cause of the dwellers' happiness effectively, and were convinced that they knew the single best way of achieving this aim.

However, functionalism à la CIAM, and most notably the rejection of the traditional notions of the city as a space of identification and representation, was not unrivalled. In the Stalinist Soviet Union, for example, after a spell of modernist experiments in the decade following the Bolshevik Revolution, the socialist-realist alternative was born. This combined rationalist principles of architecture and urban planning derived from modernism with the adoption of traditionalist patterns for the staging of the city, which was placed at the service of state representation and political propaganda. Especially Moscow, as the world capital of communism, was to be moulded into a quasi-religious sanctuary by the Bolshevik regime; it was to be a place representing a universal promise of happiness. Moscow's spectacular urban developments in the Stalinist period did not fail to arouse the interest of the Western world, notably that of left-wing intellectuals, who were tired of the capitalist systems in their home countries. In her contribution, Marina Dmitrieva examines the travelogues of foreign visitors to Moscow and other Soviet cities. Whereas in the nineteen-twenties most had focused on the old historical architecture and the exotic bazaars, at the beginning of the nineteen-thirties their general impression was that Russia was being rebuilt from scratch as a utopia turning into reality. Dmitrieva analyses the travellers' longing for a better world and their fascination with the direction Russia was taking towards the future, but also their surprise and disenchantment as the continuing discrepancies between vision and reality became apparent.

At the same time, Mussolini's Italy and Hitler's Germany were launching projects to mould Fascist ideology and aesthetics into the cityscape, regularly staging public displays of happiness, at least on ceremonial or propagandistic occasions.[10] Millions paid for the totalitarian utopia in Stalin's Soviet Union with their lives, as victims of the ideologically motivated mass murders, whilst Nazi terror and World War Two turned the better part of Europe into a burning hell. However, in the aftermath, the dream of happiness on earth resurfaced. What is more, the shock of the unprecedented destruction and barbarism experienced during this time released hopes and visions of a completely new beginning, free from the restrictions and exclusions of oppressive regimes. This affected not least the treatment of urban spaces. In retrospect, it has often been deplored that those parts of the urban heritage which had been spared by bombs in the war were subsequently cleared away by over-ambitious planners, on both sides of the Iron Curtain.

Tabula rasa attitudes such as this arose from two main sources. First, the widespread animosity of modernist architects and urban planners towards the historic city. The city of the nineteenth century was held responsible for almost all the misfortunes suffered by mankind. "Let collapse the built offences" ("Lasst sie zusammenfallen, die gebauten Gemeinheiten"), was a desire Bruno Taut had already expressed after World War One.[11] World War Two saw the realisation of this desire in numerous cities, spurring it on still further. The second source, closely connected to the first one, was the unquestioned belief in planning and its ability to construct a completely new world, unburdened by the flaws of the past and paving the way for the emergence of a new society. An impressive book edited by Cor Wagenaar demonstrates how, in the post-war decades, urban projects and the visions of cities—those that had been destroyed not less than those that had remained unscarred—were promoted all over Europe as enticing icons carrying the promise of a brighter future.[12] As Kristin Feireiss puts it in the preface to Wagenaar's book, the newly created or remodelled cityscapes served as a means of winning over the people's minds. They were particularly suited for this mission, as they were conceived as attempts to make the imagined prospects come true.[13]

This held particularly true for cities in socialist countries.[14] In contrast to the Western world, where bold projects often clashed with ownership structures, socialist regimes had the ownership of the land at their complete disposal. In our volume, this constellation is reflected in several essays relating to the socialist part of Europe. Jacek Friedrich discusses the post-war visions for a new Warsaw and their propagandistic promotion as a "great contribution in the building of a happier world." The rebuilding of the capital, which had been utterly destroyed by the German occupants, was seen as one of the central tasks of the Polish state, and even of the whole nation. The promise of fundamental improvements encompassed not only the comfort of the inhabitants, but also new aesthetic values. Thus, the Soviet-like socialist-realist splendour of the newly planned monumental buildings was praised for its "beautiful expression, characterising the new epoch of genuine humanism—an epoch defending the rights of the working man." A large number of the planned projects were actually carried out. Yet for various reasons the socialist-realist idea of "palaces for the working class" proved unfeasible after a few years. Thus, from the late nineteen-fifties onwards, small apartments in bare standardised buildings were hailed as the ultimate socialist living facility—a concept that Friedrich characterises as a modest vision of individual happiness in the privacy of one's own home.

What remained was a patronising planning ideology and practice, with the state and its representatives posing as benefactors, adopting the citizens as their beneficiaries. This imposed relationship, which can be seen as a return of pre-modern patterns of paternalism in socialist disguise, could not prevail without giving rise to a considerable amount of dissatisfaction and conflicts. Ana Kladnik focuses on the interactions between architects, planning authorities and inhabitants regarding the construction, distribution, and management of apartments in Havířov and Velenje—two newly built industrial towns in Czechoslovakia and Yugoslavia—in the nineteen-fifties and -sixties. From today's perspective, settlements such as these—characterised by the physical decay of the buildings and an ageing population—are seen as the epitome of socialist misery. As György Konrád has reminded us, however, at the time of their construction they did indeed contribute to public happiness—at least for those lucky enough to be granted one of the much sought-after apartments.[15] Kladnik reaches the same conclusion, emphasising the potential of modern appliances.

The inhabitants of the newly planned industrial cities, the majority of whom came from rural areas, often had difficulties in adapting to the urban environment or even using the facilities provided in their apartments correctly. This was all the more the case with the peasant population in remote regions of the Soviet Union, urged to move into the newly founded agro-towns set up next to collective farms. Mart Kalm traces the development of such settlements in Estonia from the nineteen-sixties to the -eighties, a period during which attempts to combine elements of urban and rural life generated massive social problems and a general sense of hopelessness. Nonetheless, the Estonian collective farms and agro-towns survived and developed as best they could, and for some people they may even have brought happiness. The happiest agro-town inhabitants, Kalm suggests, were the members of the technocratic elite, who were granted the privilege of living in a private detached house.

In Kladnik's text, as in Kalm's, the aspect of re-educating the inhabitants to use the apartments appropriately and adopt suitable behaviour within the urban community features time and again. Hence, projects in the name of public happiness often failed to take into account people's traditional habits and needs. On the contrary, people were expected to adapt to their newly built environment. One could be tempted to regard this as a typically socialist approach; however, it should rather be seen as a general pattern relating to modernism, which requires people to change in order to become "capable of happiness." Clarisse Lauras demonstrates this in the exemplary case of the creation of Firminy-Vert, a new town in the French Loire Département. Le Corbusier was significantly involved in this project, which was initiated in 1954. The auspicious concept of the city as a modernist space for happiness was presented in a booklet handed out to all its new inhabitants. The booklet also outlined some general rules regarding the use of the apartments and social coexistence within the community, the observance of which was seen as a precondition for the development of a "new way of living" along the lines of the planned vision. Firminy-Vert may have introduced many conveniences to improve the everyday life of its inhabitants, but the idea of re-educating them and transforming their cultural habits by placing them in a new urban environment once again turned out a utopian vision.

As the history of urban planning reveals, there has always been a divergence between the imagined picture of a planned urban environment and the reality of the daily life of its population. Indeed, to this very day it is a bone of contention as to whether this discrepancy is greater in the case of public projects—such as those presented by Friedrich, Kladnik, Kalm, and Lauras—or in the more market-driven undertakings of private companies. An example of the latter is investigated in the contribution by Bruno Bonomo. He focuses on the planning, promotion and appropriation of Casalpalocco, a Roman suburb developed by a leading Italian building company between the mid-nineteen-fifties and the mid-nineteen-seventies. It was conceived as an alternative to living in the overcrowded and noisy centre of the capital, thus meeting the evolving lifestyle aspirations of the Roman middle classes. The company's promotional campaign promised the prospective purchasers of the dwellings nothing short of "a home in a green environment, where you can be on holiday 365 days a year." Even though the promise expressed in this persuasive advertisement could not be fulfilled in a literal sense, Bonomo shows that certain elements of the developer's vision were in fact confirmed by the residents' perception of life in Casalpalocco, mainly during the initial stages. This relative success seems to have been rooted in the developer's recognition and fulfilment of the existing needs of a clearly defined, limited target group, also providing a certain degree of intentional social distinction and exclusivity.

Since then, this pattern has clearly gained in importance. Following the collapse of socialism and the decline of the Western welfare state, the public actors of urban planning have partly been superseded by private developers. This can be clearly seen in the expansion of privatised areas such as shopping malls and entertainment parks, and even more in the current shift from building houses for the masses to catering for higher levels of income. The egalitarian principles found in socialism, as well as in countless modernist projects in the Western world, have been replaced by planning practices that pay tribute—more or less explicitly and to varying degrees from country to country—to the commercialisation of living space(s) and a movement towards social segregation. The clearest expression of this tendency, arguably, is the recent proliferation of gated and guarded housing estates. This phenomenon has long been associated with urban developments in the Americas, where social divisions are expressed more clearly. However, gated communities have palpably spread through several European countries as well, currently mushrooming especially in the postsocialist part of the continent.

In the final contribution to this volume, Jacek Gądecki and Christian Smigiel draw attention to the rhetorical strategies used by the developers and sellers of gated communities in Bulgaria and Poland to promote their product as a comprehensive lifestyle package. Of course the promise of safety is crucial to this concept, but it is only one of several features. On the basis of a broad repertoire of cultural references, gated communities are being praised as an exclusive, almost paradisiacal living space, offering a mixture of lively urbanity and rural relaxation and thus a harmonious way of life, set apart from the threatening chaos of the rapidly changing city. The proliferation of this type of housing reflects the societal uncertainty and culture of fear which has seized the post-socialist countries. Yet gated communities may in fact be responsible for exacerbating this problem, as they blatantly reinforce the differences and antagonism that exist between the social classes.

Gated communities most clearly indicate the current trend towards a diversification of housing models and the fragmentation and privatisation of urban space. Yet, certain fields of public intervention in the urban environment have persisted, or even newly emerged, and there are still vague consensual notions striving towards sound development—above all, the notion of "sustainability." Notwithstanding this, it can safely be claimed that, in the early twenty-first century, an emphatic notion of happiness for the entire urban community is not exactly at the top of the agenda. Nor do the contemporary promises of happiness for selected parts of society have the same persuasiveness or appeal as the great visions emerging in the early and mid-twentieth century. Even the boldest of the developers' promotional advertisements cannot conceal the fact that the belief in the potential of urban planning to make people lastingly and fundamentally happy, which inspired such a great number of concepts from the Enlightenment until late modernism, has diminished. Our expectations of urban planning have basically been narrowed down to aspects such as convenience, lifestyle and sustainability. Pragmatism has finally seized victory over utopianism, and models of future urban life envisaged by "trendspotters" usually receive more attention than the visions of trained urbanists.[16]

Nonetheless: the role of architecture and urban planning in the pursuit of happiness is still a topic of discussion. Recently, some of the more well-known architects have taken an active part in such discussions, philosophising on how their projects and visions might be conducive to a happy life, whether as part of their branding strategy or out of real concern. We also witness the proliferation of new, at times megalomaniac construction sites in South East Asia or the Arab States, which imply a notion of happiness based on being secure enough to spend money at one's discretion in an environment of air-conditioned skyscrapers protected by video cameras and security guards. In Europe, which is not enchanted by such visions to the same degree, the general assumption of a close link between the design of urban environments and the prospect of happiness will, in all likelihood, also prevail. Notions of happiness in the city may well become further diversified, not only among social groups and lifestyle communities, but also according to changing needs in different phases of life. A further pluralisation and individualisation of urban spaces would be the result. But, as history suggests to us, happiness cannot be planned; thus, this must remain but an assumption for the time being.

Acknowledgements

This book originated in a panel convened by the editors for the IXth International Conference of the European Association for Urban History (Lyon, August 27–30, 2008). Thanks to the wide attention enjoyed by the venue and the support given to our session, we were able to assemble papers from considerably diverse backgrounds. Their quality and the highly inspiring discussions they incited encouraged us to turn the presentations, revised, enlarged, and with the addition of further contributions, into a collected volume. We are much indebted to all the authors for the fruitful exchange of ideas, for their great interest in the project and not least for their readiness to submit detailed contributions at a speed which was—by academic standards—quite breathtaking.

The realisation of the project was much aided by the excellent working conditions currently enjoyed by the editors. Arnold Bartetzky is indebted to the Centre for the History and Culture of East Central Europe (Geisteswissenschaftliches Zentrum Geschichte und Kultur Ostmitteleuropas) at the University of Leipzig, where he is associated to the research project "Imaginationen des Urbanen in Ostmitteleuropa. Stadtplanung—Visuelle Kultur—Dichtung" (Imaginations of Urbanity in East Central Europe. Urban Planning—Visual Culture—Literature). Marc Schalenberg, as a research fellow at the Helsinki Collegium for Advanced Studies, likewise profited from highly favourable circumstances for the rewarding, if time-consuming tasks involved in conceiving and editing a volume such as this. We are thoroughly grateful to both institutions! Generous financial support for the Leipzig research project and for the publication of this book was granted by the Bundesministerium für Bildung und Forschung (Federal Ministry of Education and Research).

If this publication has found a linguistic form to satisfy the expectations of English-speaking readers, this is mainly thanks to Louise Bromby (Leipzig), who not only edited the entire book with a great deal of patience and sensitivity, but also translated some of the texts from their original languages. It would hardly have been possible to accomplish the huge volume of editorial tasks without the untiring and professional input of Christian Dietz (Leipzig), who checked through all of the texts, took care of all aspects of formal consistency and prepared the illustrations provided by the authors for printing. Our warmest thanks to Louise and Christian!

Last but not least: we thank the team at the jovis Verlag Berlin, especially Susanne Rösler and Philipp Sperrle, not only for the fact that the book could be published so quickly, but for the high quality of its presentation and visual design. Many thanks for the professional, efficient, and pleasant cooperation!

Endnotes

1 Darrin M. McMahon, *Happiness. A History* (New York: Atlantic Monthly Press, 2006), 404.

2 McMahon, (see note 1), 12–13.

3 McMahon, (see note 1), 200.

4 Wolfgang Pehnt, *Das Ende der Zuversicht. Architektur in diesem Jahrhundert. Ideen—Bauten—Dokumente* (Berlin: Siedler Verlag, 1983).

5 Kristin Feireiss, preface to *Happy. Cities and Public Happiness in Post-War Europe*, ed. Cor Wagenaar (Rotterdam: Nai Publishers, 2004) 9; Cor Wagenaar, "Cities and the Pursuit of Public Happiness. An Introduction," in *Happy. Cities and Public Happiness in Post-War Europe* (see above), 14–23.

6 Alain de Botton, *The Architecture of Happiness* (London: Hamish Hamilton, 2006). German edition: *Glück und Architektur. Von der Kunst, daheim zu Hause zu sein* (Frankfurt a. M.: S. Fischer Verlag, 2008).

7 For an overview, see e.g.: Ruth Eaton, *Ideal Cities: Utopianism and the (un)built environment* (Antwerp: Mercatorfonds, 2001). German edition: *Die ideale Stadt. Von der Antike bis zur Gegenwart* (Berlin: Nicolaische Verlagsbuchhandlung, 2003); Charles Delfante, *Grande histoire de la ville: de la Mésopotamie aux Etats-Unis* (Paris: Armand Colin, 1997). German edition: *Architekturgeschichte der Stadt. Von Babylon bis Brasilia* (Darmstadt: Primus Verlag, 1999); Gerd de Bruyn, *Diktatur der Philanthropen. Entwicklung der Stadtplanung aus dem utopischen Denken* (Braunschweig, Wiesbaden: Friedr. Vieweg & Sohn Verlagsgesellschaft, 1996); Hanno-Walter Kruft, *Städte in Utopia. Die Idealstadt vom 15. bis zum 18. Jahrhundert zwischen Staatsutopie und Wirklichkeit* (Munich: C. H. Beck'sche Verlagsbuchhandlung, 1989); *Stadt und Utopie. Modelle idealer Gemeinschaften*, ed. Neuer Berliner Kunstverein (Berlin: Verlag Frölich & Kaufmann, 1982).

8 Gerhard Köhn, *Die Bevölkerung der Residenz, Festung und Exulantenstadt Glückstadt von der Gründung 1616 bis zum Endausbau 1652* (Neumünster: Wachholtz, 1974).

9 A good recent survey: Dieter Schott, "Die Stadt als Thema und Medium europäischer Kommunikation—Stadtplanung als Resultat europäischer Lernprozesse," in *Städte im europäischen Raum. Verkehr, Kommunikation und Urbanität im 19. und 20. Jahrhundert*, ed. Ralf Roth (Stuttgart: Steiner Verlag, 2009), 205–25.

10 Robert Graf, "Die Inzenierung der 'Reichshauptstadt Berlin' im Nationalsozialismus," in *Selling Berlin. Imagebildung und Stadtmarketing von der preußischen Residenz bis zur Bundeshauptstadt*, ed. Thomas Biskup and Marc Schalenberg (Stuttgart: Steiner Verlag, 2008), 193–208.

11 Bruno Taut, *Die Auflösung der Städte oder Die Erde eine gute Wohnung oder auch Der Weg zur Alpinen Architektur* (Hagen: Folkwang-Verlag 1920), 1.

12 Wagenaar, (see note 5); An important publication on a related topic: *Constructed Happiness. Domestic Environment in the Cold war Era*, ed. Mart Kalm and Ingrid Ruudi. (Tallinn: Estonian Academy of Arts, 2005).

13 Feireiss, (see note 5), 9.

14 Arnold Bartetzky, "Stadtplanung als Glücksverheißung. Die Propaganda für den Wiederaufbau Warschaus und Ost-Berlins nach dem Zweiten Weltkrieg," in *Imaginationen des Urbanen. Konzeption, Reflexion und Fiktion von Stadt in Mittel- und Osteuropa*, ed. Arnold Bartetzky, Marina Dmitrieva and Alfrun Kliems (Berlin: Lukas Verlag 2009), 51–80.

15 György Konrád, "Rückblick auf die Beglückung," in *Glück—Stadt—Raum in Europa 1945 bis 2000*, ed. Romana Schneider and Rudolf Stegers (Basel, Berlin, Boston: Birkhäuser 2002), 8–11.

16 In his recent outline for a comprehensive history of international planning in its various fields of application, Dirk van Laak has suggested a similar periodisation, with its intellectual origins in Europe in the Enlightenment, leading on to a "classically" modern phase of all-embracing planning between World War One and the early 1970s (across political systems) to a phase of "postmodern pragmatism," characterised by cautious "projects" rather than by valiant "planning"; Dirk van Laak, "Planung. Geschichte und Gegenwart des Vorgriffs auf die Zukunft," *Geschichte und Gesellschaft* 34 (2008): 305–26.

"GLÜCKSELIGE STÄDTE"

Johann Peter Willebrand's Conception
of Urban Happiness

Mascha Bisping

In Early Modern times, the question of how it might be possible for a city to be happy would have been considered rather a strange one. Utopian texts dating from that period, describing visions of cities, were always concerned with exemplary cities that would work well because they were well governed and designed according to ideal forms. However, since the early Enlightenment, the question of how the people living in a city and the state governing them could be made happy was an issue of increasing importance. In the discourse surrounding the German Enlightenment the term *Glückseligkeit* was used more and more, describing a whole set of political, economic, and social practices.

Towards the end of the eighteenth century, a German author developed a concept of Glückseligkeit for the city. The city, as a place of social densification, was the most important field for these practices.

The author, Johann Peter Willebrand (1719–1786), was quite widely known in the later part of the eighteenth century—as reflected by the wide presence of his works in libraries and the attention contemporary literary journals paid to them.[1]

Willebrand was not an architect or an engineer but a scholar of law, who first practiced as a solicitor, later as a counsellor of justice and, in the last third of his life, mainly as a free writer of historical and travel literature. The concern for the order of the polity permeates his entire work. In 1765 he published an *Abrégé de la police*[2] and in 1771 a curious book entitled *Grundregeln und Anleitungssätze zur Beförderung der gesellschaftlichen Glückseligkeit in den Städten* (Basic Rules and Instructions for Enhancing Social Happiness in the Cities).[3] This work cannot be seen as a proper treatise. The author himself later called it a "List of categories on the requirements of city police."[4] Rather it must be seen as the list of contents or plan for a much larger publication on the subject of how civil society should be organised. The first part of Willebrand's opus, entitled *Grundriss einer schönen Stadt Vol. I* (Outline of a Beautiful City), was published in 1775; parts two and three followed a year later.[5] This work was still considered worthy of mention by two of the founders of the modern discipline of urban planning, Joseph Stübben and Albert Erich Brinckmann, and in fact it was the only German theoretical treatise on the city from the eighteenth century with encyclopaedic pretensions.[6] The *Grundriss* seems to represent a practical short version of the large publication enterprise envisaged by the *Grundregeln*. In the following three sections, and especially in the third, I will refer mainly to the *Grundriss*.

First there is the international and national context of Embellishment, Improvement, and the cameralistic theory of the police. The work can be seen as a German contribution to the European discourse on the improvement of cities. The term Grundriss must be read in a metaphorical sense; the work does deal with questions of aesthetics, but these are included in a much broader concept of city design. The petrified form, the "architecture of the city" (Aldo Rossi) is not considered as secondary, but as the very framework upon which the real beauty of the city is based, which, in an overall conception of political order, entails far more than a mere visual quality.

Johann Peter Willebrand
K. Dän. w. Justizrath

Grundriß
einer schönen Stadt,

in Absicht ihrer Anlage und Einrichtung
zur
Bequemlichkeit, zum Vergnügen, zum Anwachs und
zur Erhaltung ihrer Einwohner,
nach bekannten Mustern entworfen.

Nebst einer Vorrede
von der Wirkung des Clima auf die Gesinnung
und Gesetzgebung der Völker.

Erster Theil.

Hamburg und Leipzig.
Zu Hamburg in der Bohnschen Buchhandlung und im Adreß-
Comtoir, zu Leipzig in der Hilscherschen Buchhandlung
und im Intelligenz-Comtoir zum Verkauf. 1775.

1   Front page of *Grundriss einer schönen Stadt, Vol. I.*

The second part of the essay will deal with the various ideas of happiness found in philosophical and political discourse in the eighteenth century. In Willebrand's *Basic Rules and Instructions* we find the keyword Glückseligkeit in the title. This term is actually predominant in all writings by the author. In order to understand the complex texture of the "beautiful city," it is necessary to understand what Glückseligkeit generally implied at that time and in Willebrand's thinking in particular: while the English term "happiness" suggests an individual right to ambition achieved by means of personal or collective engagement, the German term describes a "state of order" achieved by a well-organised government and inhabitants who are virtuous as well as wealthy.

The third part of the paper will describe and examine the *Grundriss einer schönen Stadt* as a spatial vision of Glückseligkeit. Central to Willebrand's writings is an emphasis on order, regulation and systematisation as the most important preconditions for Glückseligkeit. These must be fulfilled within the actual form and life of the city and are part of the Enlightenment discourse in general.

Willebrand's works represent a significant German contribution to what Michel Foucault evaluated as the birth of "governmentality" and "biopolitics."[7] The term governmentality was used to describe "a complex of techniques of governing and modes of thought, which gradually developed along with the emergence of modern (biopolitical) statehood and became institutionalised in this modern state."[8] "Biopolitics" are those techniques and practices of governing aimed at the administration and regulation of life. Since the former subjects of a state had been transformed more and more into a "population" and as such possessed an economical value, the authorities were no longer faced with the task of simply dominating and governing a worthless and replaceable mob, but of increasing and maintaining this economically important factor. Statistics, hygiene, health, and everything that could increase the pleasure of life within a certain state became a central concern of government.

Willebrand's work, notably the *Grundriss* (▶ 1), has to be comprehended within the context of this contemporary political shift. As a model developed under the influence of cameralism, it can be seen as a specific German effort to give biopolitics a spatial form by providing a tangible vision for the Glückseligkeit of a beautiful city.

The Improvement of Cities: Police and Cameralism in the Eighteenth Century

The issues addressed by Willebrand, such as improving, bettering and beautifying cities, were amongst the main topics of Enlightenment discourse in Western Europe. The city became the subject of theoretical reflection in a novel way (e.g., Voltaire, Marc Antoine Laugier, Pierre Patte, Francesco Miliza, later especially John Claudius Loudon).[9] Enlightenment theorists made the human individual with his perceptions and needs (daily life, health) the measure of urban qualities rather than an abstract order that symbolically represented the form of the society, the regime or the state. A crucial aspect of the new urban discourse was the fact that it dealt with the question of how existing cities could be made beautiful or more beautiful by applying general principles. Beauty no longer depended on a precisely defined and predetermined form. Before 1700, in contrast, urban theory had usually taken place on the plain field of *a tabula rasa*.[10] Problems seen by critics, especially in the existing (medieval) cities, were their complexity of design which led to confusion, narrowness, lack of hygiene, and poor functionality. They demanded a new order for the cities as regards urban design, technology (especially concerning fire prevention), hygiene, and also legislation. But apart from these common issues, in the eighteenth century every state had its own specific problems. Each of them had distinct philosophical and political traditions and individual priorities as far as the development of urban and sociological structures was concerned.

The English "improvement" efforts focused on aesthetic forms and tools derived from the English garden theory and the new theory of perception. One of the main subjects was the provision of urban green spaces, both private and public.[11] At the same time English urban planning was rather pragmatic and always paid great attention to rights of property and economic considerations. The squares and circles that were built and rebuilt after the great fire of London were the direct result of such imperatives.

French *embellissement*, by contrast, placed emphasis on the grand form, prestige, capaciousness and functionality of the city (Marc Antoine Laugier). The design and construction of the street as a public space, as well as technical questions, were the most important topics here (Pierre Patte).

In the German states the problem of old, narrow and dirty cityscapes was evident. Although people knew about the English and French discourse, there was almost no literary theoretical reflection on the subject of *Verschönerung* in German until about 1800. One reason for this was that the German elite read and corresponded in French anyway (see Willebrand's *Abrégé*) so that there was no need for translations or special publications in German. Some of the discussions were taking place in German aesthetic journals. Another reason was that the problems in German cities and states were fundamentally different from those of the other European states. The few larger cities in the German territories were much smaller than Paris or London, and industrialisation developed much later than in England. The German princely states, in the late eighteenth century still suffering from the repercussions of the Thirty Years' War and the Seven Years' War, were mainly faced with the challenge of building new residences, improving country areas and smaller cities, rebuilding the cities that had been devastated or burned down—the so-called *Retablissement*[12]—and building up new cities and colonies on wasteland. The bigger cities, often self-governing (the so-called *Reichsstädte*), mostly expanded rather than producing new strategies of order in the old texture of the city. The most important changes were carried out at the borders: many cities broke down the old ramparts in the eighteenth century and replaced them with boulevards.

Willebrand's ideas concerning the material form of a city are not uncommon for the time. The uniqueness of his work lies in the systematic presentation of an overall concept for the city in terms of the design of urban society by the *Policey* (police), and in the fact that this concept touched on any aesthetic issues at all. During the second half of the eighteenth century *Policeywissenschaft* (science of the police)[13] encouraged the implementation of the theory of cameralism in the German states. The police was generally an important subject in European Enlightenment discourse, but within German political theory the Polizey became an integral part of the economical-political science of cameralism.[14] Polizey could refer to anything that affected daily life in the city, supporting the intentions of cameralism.[15] Foucault calls the police "the prerequisite of the existence of urbanity."[16] The impact of cameralism was to systematise all aspects of state and society with regard to their economic benefits. The main ambition of this doctrine was to permeate society in a thoroughly economic way in order to secure the welfare of the state.[17] An important device used in cameralism to attain welfare, as in the French theory of physiocracy, was circulation. According to this theory, in order to increase circulation it was necessary to increase the number of inhabitants living in a state or a city. Thus the main goal of political practices was so-called *Peuplierung* (population growth).

Another precondition for circulation was the difference between urban and rural economy, and here an important distinction between cameralism and French physiocracy must be made.[18] While physiocratic theory considered the country to be the only place where happiness and real wealth could be achieved, the city being a mere necessity for the purposes of commerce and trading, cameralistic theory pointed out that the countryside needed wealthy cities and vice versa. In contrast to physiocracy, cameralism also thought luxury goods to be useful within commerce.

The central concern of Willebrand's writings on urban design is not only to increase population in the cities and make people stay, but also to keep moral and health standards high, so that the population's abilities could be put to use for economical purposes on a permanent basis. The complete title of the *Grundriss einer schönen Stadt* therefore is: ... *to the purpose of its layout and arrangement to ensure the comfort, joy, preservation and increase in number of its inhabitants designed according to well-known models.*[19]

By composing his *Grundriss* according to "well-known models" Willebrand's approach is similar to that found in the French and English discourse referring to the improvement of existing cities. But while French publications especially focused on the improvement of the city of Paris, Willebrand names many cities from the Holy Roman Empire and abroad. He refers to the good or bad governments, installations, institutions, facilities, or structures of the examples chosen. The introduction to the first part of the book begins with short tributes to the cities Willebrand judges to be ideal models: "flourishing" Petersburg, Berlin as "the queen among the cities in Europe," Copenhagen where the "bricks have been transformed into marble," Mannheim as "the most regular city in the world," the *Neustadt* of

Kassel "a model for the new colonies," London with its "Roman spirit," Vienna, Potsdam, and Brunswick. In the following chapters Willebrand continues to refer to these cities as examples of "greater perfection than my summary could depict."[20]

Glückseligkeit versus the Pursuit of Happiness

Central to all cameralistic objectives was a philosophical reformulation of the eudemonistic idea concerning the state. Johann Heinrich Gottlob von Justi declared "gemeinschaftliche Glückseligkeit" (common felicity) to be the "Endzweck des Staates" (ultimate purpose of the state).[21]

The meaning of the English "pursuit of happiness," derived from Adam Smith's theory and adopted in the American Declaration of Independence, is basically different from that of the German term Glückseligkeit. The latter is sometimes translated as "felicity." However, the English term felicity tends to describe individual experience. Glückseligkeit has intrinsically more in common with the theological term *beatitudo* or "beatitude." It implies the secularised form of a state of eternal quiet and peace, achieved by following the virtuous principles of Protestant ethics, although Willebrand generally favoured religious liberty.

The Anglo-Saxon concept describes the pursuit of each individual within (a democratic) society, implying the "unalienable" right to individual as well as to social behaviour; it is the happiness of every individual that contributes to the happiness of society. The state of Glückseligkeit on the other hand requires an authoritarian government issuing governmental commands and the observation of these commands by the subjects. It was Martin Luther who first established a theologically founded duty on the part of the authorities to take care of the mental, spiritual, and material welfare the subjects.[22] In cameralism we meet the secularised form of these ethics. Christian Wolff, the most influential philosopher for the cameralistic view of the world, originally defined Glückseligkeit as a "Zustand einer dauerhaften Freude" (state of permanent joy) that could be created by rational and virtuous actions in conformance with nature.[23] It is the natural order that provides the basis for Glückseligkeit, which is intrinsically meant as an "Ordnungszustand" (state of order).[24]

In this way, the interrelationship between social and personal happiness is diametrically opposed in both conceptual traditions: the Anglo-Saxon term "happiness" stresses the personal pursuit of happiness, which essentially contributes to common happiness and therefore makes individuals worthy of being granted positions in law. According to the German concept of Glückseligkeit, people had to subordinate their own needs to the happiness and welfare of the general public in order to live happily. Justi assumed that one could be "glückselig" without being happy or even satisfied.[25] He differentiates "Glück" and "Glückseligkeit": personal Glück could be derived from just having enough to eat. Glückseligkeit, in contrast, is a state whose objective content is determined by general criteria a priori. It aims to be a component of beatitude within the broader contextual setting of state and society. With respect to the social dimension, the concept is similar to that found in Rousseau's *Contrat social*: happiness is more than the sum of individual concerns. But whilst Rousseau's idea was to strengthen the subject against the state and install the term of the sovereignty of the people, cameralistic theory never challenged the sovereignty of the monarch, but rather tried to find a new means of reinforcing and stabilising state power and welfare.

As an economically motivated key term in cameralism, Glückseligkeit is said to be a significant factor as far as two changes in the eighteenth century are concerned: the "general secularisation of the concepts of life and the purpose of government," and the "improvement of governmental competence within welfare."[26] The process of making divisions between state and society, which began in the seventeenth century, was continued in cameralism. The police must provide the necessary apparatus to bridge the new gap between state and society. In this sense the police is the vicarious agent of a grand plan. In cameralism the state was to "be made available for 'technical planning' to a far greater extent than ever before."[27] Underlying this project was a strong belief in the feasibility of planning, economic success, and hence in a perfectly working society. This is the most important difference as compared with mercantilism, which was confined to certain economic methods. Cameralism demanded an overall shaping of society with the final goal of establishing Glückseligkeit and welfare as economically vindicated values.[28]

Glückseligkeit served as a kind of binding link between state and society: the strength of the state should emerge from the happiness of the people,[29] and this was only possible if the people were reconciled with disciplinary power, security institutions, and the economic and territorial practices of the state. Everyone who moved and behaved within the framework of norms and regulations set by the police was promised the reward of participation in social Glückseligkeit, as a secularised form of salvation. First and foremost, however, not only the subjects must act in a responsible manner if Glückseligkeit is to be achieved. Willebrand explicitly urges the authorities to fulfil their duty first: only he who creates reasonable rules and norms and conforms to them can successfully "sell" and maintain the perspective of Glückseligkeit.

Thus, in the name of Glückseligkeit, the city itself had to be transformed into a principally economic space of action and thus became subject to planning just as the state was. In consequence every person, every house, every street, and every place, every public institution, every interaction, and every activity was assumed to serve economic purposes.

Spatialising Glückseligkeit in the Beautiful City

How could Glückseligkeit be realised in the physical space of a city? This is actually the main question behind the work of Johann Peter Willebrand, who tries to find a popular and a readable form for the presentation of a rather technical matter. Hence the *Outline of a Beautiful City* follows the image of a city step by step, with the intention of reaching the inner eye of the reader and constructing an ideal. The author works his way through all parts of the polity and defines the present conditions, nuisances and needs, subsequently listing all the installations, changes, rules, and norms that are required. In this way, *Policeywissenschaft* becomes a science of the city.

Willebrand's *Grundriss* is multidimensional, i.e., it is a formation to be realised in space and time and on a social level. It is significant that the dramaturgical structure of the first part follows a progression from the outside to the inside, starting from an overall view and progressing to smaller units, from broader categories of space (location, territory of the city, periphery, suburb, city) to details (main buildings, sites of pleasure and amusement, infrastructures such as post office or inn, and also non-spatial infrastructures such as public clocks that contribute to the orderly life of the city). It is a structure inspired by the way a stranger arrives in a city and becomes familiar with it. And, according to Willebrand, the impression a stranger gains of a city is actually an accurate measure of its beauty. Within this complex interaction, architecture and urban form are equally valid parts of his concept, although they are not the most important ones. Real "beauty" is created by means of social, economic and architectural activities.

The most important factor with regard to Glückseligkeit is also the logic of the economy when it comes to urban design. On the one hand, the economic system is sustained by committing desired groups of inhabitants to the city, e.g., by initiating activities such as building well-proportioned architecture. On the other hand, passive tasks such as standardisation, control, and observation must be undertaken to support the active tasks and ensure that their effects are long-lasting, for example by introducing building regulations and a building police, in the form of a commission responsible for the authorisation of workers, plans, buildings, and the alteration of buildings.

The central idea in the matrix of Willebrand's urban cameralism is a hierarchical structure incorporating all the elements of the city. In his general introduction, the most important prerequisites for a beautiful city are defined as "Wille und Vermögen" (will and funds) and an efficient police force, good laws, inhabitants who think and live in a moral way, good administration and justice. Other necessities are appropriate taxes, an efficient and regular census of the people in the form of a "registry of persons," and last not least *Subordination,* which literally means a strict hierarchical apparatus of administration.[30] He concludes that "subordination is the soul of every good civil institution, and along with that one of the most important requirements of a good city."[31]

The "outline" of the beautiful city is, as mentioned above, not a specific set of instructions for building a city. The author even states that the form of the city is not very important:

> What form a new city should have, and how the city should be divided into alleys, or in
> how many boroughs it is to be intersected, this is arbitrary to the ruler who orders a city
> to be built and established, so that it is superfluous and negligible to mention anything
> about that. But this I may remind you of, that according to its nature a circular city is
> seemingly more comfortable than a city that is built in a square or longish shape.[32]

He gives no reasons for the statement made in the last sentence, and is far more concerned with improving and expanding existing cities. Nevertheless, misunderstanding Marc Antoine Laugier's intentions to compare the city to a park,[33] Willebrand reminds the reader of the chessboard pattern as it had been realised in many new cities like Potsdam and Mannheim as a model for the city: he advocates that the streets should be "perfectly straight and regular" as they were in these cities and concludes that "generally it is a rule that the alleys in a city must look like a sectioned-off park, whose main paths usually all lead to a wide regular place at the centre."[34] But still the contents of the city (buildings, streets, people, government) and the functionality of these contents is considered much more significant than its layout as far as the Glückseligkeit of a city is concerned.

For the same reason, strong military fortifications surrounding the "beautiful city" do not only become superfluous, but are ideally to be replaced by a good government and the levelling morality of civil society.[35] It was a commonly shared view that the enormous city walls of early modern times were often targeted inwards towards the city's own inhabitants rather than against foreign enemies who might attack the city from the outside. In the embellished and well-ordered city this function is unnecessary. Enlightenment discourse considers the walls "barbaric" (Georg Forster) and unhealthy because they keep bad air in the city. But at the same time a city without any form of guarded boundary is not yet favoured by Willebrand because, according to the cameralistic theory, it is necessary to keep the "Landwirthschaft" (rural economy) and the "Stadtwirthschaft" (economy of the city) separate. A certain difference must be maintained between the two in order to stimulate the circulation of things, money, and people.[36] That is why he is greatly concerned with the city walls, manned gates and customs staff.[37] He is also a supporter of walkways along the modern ramparts, which are only built to guard against unnoticed invasion from outside, which he calls "Anlauf."[38] Willebrand's remarks imply the idea of a city space that opens up from the inside, as a reflection not only of the city, but of society as a whole.

For the organisation of the city there must be a certain structure of parameters available within its order: a huge part of Willebrand's book is dedicated to the classification of different sorts of people, activities, laws, climatic circumstances, businesses, and manners. His general statement on this enterprise reveals all the hierarchical and segregational characteristics of the theory:

> Wise rulers of a city only recognise its growth as valuable to the enhancement of the Glückseligkeit of their society, if it consists of human beings who are fruitful to common welfare by their industriousness and wealth, and who are willing to accept the limits set by the authorities, whereby tranquillity and concord are maintained. It might well be impossible for me to mention all kinds of human beings who are apt to support this ultimate purpose of civil society; meanwhile I will do my best to classify them in the following to the best of my ability.[39]

Grundriß einer schönen Stadt,

oder

Bemerkungen, was zum Anwachs und zur Erhaltung der Städtischen Einwohner dienet.

Nebst Verfolg der Vorrede
von der Wirkung des Clima auf die Gesetzgebung u.s.f.

REIPUBL. SALUTI
SUAVITATE
HUMANITATE
INDULGENTIA CURAQUE
CONSULENDO.

Zweyter und dritter Theil.

Hamburg und Leipzig.
Zu Hamburg in der Bohnschen Buchhandlung und im güld-
nen A B C, zu Leipzig in der Hilscherschen Buchhandlung,
auch in beyden Städten in den Adreß-Comtoiren
zum Verkauf. 1776.

As well as economic concerns, disciplinary order and security are omnipresent in every field of activity, every single action, every business transaction, and every field of social life that can be publicly regulated. But economy, discipline, and security also intrude far into the workings of individual households. At the same time, the intention is not to establish any despotic order, but to develop all the profitable abilities of every individual to the full. Hence the term "Freyheit" (freedom) has a certain place in the theory of cameralism. Willebrand points out that to "guarantee the freedom of property" would be highly recommendable for a city wishing to attract wealthy residents. Still, he warns against dissipated freedom that undermines strong morals and drives desirable inhabitants away.[40] Interestingly late cameralism, of which Willebrand is a representative, is far closer to liberalism than to mercantilism with regard to freedom, particularly the freedom of property. The latter tended to constrain liberties, whilst cameralism supported them up to a certain point.

The second part of Willebrand's *Grundriss* (▶ 2) mainly contains considerations on demographic politics and specific economic ideas to attract good citizens. In the second volume, containing parts two and three, he deals with the special demands of hosts and future residents from all social classes.

Good residents, according to the *Grundriss,* are the "Schätze der Städte" (treasures of cities),[41] the core of the "beautiful city." They are wealthy, but above all hard-working, industrious, skilled, and therefore profitable inhabitants. Quality and qualifications are more highly valued than financial capital, origins, and social background, which were formerly so important in a feudal system. The increasing appreciation of quality and qualifications in the Enlightenment leads to new concerns such as the fostering of children and education, the freedom of religion, the suspension of constraints imposed by guilds, and the founding of qualified administrative units. A good city had to mirror these requirements by providing and maintaining the appropriate institutions.

For Willebrand, an essential quality with regard to Glückseligkeit is "Gemütsruhe" (peace of mind). In the third part of the *Grundriss,* Gemütsruhe is introduced as an important criterion for the beauty of the city. Peace of mind would primarily be the result of education, morality, obedience, practised religiousness and the avoidance of moral conflicts. Altogether mental hygiene is encouraged in order to preserve economic productivity.[42]

Willebrand uses the term "Schönheit" (beauty) to describe far more than mere aesthetic concepts such as the *line of beauty* or the rules governing the proportions of columns. Beauty is to be seen as a corollary to Glückseligkeit, together they both form an inseparable unit, a semantic system derived from mutual support of ideal conditions and useful institutions. Although beauty and Glückseligkeit are not congruent, they are unconditionally dependent on each other. Glückseligkeit as a state of order that is mainly produced by biopolitics can only be developed in the "beautiful city." The "beautiful city" is the outcome of Glückseligkeit. Implicitly, Willebrand creates the aesthetics of biopolitics.

One could read *Grundriss einer schönen Stadt* as a utopian text. The "beautiful city" is actually made up of the many existing model cities he mentions, and it is an urban ideal. But at the same time it certainly seems to be feasible. Personal happiness cannot be planned by individuals, but Glückseligkeit, as a purpose of the state, a secularised, Protestant version of paradise, actually can.

While Willebrand maintains a strong disciplinary and systematic perfectionism in the setting up of an ideal community, he also modifies this by stating that many cities were already quite satisfactory although all the institutions he described could not yet be found there. Eventually the author himself makes an effort to practice the virtue of modesty, since he does not expect to find "perfect institutions in cities of imperfect people."[43] Willebrand's effort to systematise and regulate the city by means of a complex treatise is hence a unique as well as significant phenomenon in the late Enlightenment.

Conclusion

The philosophical difference between the German Glückseligkeit provided with the support of the authorities and the concept of happiness pursued by the individual has important implications for the planning of a city. Whilst the first is seen from the perspective of an absolute ideal that can be planned and achieved and is mainly social in nature, the other implies only the freedom to pursue an ideal, whether personal or social. The first entails imposing rather restrictive norms in urban planning and a distinctive framework for individual initiatives. Although it promotes a consistent image of the city that might be perceived as beautiful, it contains the risk of appearing too "cool," over-restricted, lifeless, or even dead. The lack of flexibility to react to changing circumstances might also endanger prosperity. The other, more "liberal" way could provide the framework for a freer development based on individual rights and responsibilities with a minimum of restrictions. The outcome may or may not be a pleasing one. The visible qualities of a completely liberal city "planning" would depend on the inhabitants' different individual ideas of happiness. This liberal city would present itself as an arbitrary compilation of individual actions and building activities. The coherence or incoherence of the cityscape would mainly be left to chance.[44]

In this respect, it may be no coincidence that Willebrand was read again by Joseph Stübben or Albert Erich Brinckmann towards the end of the nineteenth century, in an era of reformism and at the dawn of modernism. This was an era when liberalism in urban planning was at its peak, resulting in the worst conditions for the lower classes. Stübben and Brinckmann only mention Willebrand briefly. We do not know their thoughts on the social implications of the eighteenth-century theorist's opinions. But actually the enlightened concept of Glückseligkeit, beyond absolutism and cameralism, could have paradoxically inspired an ideal of public welfare in an overall spatial "design" aimed at providing a form of happiness that did not only apply to the happy few with the knowledge and the financial means to pursue it.

Beyond their historical value as documents on cameralistic ideas of biopolitics and the problems of cities in the eighteenth century, the works of Johann Peter Willebrand are to be seen as rigid but necessary categorisations contributing to the evolution of modern city planning.

Since the Enlightenment, the details of our understanding of what happiness means with respect to urban planning and urban life have changed. But the various discourses that took place in the Enlightenment paved the way for modern traditions in the field of urban planning, not least the discussion on how much freedom and how many restrictions are necessary in architectural and urban design, a discussion that remains an ambivalent and controversial one up until today.

Endnotes

1 Particularly there are several reviews of the *Grundriss einer schönen Stadt* (for bibliographical information see note 5) by well-known personalities in two of the most important journals of that time: Christoph Martin Wieland, review of *Grundriss einer schönen Stadt vol. 1*, by Johann Peter Willebrand, *Der Teutsche Merkur* (1775:2), Quartier: 190–92; Friedrich Arnold Klockenbring, review of *Grundriss einer schönen Stadt vol. 1*, by Johann Peter Willebrand, *Allgemeine deutsche Bibliothek* 27 (1775), part 1, 55–60; Friedrich Arnold Klockenbring, review of *Grundriss einer schönen Stadt vol. 2*, by Johann Peter Willebrand, *Allgemeine deutsche Bibliothek* 35 (1778), part 2, 616–17; eventually the author himself presented his book "critically": Johann Peter Willebrand, review of *Grundriss einer schönen Stadt vol. 2*, by Johann Peter Willebrand, *Der Teutsche Merkur* (1776:3): 178–81.

2 Johann Peter Willebrand, *Abrégé de la police, accompagné de réflexions sur l'accroissement des villes* (Hamburg: Estienne und Sohn, 1765).

3 Johann Peter Willebrand, *Grundregeln und Anleitungssätze zur Beförderung der gesellschaftlichen Glückseligkeit in den Städten, mit Verzeichniss der zur Erklärung erforderlichen Hülfsmittel; nebst einer Vorrede, von der edlen Einfalt der gesellschaftlichen Einrichtung der alten Deutschen* (Leipzig: Heinsische Buchhandlung, 1771).

4 "Rubriken-Verzeichnis der Erfordernisse einer Stadt-Polizey": Johann Peter Willebrand, *Grundriss einer schönen Stadt. vol. 1* (Hamburg: Bohnsche Buchhandlung; Leipzig: Hilschersche Buchhandlung, 1775), introduction, 3.

5 Johann Peter Willebrand, *Grundriss einer schönen Stadt in Absicht ihrer Anlage und Einrichtung zur Bequemlichkeit, zum Vergnügen, zum Anwachs und zur Erhaltung ihrer Einwohner, nach bekannten Mustern entworfen. vol. 1* (Hamburg: Bohnsche Buchhandlung; Leipzig: Hilschersche Buchhandlung, 1775); parts two and three were published in one volume under the title: *Grundriss einer schönen Stadt oder Bemerkungen, was zum Anwachs und zur Erhaltung der Städtischen Einwohner dient* (Hamburg: Bohnsche Buchhandlung, güldenes ABC; Leipzig: Hilschersche Buchhandlung, 1776). In the following the two volumes are cited as Willebrand, *Grundriss I* (1775), and Willebrand, *Grundriss II* (1776).

6 Francesco Finotto, "I fondamenti della bella Città nella teoria di J.P. Willebrand," in *Storia urbana. Rivista di studi sulle trasformazioni della città e del territorio in età moderna* 19 (1995:3): 21–39, 22.

7 Michel Foucault, *Sécurité, territoire, population. Cours au Collège de France (1977–1978)*, ed. Michel Senellart (Paris: Gallimard/Seuil, 2004); Michel Foucault, *Naissance de la biopolitique. Cours au Collège de France (1978–1979)*, ed. Michel Senellart (Paris: Gallimard/Seuil, 2004). In the following I will mainly refer to the German edition: Michel Foucault, *Sicherheit, Territorium, Bevölkerung. Geschichte der Gouvernementalität. vol. 1* (Frankfurt a. M.: Suhrkamp, 2006); Michel Foucault, *Die Geburt der Biopolitik. Geschichte der Gouvernementalität. vol. 2* (Frankfurt a. M.: Suhrkamp, 2006).

8 "*Gouvernementalität* bezeichnet … einen Komplex aus Regierungstechniken und Denkweisen, die sich mit dem Auftauchen moderner (biopolitischer) Staatlichkeit allmählich durchgesetzt und in dieser erst institutionalisiert hat.": Martin Saar, "Macht, Staat, Subjektivität. Foucaults Geschichte der Gouvernementalität im Werkkontext," in *Michel Foucaults 'Geschichte der Gouvernementalität' in den Sozialwissenschaften. Internationale Beiträge*, ed. Susanne Krasmann and Michael Volkmer (Bielefeld: transcript, 2004), 23–45, 30.

9 Mascha Bisping, "Die ganze Stadt dem ganzen Menschen? Zur Anthropologie der Stadt im 18. Jahrhundert," in *Die Grenzen des Menschen. Anthropologie und Ästhetik um 1800*, ed. Maximilian Bergengruen, Roland Borgards, and Johannes F. Lehmann (Würzburg: Königshausen & Neumann, 2001), 183–203.

10 The emphasis lies on "theory," understood here as a rather "narrow" term that comprises only theoretical treatises published to distribute general principles of city planning. This is a theoretical tradition deriving from Vitruv's "De Architectura." The actual planning practice and also the discourse concerning building regulations, letters, instructions, memoranda, etc. practically always dealt with changes and improvements in existing cities and adaption to environmental circumstances. But even these sources tend to take their main ideas from the ideal of a perfect city planned on an open space and even terrain; see: Eva-Maria Seng, *Stadt-Idee und Planung. Neue Ansätze im Städtebau des 16. und 17. Jahrhunderts* (Munich, Berlin: Deutscher Kunstverlag, 2003).

11 See e.g., Todd Longstaffe-Gowan, *The London town garden 1740–1840* (New Haven/CT: Yale University Press, 2001).

12 The terms "Meliorationen" and "Retablissement" mainly derive from the Prussian practice. See: Ralph Jaeckel, "'Bauen wie auf der Friedrichstadt'— Das Retablissement der brandenburg-preussischen Provinzialstädte im 18. Jahrhundert," in *Mathematisches Calcul und Sinn für Ästhetik. Die preussische Bauverwaltung, 1770–1848*, exhibition catalogue of the Geheimes Staatsarchiv Preussischer Kulturbesitz in collaboration with the Kunstbibliothek der Staatlichen Museen zu Berlin, Preussischer Kulturbesitz (Berlin: Duncker und Humblot, 2000), 11–24.

13 For *Policeywissenschaft* as a German speciality see also: Foucault, *Geschichte der Gouvernementalität. vol. 1*, (see note 7), 458.

14 While mercantilism was a group of heterogeneous economical theories, cameralism was grounded on mercantilism but gained homogeneous standardisation due to the establishment of university chairs. The first chair for cameralism was established at the Prussian university of Halle in 1727.

15 Johann Heinrich Gottlob Justi defined the *Polizey* as the totality "of laws and rules, that affect the internal politics of the state and support the strength and accumulation of stately power, and whose goal it is to use its potential in the right way." I.e., "die Gesamtheit von 'Gesetzen und

Regelungen, die das Innere eines Staates betreffen und die Kräftigung und Steigerung der Macht dieses Staates verfolgen und deren Ziel es ist, seine Kräfte richtig zu gebrauchen.'": Johann Heinrich Gottlob von Justi. *Grundsätze der Policey-Wissenschaft* (Göttingen 1756), cited from Michel Foucault, *Geschichte der Gouvernementalität I*, (see note 7), 452.

16 "Die Polizei als Existenzbedingung der Urbanität": Foucault, *Geschichte der Gouvernementalität I*, (see note 7), 483.

17 See particularly: Thomas Simon, "*Gute Polizey*" *Ordnungsbilder und Zielvorstellungen politischen Handelns in der Frühen Neuzeit* (Frankfurt a. M.: Vittorio Klostermann, 2004); Marcus Sandl, *Oekonomie des Raumes. Der kameralwissenschaftliche Entwurf der Staatswirtschaft im 18. Jahrhundert* (Cologne, Weimar, Vienna: Böhlau, 1999).

18 Marcus Sandl, "Landeskultivierung und Raumkoordination. 'Landschaft' im Spannungsfeld von 'Polizey' und 'Oeconomie'," in *Der imaginierte Garten*, ed. Günter Oesterle and Harald Tausch (Göttingen: Vandenhoeck & Ruprecht, 2001), 73–91, 83.

19 For the complete bibliographical reference see above: (note 5).

20 Willebrand, *Grundriss I*, (see note 5), 1–3 (accentuations in italics added by MB to indicate the cited segments): "Wo ehemals ein grosser Peter sich ein Feld erwählte, um das, jetzt unter dem sanften Scepter der glorreichen Kaiserin Catharina *blühende Petersburg* darauf anzulegen. Wo ein Churfürst Friederich der dritte einen Platz um *Berlin* antraf, darauf die Stadt aufzuführen, die unter den Händen noch grösserer Nachfolger *die Königin der Städte in Europa* geworden. Wo Friederich der fünfte, wie vor Zeiten August zu Rom, *die Ziegelsteine der Stadt Copenhagen in Marmor verwandelte*; und wo Philipp Carl, *Mannheim zur regelmässigsten Stadt der Welt*, und ein glorwürdiger *Wilhelm von Cassel die französische Neustadt zum Model neuer Colonien machte*; da waren Felder und Plätze, wo Plane zu schönen Städten ausgeführet werden konnten. Aber auch da, wo die schöpferischen Geister Josephs des Allgeliebten [Emperor Joseph II], Friedrich des Helden [Frederick

II of Prussia], und des königlich denkenden und handelnden Carl von Braunschweig ; oder da, wo der auf den Britten ruhende *Römische Geist in London*, wie dort in *Wien, Potsdam* und *Braunschweig*, alte Städte zu neuen schönen Wohnungen umschaffen, da siehet man Städte *in grösserer Volkommenheit, als sie mein Abriss in folgenden Blättern schildert.*"

21 "Dieser Endzweck (des Staates; MB) ist die gemeinschaftliche Glückseligkeit.": Johann Heinrich Gottlob von Justi, "Kurzer systematischer Grundriss aller Oeconomischen und Cameralwissenschaften (1759)," in *Gesammlete politische und Finanzschriften über wichtige Gegenstände der Staatskunst, der Kriegswissenschaften und des Cameralund Finanzwesens, vol. 1/3* (Copenhagen: Rothensche Buchhandlung 1761/64), 504–73, 505; see also: Ulrich Engelhardt, "Zum Begriff der 'Glückseligkeit' in der kameralistischen Staatslehre des 18. Jahrhunderts (J.H.G. von Justi)," *Zeitschrift für Historische Forschung* 8 (1981): 37–79, 47–48: "Nach Justi und … nach Auffassung fast aller Kameralisten liegt der 'Endzweck des Staats' bzw. Gemeinwesens in der Tat in der 'gemeinschaftlichen Glückseligkeit' der (als Einheit begriffenen) 'Untertanen und des gesamten Staats.'"

22 Engelhardt, (see note 21), 40.

23 Engelhardt, (see note 21), 41.

24 Simon, (see note 17), 511.

25 "Diejenigen, welche glauben, dass die Zufriedenheit auch bei der blossen Notdurft des Lebens glücklich machen könne, verwechseln diesen Begriff mit glückselig. Man kann alsden glücklich, aber nicht glücklich sein." Johann Heinrich Gottlob von Justi, *Gesammlete politische und Finanzschriften, vol. 3/3,* (see note 21), 27–28 cited from Engelhardt, (see note 21), 61.

26 "Die Kameralistik kann daher in zweifacher Hinsicht als bemerkenswerter Indikator verstanden werden: 1. für die *allgemeine Säkularisierung* der Lebens- und Staatszweckauffassung im 'Zeitalter der Aufklärung' und 2. für die eingangs erwähnte Steigerung *staatlicher*

Wohlfahrtskompetenz im politischen System 'des' aufgeklärten Absolutismus.": Engelhardt, (see note 21), 43 (accentuation in italics according to original source). Simon, (see note 17), 514–15, differentiates this perspective (516 in particular).

27 "In bisher unbekanntem Ausmass wurde der Staat für 'technische Planung' verfügbar.": Engelhardt, (see note 21), 45.

28 Simon, (see note 17), 14.

29 Foucault, *Geschichte der Gouvernementalität I*, (see note 7), 470 in particular.

30 This is an abstract of a more detailed and extended sequence of paragraphs in: Willebrand, *Grundriss I*, (see note 5), 3–23.

31 "Die Subordination ist endlich die Seele einer jeden guten bürgerlichen Einrichtung, mithin noch eine der wichtigsten Erfordernisse einer guten Stadt.": Willebrand, *Grundriss I*, (see note 5), 17.

32 "Welche Form eine neue Stadt haben müsse, und wie eine Stadt durch Gassen abgetheilet werden soll, oder in wie viele Bezirke man sie abtheilen will, dieses ist so willkührlich für denjenigen Beherrscher, der es befiehlet, eine Stadt zu bauen und anzulegen, dass es sehr überflüssig und nichts bedeutend sein würde, hievon etwas anzuführen. Dieses aber darf ich noch wohl erinnern, dass ihrer Natur nach eine Stadt, welche in der Ründe liegt, allem Ansehen nach für die Bewohner bequemer seyn muss, als eine ins Gevierte oder in der Länge erbauete Stadt.": Willebrand, *Grundriss I*, (see note 5), 126.

33 Marc-Antoine Laugier, *Essai sur L'Architecture* (Paris: Duchesne, ²1755 [1753]), 222.

34 "… schnur gerade und regelmässig … Ueberhaupt aber ist es eine Regel, dass die Gassen in einer Stadt einem durchgehauenen Thiergarten ähnlich sehen müssen, dessen Hauptwege alle auf einen grossen regelmässigen Mittelplatz zu führen pflegen.": Willebrand, *Grundriss I*, (see note 5), 127.

35 "Starke Mauern und dauerhafte Vestungswerke können durch eine grössere Macht umgeworfen und überwältiget werden; Aufrichtigkeit aber und Gerechtigkeit bevestigen den innern Frieden einer Stadt, und erwecken das Vertrauen der Nachbaren.": Willebrand, *Grundriss I*, (see note 5), 9-10.

36 Sandl, (see note 18), 73–91, for *Stadt-* and *Landwirthschaft* see: 83–84.

37 Willebrand, *Grundriss I*, (see note 5), 32–35.

38 Willebrand, *Grundriss I*, (see note 5), 166–178.

39 "Weise Vorgesetzte einer Stadt erkennen also nur den Zuwachs zu Beförderung der *Glückseligkeit* ihrer Gesellschaft für rüchtig, der aus Menschen bestehet, die durch ihren Fleiss und Vermögen der gemeinen Wohlfahrt erspriesslich sind, und die sich durch obrigkeitliche Anordnungen die Gränzen willig bestimmen lassen, wodurch Ruhe und Eintracht unterhalten werden. Es dürfte mir unmöglich fallen, alle Arten der Menschen zu nennen, die geschickt sind, diesen Endzweck in der bürgerlichen Gesellschaft zu befördern; inzwischen werde ich mich befleissigen, sie unten nach bestem Vermögen zu classificiren." Willebrand, *Grundriss II*, (see note 5), 10.

40 "Der Genuss der gesetzlichen Freyheit unterscheidet glückliche Bürger von elenden Sclaven, die in Ketten des Despoten seufzen: und diese Freyheit muss man jeden Fremden von einer Stadt versichern können; weil die *Versicherung von Freyheit und Eigenthum* sehr empfehlend ist.": Willebrand, *Grundriss II*, (see note 5), 20–21.

41 Willebrand, *Grundriss II*, (see note 5), 2.

42 For *Gemütsruhe*: Willebrand, *Grundriss II*, (see note 5), 188–207.

43 "Ferner, dass ich nie in Städten unvollkommener Menschen vollständige Einrichtungen erwarte.": Willebrand, *Grundriss I*, (see note 5), Vorbericht, fol. 3.

44 Mascha Bisping, "'Manufaktur' oder 'Garten'. Krefeld im Prozess der Verlandschaftung zwischen kameralistischer und liberalistischer Raumordnung" in *Räume der Stadt - Von der Antike bis heute*, ed. Cornelia Jöchner (Berlin: Reimer, 2008), 199–220.

THE CHANGING PATTERN

of Urban Form in Relation
to the Perception of Happiness
in Georgian Birmingham

Mohsen Aboutorabi,
Andreas Wesener

Introduction

This paper examines the urban development of Birmingham in relation to the changing social, economic and cultural environment in the context of the city during the eighteenth and early nineteenth centuries. It raises the question of whether these changes corresponded to a particular notion of happiness, and how this notion was perceived and interpreted by the different social actors in Georgian Birmingham. The expansion of industrial development and the economic growth during the eighteenth century have been associated with the city's social structure: the emergence of a working and middle class alongside the affluent.

The pursuit of happiness could be recognised among all social classes, but it was perceived differently by each social group. While amongst the working and lower middle classes access to work, urban well-being, and the opportunity to start up as independent small industrial masters were indicators of social ascent and personal growth, the upper middle class had aspirations for social status through moderate prosperity and privileges such as spatial separation from the polluted and overcrowded industrial quarters. The third social group, referred to as the affluent class in this paper, had attained their privileges through professional accomplishments rather than hereditary rights. Although they did not formally belong to the upper class, their exceptional success distinguished them from the upper middle class in terms of social status, wealth, and political influence. Their protagonists—personalities such as Matthew Boulton, James Watt, or Joseph Priestley—had achieved prominent status through their involvement in industrial activity, technological progress, and partly through their influential activity within the Lunar Society. They enjoyed their uniqueness by following widely accepted ideals based on Greek and Roman virtues, and their status was represented by their properties, situated in pleasant and quiet suburban areas separated from the lower classes.

The paper suggests that the perception of happiness, interpreted and applied in different ways by the dominant social classes, had an increasing influence on the development and changing pattern of urban form in Georgian Birmingham. While the upper middle and the affluent classes used their financial means to establish residences outside the city, the working and lower middle class continued to live next to their industrial work places. However, the expansion of industrial activity transformed the social geography of the city to a great extent.

THE GEORGIAN PERIOD

The Georgian Period in Britain (1714–1830) commenced with the accession of George I (1660–1727) as King of Great Britain and Ireland on 1 August 1714 and ended with the death of George IV in 1830. Although the period is defined by the reign of four kings, important socioeconomic processes such as industrialisation, the emergence of new social classes and the rapid growth of population, started before 1714 and continued far into the

Victorian Age. The sociopolitical environment of the Georgian Period was characterised by violent events such as political rebellions (Jacobite uprisings in 1715–16 and 1745–46), frequent riots due to bad social conditions, and wars with France and Spain (Napoleonic wars 1793–1815). Britain was about to become a world power, the leading nation in terms of economic and military force with world-wide trade connections. The growing demand for industrial workers made people leave the rural areas to try their luck in the new industrial cities. In pursuit of job opportunities offered under the worst conditions men, women, and children worked long hours in mines and factories. The living environment of the new working class was dominated by poor housing, a lack of proper sanitation, which frequently caused the spread of epidemic diseases, and hunger due to economic slumps and the increasing costs of war. The Georgian cities have been described as places of cruelty and indifference:

> Crowds went to watch the execution of criminals, and death was the penalty for many offences which would now be considered trivial. Other entertainments were the baiting of animals, cockfighting, and even observing the behaviour of lunatics in Bedlam. Gin was cheap, and squalid addiction to it was not uncommon.[1]

The affluent class developed a preference for the cultural, social and political model of the Athenian democracy and the Roman Republic. This may have been rooted in a general distaste for absolutist France or a romanticised vision of ancient virtues, perceived by the educated citizens through their study of Greek and Roman classical literature.[2] However, the rejection of the prevailing European style influenced by French taste, especially Baroque and Rococo, allowed Georgian design to emerge as "self-consciously anti-European."[3] For the 'proper' Georgian citizen, who had the privilege of living away from the pollution and poverty of the overcrowded industrial areas, and had butlers, cooks, housemaids, housekeeper and several other servants,[4] social ideals might have been a topic for intellectual discussion amongst gentlemen, while those without financial means found themselves in a situation similar to that of the Athenian slaves.[5] Industrialisation and the rapid growth of the urban population created a massive demand for new property development and a promise of good profits for speculative builders, so that "beneath the high ideal of the Georgian City there lay a reality that was hard-headed, sometimes sordid, and almost always concerned with money."[6] While the Georgian elite romanticised the political and social ideals of an ancient society, their cities were developed by speculative builders in response to a property market situation based on the demands of the Industrial Revolution and its protagonists.

PERCEPTION OF HAPPINESS

Happiness, as a state of mind, is difficult to define. We often experience it as an intangible quality, or, as "an abstraction out of reach of measurement or calculation … It depends in a great measure on temperament, on the capability of enjoyment, on the depth or shallowness of each individual's philosophy."[7] One possible methodological approach to categorise the different aspects of happiness is the focus on factors that determine the subjective perception of life satisfaction. Happiness is hereby related to a favourable balance of pleasure and pain. The evaluation is based on the self-assessment of feelings and it focuses on factors that determine individual pleasure and satisfaction.[8] Another possible approach to happiness is related to personal growth and the notion of a 'good life.' The ancient Greek philosophers agreed that "happiness is mostly, if not totally, dependent on the choices we make in life"[9] with the consequence that the degree of happiness depends on how we appraise our own decisions and how our choices are valorised by others. Athenian society broadly identified six aspects (goods) that were needed for a happy life: financial property, physical well-being, social status, good fortune, fairness and courage, and wisdom.[10] At least four of these six aspects depend on one's own choices in life and, in the best case, making the right choices would lead to happiness as defined by quality of life in terms of financial and social status, character development, and intellectual growth.

The Athenian definition of happiness can be associated with a more recent concept, the theory of basic needs, known as Maslow's Pyramid.[11] Here, a hierarchy of physiological and psychological needs is defined in relationship to the basic desires humans generally seek to satisfy. These include basic physiological and safety needs such as food, water, air, security, shelter, stability, etc., and growth needs such as love and belongingness, self-esteem and self-fulfilment including truth, individuality, and meaningfulness. Maslow's theory is loosely based on Aristotle's conception of happiness,[12] but he criticises certain aspects of it, such as the acceptance of slavery and the assumption that a slave would have a slave-like nature and therefore accept his destiny.[13] From the affluent Georgian citizen's point of view, this particular aspect of Aristotle's conception might even have reassured him in his belief in a political and social ideal which justified his exposed social position and supported "… the common notion, that the happy man lives well and does well …."[14]

This raises the question of whether personal growth as a possible interpretation of happiness had an influence on the socioeconomic development in Birmingham during the Georgian period and whether this influence effected the development and changing pattern of urban form. Personal growth has been associated with economic prosperity and social status, and all social classes seem to have shared this particular interpretation. However, only the affluent classes had the financial means to achieve an extended understanding of the 'good life' described in Maslow's concept of self-fulfilment. The study of the classics became a familiar intellectual task for the educated Georgian citizen, and ancient Greece enjoyed widespread popularity.[15] Economic prosperity enabled the affluent class to go beyond the basic notion of personal growth and to live in response to widely accepted moral and aesthetic standards. This might have helped them to perceive their lives as meaningful and fulfilling.

The Pursuit of Happiness and its Influence on Socioeconomic Processes and the Development of Urban Form in Birmingham

THE DEVELOPMENT OF THE MANUFACTURING INDUSTRY

Birmingham has a long history in metal manufacturing and early traces of this industry, which has become so intrinsically connected with the city's development, can be found in early fourteenth century sources in which the 'Birmingham Pieces' are mentioned.[16] Several reasons for the early development of the metal manufacturing industry have been suggested, including the availability of iron ore and coal from the nearby mines in South Staffordshire and East Worcestershire, the lack of a charter and the absence of privileged guilds, the existing tradition and skills in working with iron, the long-established trading connections with London, and Birmingham's central position which enabled manufacturers to recruit immigrant labour from the surrounding areas.[17] During the sixteenth and seventeenth centuries, two of the industries that were later to dominate in Birmingham started to bloom: the gun manufacturing industry and the toy industry (the manufacture of small metal items), which was the predecessor of the famous jewellery industry. Nevertheless, Birmingham remained comparably small; the big expansions in terms of industrial production and urban development came with the onset of the Industrial Revolution in Britain at the beginning of the eighteenth century.

The estimated population growth in Birmingham from 11,400 inhabitants in 1720 to 52,250 inhabitants in 1785[18] reflects the growth of industry and the need for labour at that time. Unlike other industrial centres, such as Manchester or Leeds, Birmingham's metal industry did not grow on the basis of new technological innovations or the introduction of large factory systems. Birmingham's industry was mainly based on a large number of small-scale workshops and highly specialised manual labour.[19] The majority of workers were employed by small- and medium-sized companies.[20] Industry cumulated in areas which had already been the centre of metal manufacturing since medieval times: the city centre and the areas around Digbeth and Deritend, south of the centre. At the beginning of the eighteenth century migration from the surrounding countryside increased rapidly. The promise of finding a job in the fast-growing metal manufacturing industry made many young men, often with their families, leave the countryside in order to escape poverty and to seek new perspectives for a better life. In this period, new social classes emerged: a lower middle class, mostly industrialists who owned small and medium-sized family enterprises; and a working class, often skilled in metal manufacturing, to provide the necessary labour force for the new industries. During the eighteenth century, both classes lived and worked together next to their workplaces in the overcrowded central areas of Birmingham. The small-scale, family-owned workshops prevented social differences between the small industrialists and the skilled workers from arising. This particular quality of Birmingham's industry continued far into the nineteenth century.[21]

1

THE EMERGENCE OF THE RESIDENTIAL GEORGIAN SUBURB

In the first half of the eighteenth century, the situation in the overcrowded industrial areas of the city centre had worsened due to the precarious sanitary conditions for both workers and small entrepreneurs. In 1713, the landowner John Pemberton released land for a new residential development which included a Georgian square—'The Square'—and several new streets (▶ 1). Industrial use was prohibited by covenants attached to the leases. This prevented the migration of small industrialists from the overcrowded industrialised central areas into the first Georgian suburb, since their domestic-cum-industrial units were not permitted.[22] The attempt to exclude the industrial lower middle class from the amenities of a new and quiet suburban neighbourhood increased the social status of those who were able to move there. It can be assumed that the upper middle class—lawyers, doctors, merchants, etc.—manifested their privileged position by escaping from the unhealthy conditions of an industrial environment and by keeping their distance from the small masters, their workers and their accompanying businesses. To live in a pleasant environment among other members of their privileged social class was perceived as a favourable condition, with the consequence that a growing industry was obliged to remain in its original overcrowded confinements. Thus the development of urban form was controlled by one particular privileged social group, their needs and their perception of a 'good life'.

1   Birmingham, 'The Square' (now 'Old Square'), engraving by William Westley, ca. 1730.

In the seventeen-thirties and seventeen-forties, two new large estate developments became suitable for industrial settlements: Weaman Estate or St. Mary's district—later known as the Gun Quarter—and Colmore Estate, which would become the Jewellery Quarter by the end of the eighteenth century. Although both new developments were originally designed as residential suburbs for the wealthier classes, the lack of restrictive covenants[23] created an opportunity for small industrialists. These small masters, who belonged to the metal or gun manufacturing industries, migrated to St Mary's district immediately after its opening.[24] Westley's map of Birmingham (▶ 2), dated 1731, illustrates the medieval core around St. Martin's church, the industrial core areas in Digbeth and Deritend, the new St. Philip's cathedral with its surrounding residential settlements, and the new Georgian quarter around 'The Square,' marked in dark-grey. St. Mary's district, north of 'White Hall' can be observed in the early stages of its development with a few leases of land already built upon. The lease-holders were under obligation to build their own houses, and the lack of restrictions for industrial use allowed the immediate erection of domestic premises with adjacent workshops in the gardens to the rear.[25]

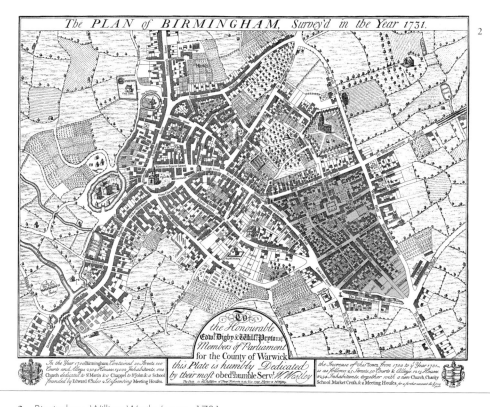

2 Birmingham, William Westley's map, 1731.

The second new development, the Colmore Estate, released a large plot of land by a private act of Parliament in 1746.[26] The land was divided into plots for houses with small frontages (4.6 meters) and large gardens,[27] and as in St. Mary's district, the lack of restrictions for industrial purposes encouraged a residential-cum-industrial development with domestic houses to the front and added workshops in the gardens to the rear.[28] Colmore Estate was a typical Georgian development, like many others in Britain at that time, based on a rectangular grid with regular plots of land for building leases and a new square around St. Paul's church.

THE SYSTEM OF BUILDING LEASES AND SPECULATIVE BUILDING

The system of building leases had been introduced by Lord Southampton in the seventeenth century to develop Bloomsbury Square in London, and it became a common method for building town houses in the Georgian Period. Lease-holders could build houses for themselves or third parties by paying a ground rent to the landowner. The property would be returned to the owner after the lease expired. Proprietors received a regular rent while builders could speculate on a quick profit after completing the basic construction.[29] They would build the load-bearing structure of the house as quickly as possible, design the façade with the help of predetermined patterns, and sell the house to its new occupier who could then design the interior according to his own taste. Despite the rapid increase in population in the eighteenth century and the concomitant demand for new buildings, this system was not without risk for the builder. Housing slumps or the emergence of negative reputations in particular areas could make properties unmarketable, leaving speculative builders with unfinished houses and debts.[30] In Birmingham, this happened to the speculative builder of Birmingham Crescent, a stylish Georgian townhouse development designed by John Rawsthorne and Charles Norton, where construction began in 1795. The builder went bankrupt after he had constructed a few buildings because the area had become unfashionable.[31] The building was left uncompleted and later abandoned.

THE DEVELOPMENT OF COLMORE ESTATE AND ST. MARY'S DISTRICT

The building leases of the Colmore Estate[32] reveal that building activity must have started immediately after the new estate was released, and that some of the new building leases were taken by small industrialists who built their own houses for residential purposes along the streets with workshops in the gardens to the rear.[33] The remainder of the leases went to speculative builders, for example bricklayers. For the small industrialists, the main motivation for moving into the new quarter was a wish to escape from the overcrowded central areas in order to gain more space for themselves, their families, and their businesses. The concept of 'domestic-cum-industrial' mixed land use was of great importance for business development and enabled small industrialists to live next to their manufacturing businesses. For them, the separation of living and working space was either not affordable or not practical. Those who could afford to move away and live outside the industrial areas did so. Their higher social status was reflected in the location, size, and quality of their homes reflecting their distinctive position and status in society. From the seventeen-seventies onwards the further development of the Colmore estate, especially around St. Paul's Square, reflects the endeavours of Birmingham's elite to live at a distance from the growing number of low-status domestic and industrial buildings that had stretched out in the previous three decades over a larger area in the southern part of Colmore Estate.[34] The section of Bradford's 1751 map (▶ 3) illustrates the embryonic state of the two new Georgian Quarters, still without the squares and churches. Colmore Estate lies in the south-west area of Snow Hill; only five years after its release new streets had already been built and building activities begun on numerous new plots of land. To the northeast of Snow Hill the new St. Mary's district started to grow, but the comparison of land use between 1731 and 1751 reveals that building activ-

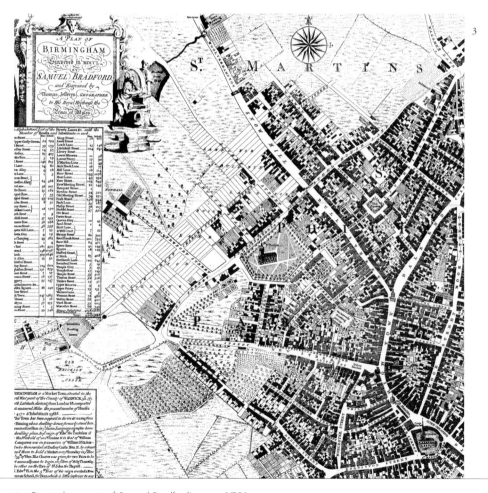

3   Birmingham, part of Samuel Bradford's map, 1751.

ity must have slowed down. The depicted part of Hanson's 1778 map (▶ 4) illustrates the spread of industry throughout the southern part of the two new quarters. Two new churches and squares—St. Paul's and St. Mary's—and an expanded rectangular grid of new streets are already displayed.

THE PURSUIT OF HAPPINESS FOR THE AFFLUENT AND UPPER MIDDLE CLASSES

In the northern part of Colmore estate, members of the affluent class were able to pursue their concept of happiness. Aristotle had considered property as a prerequisite of personality and a fundamental quality for leading a 'good life.' The Greek household (*oikos*) provided authority and autonomy, necessary conditions to develop 'virtue' and to act within the political and social sphere. Possession was not so much considered as an economic asset, but as a sign of citizenship.[35] The other cultural ideal of the Georgian era was the Roman

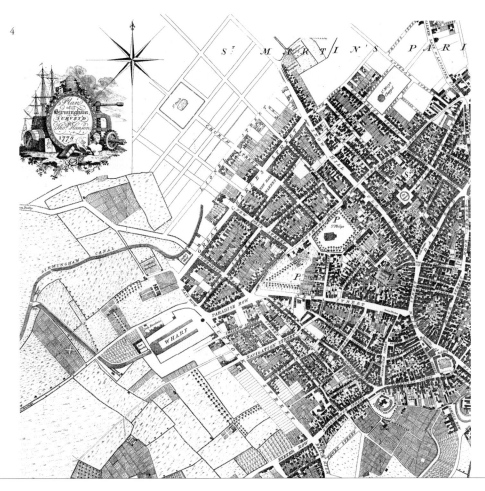

4

4   Birmingham, part of Thomas Hanson's map, 1778.

Republic and the type of residence considered appropriate for the qualified citizen was the detached villa within a rural or suburban environment. The Western-Roman tradition, continued from Aquinas to Locke, understood property not only as a prerequisite of personality but as a natural right; something characteristic of the person who owned it. This particular relationship between right and ownership made property legally important for political relationships and the notion of the 'good life': "Since the law defined justice in terms of *suum cuique*, it was possible to define the good life in terms of property relations, or of human relations as the notion of property served to define them …"[36] The country house and the "villa type, associated with Pliny"[37] became a symbol of social status in terms of prosperity, taste, virtue, and rights; a place where the owner could offer hospitality, cultivate friendships, and enjoy his leisure time. These early suburban villa developments reflect the attempt of affluent citizens to live in pleasant surroundings away from industry but within commuting distance of their businesses.[38] The owner of such a house had achieved wealth, status and good fortune by making the right choices in life. He lived in a healthy

5 Birmingham, Georgian townhouses, 12–14 St. Paul's Square, photograph 2008.

6

environment and showed taste, intellectual capacity, and political power by living according to the standards of an idealised and widely accepted model of the perfect society. Surviving examples of this type of building, now mostly surrounded by industrial extensions, can be found in the Jewellery Quarter; for example, in Frederick Street, Camden Street, and Summer Hill Terrace.

While the suburban villa remained a privilege of the affluent class, successful professional middle-class families such as doctors, lawyers, or merchants pursued their concept of happiness in townhouse developments around the new St. Paul's Square and the streets adjacent to it.[39] The idea of the quiet, socially homogeneous suburban neighbourhood at a distance from the polluted industrial or domestic-cum-industrial developments seems to have been the dominating reason for the upper middle class to settle in the new quarter. The size of these townhouses was moderate, and the formal design conventions were restrained and reflected the moral and aesthetic values of the time and therefore the social status of its inhabitants. Nos. 12–14 (▶ 5) and 35 St. Paul's Square are surviving examples of Georgian middle-class townhouses in Birmingham. "The desire of each level of society to ape the one above it made the pursuit of gentility a moral virtue and helped to raise and maintain standards of design."[40] Personal growth in the form of social status was seen as a primary objective. This did not only require financial success and material wealth, but also achievements that reflected the ideal of an elegant and well-mannered society, including the knowledge and appreciation of the formal values which were widely recognised as 'taste.' Like charity, 'taste' was perceived as a universal and essential virtue, an ideal derived from three concepts:

6   Birmingham, Jewellery Quarter, two-storey workshop range added to the rear of a former house at No. 45 Warstone Lane, photograph 1999.

decorum, conformity, and tradition.[41] The definition of 'taste' remained deliberately vague as part of an exclusive culture considered and understood only by those with the "most re-fined intellect and sensibility."[42] This helped—at least in the case of Palladianism—to keep cultural authority within a small group of elitist connoisseurs. However, this exclusive claim could not be retained for long; with the publication and widespread use of design manuals and pattern books, Georgian design and architecture became a mass market product widely accepted by all social classes. The underlying design principles became comprehensible and well known, so that they could be easily applied by any builder.[43]

THE PURSUIT OF HAPPINESS FOR THE LOWER, MIDDLE, AND WORKING CLASSES

After the release of the two new estates, Birmingham's size rapidly increased and, unlike other industrial towns in Britain such as Manchester, there were no visible signs of housing shortage despite the massive growth in population. Between 1781 and 1791 the population grew by about 46 per cent, but the newly-built housing stock had an even higher growth rate at about 51 per cent: "In this period the town greatly expanded itself south-eastwards as far as, and beyond, the River Rea; nearly all the remaining land on the main block of the Colmore Estate on the north-west of the town was covered with houses."[44] The first census data from 1801 lists 73,670 inhabitants,[45] which represents a population growth of almost 500 per cent compared to the estimated number of 15,032 at the beginning of the eighteenth century.[46] In most areas, restrictions in terms of building control did not exist, and the only attempt to influence the quality and design of the new houses was concerned with the minimum amount to be spent on construction, the number of storeys and the alignment along the streets.[47]

The lack of restrictions for industrial activity made small industrialists and their workers move into those areas which were originally intended as residential neighbourhoods for wealthier citizens. Small and medium industrial masters erected modest semi-detached or terraced houses for themselves and their families with workshops to the rear (▶ 6), and the number of these dwellings was a reflection of the increased industrial growth in the area.[48] The growing number of workers lived close to their work places, due to the lack of transport links. This led to the development of enclosed courtyards behind the front of terraced hous-es with groups of low-quality back-to-back houses along the boundaries. The working class could not afford to move away from the industrial areas. Many of them lived in poor sani-tary conditions and in overcrowded houses, often inhabiting only one room with the entire family. They were casual unemployed labourers, and often perceived as frightening, drunk, and anti-social by the wealthier part of the population.[49] For the majority of small industri-alists and workers, the definition of happiness as "… living a truly fulfilling and meaningful life"[50] would have sounded rather cynical, considering the fact that their basic physiological and safety needs were hardly satisfied. Nevertheless, the possibility of economic and social success did also arise among skilled workers in the metal and jewellery industries, with the opportunity to start their own businesses. The initial investment in machinery was relatively low, and new masters could use parts of their domestic premises, such as attics, outbuildings within courtyards, or back rooms, for industrial purposes.[51] With the economic boom in the eighteen-thirties and a growing specialisation process, the number of small businesses increased as specialised workers left their masters in order to set up their own companies.[52] This entrepreneurial spirit amongst the working class reflects their aspiration to improve their socioeconomic situation through personal growth. They made their own choices to achieve economic stability, social status, and perhaps a meaningful life.

THE SOCIAL AND PHYSICAL TRANSFORMATION OF THE NEW GEORGIAN QUARTERS

Both new Georgian quarters, Colmore Estate and St. Mary's district, went through a physical and social transformation when industry spread into the wealthier residential areas from the late eighteenth century onwards. This created, at least at the early stage of the process, a mixed-use, socially diverse neighbourhood where the wealthier residents started to live in the midst of a growing industrial landscape of factories, workshops, and workers' houses.[53] The villas of the affluent class, protected by their surrounding gardens, "were able to survive

7   Birmingham, Heaton House, Camden Street, surrounded by industry, photograph 1999.

8   Birmingham, part of Pigott-Smith's map, 1828.

for a time as oases of gentility, as examples of *rus in urbe*, which express the idea of gracious living within an urban context."[54] However, the difference in income, social class, and lifestyle made the affluent classes leave their quarters and move on into newly developed residential suburbs such as Edgbaston. In St. Mary's district, the majority of leases were taken by small industrialists; in response to the high demand for industrial premises, the conversion of houses into workshops began within a short period of time. Industrialisation contributed to the social decline of the area and the departure of the wealthier residents by the end of the eighteenth century.[55] The wealthy northern parts of Colmore Estate went through a similar process half a century later. The idyllic resorts of the affluent classes were literally surrounded by industry, and detached villas were incorporated into industrial estates. An example of this development is Heaton House, built around 1823 for William Cotterill, a Birmingham merchant, which is closed in by industrial buildings (▶ 7).

The depicted section of Pigott-Smith's 1828 map (▶ 8) illustrates the growth of the new quarters, marked in dark-grey, by the end of the Georgian Period. It is noticeable that the rectangular street layout from the eighteenth century had not been continued as originally planned. This could be linked with landownership issues, but changing fashions may also have played a part. From the late eighteenth century onwards, 'natural layouts' and curved building geometries such as the 'Crescent' became popular in Britain.[56] Domestic-cum-industrial premises, recognisable through the long workshop extensions in the rear gardens, had spread from the south into the wealthy areas. The detached villas of the affluent class are situated to the north and west of Colmore Estate along Summer Hill Terrace, Camden Street and Frederick Street.

Conclusion

The paper has analysed the economic and social development of Birmingham during the Georgian period by asking if and how the perception of happiness influenced the development and changing pattern of urban form. The Georgian era was marked by rapid industrialisation, a massive growth in the urban population and the emergence of a new social class system. The ancient Greek concept of a 'good life' was explored and its similarities with a more recent interpretation, Maslow's theory of basic needs, were discussed. The concept considers personal growth in terms of prosperity, physical well-being, social status, and self-realisation as a possible interpretation of happiness. The educated citizens' familiarity with the classics and their admiration for ancient Greek and Roman virtues as a utopian ideal were considered as indications for an extended understanding of personal growth beyond financial means.

The development of Birmingham's first Georgian quarter incorporated explicit aspects of social segregation: the prohibition of industrial activity prevented the lower social classes from moving into the new suburb. The confirmation of social status through spatial segregation was regarded as an exclusive privilege of the affluent and upper middle classes. The detailed analysis of two new Georgian quarters—Colmore Estate and St. Mary's district—showed that these were originally planned in a similar way as the first Georgian suburb. However, the absence of restrictions for industrial use allowed the lower middle and working classes to pursue their own ambitions. Amongst these classes, basic deficiency needs had to be satisfied first, before aspirations for personal growth led them to attempt to achieve economic solidity, independence and social status. This could be observed when workers sought independence by leaving the employment of their masters to start up their own businesses, and this was reflected by their modest domestic-cum-industrial properties. The upper middle class expressed themselves through moderate and restrained townhouse developments at a distance from the lower social classes to indicate their higher social status. The affluent class had already achieved economic prosperity and manifested its status in terms of social segregation, taste, education, virtue and rights in large villa-type properties in the suburban residential areas of Birmingham. They were in a position to interpret personal growth beyond its basic notion in terms of truth, individuality, perfection, order and meaningfulness, based on widely accepted virtues during the Georgian era.

The pursuit of happiness in terms of personal growth and the 'good life' emerged throughout all social classes. It was perceived and interpreted by different actors in accordance with their individual aspirations in terms of economic prosperity, social status, and self-realisation, with a direct influence on the development of urban form in Birmingham. This development was not characterised by distinctive urban design or planning strategies. Social phenomena such as the idealisation of ancient Greek and Roman virtues neither resulted in *Leitbild*-oriented or utopian urban models, nor in significant interferences by the government or local authorities. Urban development in Georgian Birmingham was based on socioeconomic processes related to the needs and aspirations of the different actors on the property market. The detached villas of the affluent and the residential townhouses of the upper middle class demonstrate the endeavour of an affluent minority to display their social position. However, the lack of planning restrictions and the successful performance of a less affluent majority resulted in the spread of industry into the wealthy residential neighbourhoods, making the upper middle and affluent classes leave the area. The historical maps of Birmingham illustrate the social and physical transformation of two Georgian quarters; the surviving streets and buildings in the Jewellery Quarter in Birmingham are the silent witnesses of the great economic and social changes influenced by the pursuit of happiness among the different social classes.

51

Endnotes

1 Kerry Downes, *The Georgian Cities of Britain* (Oxford: Phaidon, 1979), 23–24.

2 Downes, (see note 1), 16.

3 G. J. Ashworth, "The Georgian City: The Compact City as Idealised Past or Future Ideal," *Global Built Environment* 4 (2005:3): 41.

4 James Stevens Curl, *Georgian Architecture* (Newton Abbot: David & Charles, 2002), 189.

5 Downes, (see note 1), 22.

6 Downes, (see note 1), 6.

7 Thomas Colley Grattan, *Civilized America, Vol 1+2* (London: Bradbury and Evans, 1859), 312.

8 Daniel Kahneman, Amos Tversky, and Foundation Russell Sage, *Choices, Values, and Frames* (Cambridge: Cambridge University Press, 2000).

9 Raymond J. Devettere, *Introduction to Virtue Ethics: Insights of the Ancient Greeks* (Washington, D.C.: Georgetown University Press, 2002), 55.

10 Devettere, (see note 9), 87–88.

11 Frank G. Goble, *The Third Force: The Psychology of Abraham Maslow* (New York, Grossman, 1970), 50–67.

12 Aristotle and Drummond Percy Chase, *The Nicomachean Ethics of Aristotle.* (Oxford: Henry Hammans, 1861).

13 Goble, (see note 11), 67.

14 Percy Chase, (see note 12), 19.

15 R. M. Ogilvie, *Latin and Greek: A History of the Influence of the Classics on English Life from 1600 to 1918* (London: Routledge & Kegan Paul, 1964), 77.

16 Shena Mason, *Jewellery making in Birmingham 1750–1995* (Chichester: Phillimore, 1998), 2.

17 Eric Hopkins, *Birmingham: The First Manufacturing Town in the World, 1760—1840* (London: Weidenfeld & Nicolson, 1989), 4-5.

18 Hopkins, (see note 17), 118.

19 Hopkins, (see note 17), 35.

20 John Cattell, Sheila Ely and Barry Jones, *The Birmingham Jewellery Quarter: An Architectural Survey* (Swindon: English Heritage, 2002), 4.

21 Asa Briggs, *History of Birmingham Vol. II: Borough and City 1865–1938* (London: Oxford University Press, 1952), 55.

22 Margaret Hassall, "The Gun Quarter in Birmingham" (M.A. diss., University of Birmingham, 1997), 14.

23 D. M. Smith, "Birmingham's Gun Quarter and its Workshops," *The Journal of Industrial Archaeology* 1, (1964:2): 112.

24 M. J. Wise, "On the Evolution of the Jewellery and Gun Quarters in Birmingham," *Institute of British Geographers: Transactions and Papers* 15 (1949): 66.

25 Hassall, (see note 22), 14–15.

26 England. Parliament, *An Act to Impower Anne Colmore, Widow, and Her Assigns, During the Life of Thomas Colmore, Merchant, to Make Building-Leases of Land* (London: (20 Geo. II) c. 16 (Priv. Act), 1747).

27 C. W. Chalklin, *The Provincial Towns of Georgian England: A Study of the Building Process 1740–1820*, Studies in urban history (London: E. Arnold, 1974), 81.

28 Cattell/Ely/Jones, (see note 20), 4.

29 Downes, (see note 1), 41–42.

30 Curl, (see note 4), 172.

31 Downes, (see note 1), 52–53.

32 Colmore Family, ed., *Calendar of Deeds, Maps and Other Documents Relating to the Colmore Estates in Birmingham and Elsewhere in the County of Warwick and in the Counties of Gloucester and Salop, Compiled from the Originals* (Birmingham: Colmore Family, 1934).

33 Samuel Timmins, *The Resources, Products, and Industrial History of Birmingham, and the Midland Hardware District* (London: R. Hardwicke, 1866), 223.

34 Cattell/Ely/Jones, (see note 20), 8.

35 J.G.A. Pocock, *Virtue, Commerce, and History: Essays on Political Thought and History, Chiefly in the Eighteenth Century* (Cambridge: Cambridge University Press, 1985), 103.

36 Pocock (see note 35), 104.

37 Curl, (see note 4), 190.

38 Cattell/Ely/Jones, (see note 20), 11.

39 Cattell/Ely/Jones, (see note 20), 8–10.

40 Downes, (see note 1), 37–38.

41 Downes, (see note 1), 36–37.

42 Peter Borsay, *The English Urban Renaissance: Culture and Society in the Provincial Town, 1660–1770* (Oxford: Oxford University Press, 1989), 307.

43 Ashworth, (see note 3), 46.

44 Chalklin, (see note 27), 275.

45 Census of Great Britain, "Abstract, Presented to the House of Commons, of the Answers and Returns Made to the Population Act of 41st Geo.III &c," (London: British Parliamentary Press, 1801).

46 William Westley, *The Plan of Birmingham, survey'd in the year 1731* (Birmingham: T. Richards, 1789).

47 Chalklin, (see note 27), 89.

48 Cattell/Ely/Jones, (see note 20), 16.

49 Curl, (see note 4), 187.

50 Devettere, (see note 9), 52.

51 Hopkins, (see note 17), 57.

52 Cattell/Ely/Jones, (see note 20), 50.

53 Cattell/Ely/Jones, (see note 20), 23.

54 Cattell/Ely/Jones, (see note 20), 12.

55 Hassall, (see note 22), 22.

56 Downes, (see 1), 49–53.

"LIFE, LIBERTY, AND THE PURSUIT OF HAPPINESS"

Liberalism and the Image
of the City in German
Planning Theory around 1870

Christa Kamleithner

The self-perception of city and regional planning is mainly defined as representing a counterforce to the market. This particular image of urban planning evolved at the beginning of the twentieth century, when the municipalities started to intervene in market forces in order to solve the housing question. The planners saw themselves as "precursors of order in a world of laissez-faire,"[1] whereas a liberal policy had been the rule prior to their intervention. Gerd Albers describes these liberal beginnings in modern planning in the nineteenth century as "adjustment planning";[2] as a policy which, simply following urban development and concerned only with danger prevention, was not really creative. However, a distinction must be made between practice and theory, as planning theory certainly succeeded in creating a new image and model for the city. This model is a liberal one; rather than being conceived in opposition to the market, it opposes excessive planning, especially the outdated model of planning rooted in eighteenth-century absolutism and unable to cope with contemporary conditions. This new model embraces the main features of liberal economic development and attempts to provide them with a definite form. In his history of the beginnings of the new discipline, Werner Hegemann describes a "battle of order against chaos," referring to a "struggle between … a creative power not rooted in the new circumstances on the one hand, and on the other a new economic power that destroys old forms, yet is eager to create new ones."[3]

The concepts of liberalism and planning do not, in fact, oppose one another. The idea of laissez-faire never implied the entire absence of the state or other tools of order; both the eighteenth-century physiocrats who initially created the concept and the nineteenth-century advocates of free market policy believed in the necessity for a governmental framework enabling and enhancing free trade. The main goal was to restrict direct governmental interventions and allow a "natural" order to emerge—in contrast to the caprices of governing princes in earlier times or the imperfections of the apparatuses of the public authorities in the nineteenth century. All in all, liberal governance should be based upon an accurate knowledge of "reality"; the emergence of modern social sciences goes hand in hand with the idea of a liberal regime.[4] For some years, studies analysing liberal forms of government and their techniques have been evolving, following on from the work of Michel Foucault. This discourse could also be interesting for urban and planning history.[5] Based on these studies, the following text analyses the early theories of urban planning, with the aim of elaborating upon the liberal modes of argumentation and the image of the city they infer. Modern urban planning does not arise from opposition, but is founded on the basis of liberal thinking. It creates an image of the city based on the idea of free movement and the individual pursuit of happiness, which is considered possible to be scientifically explored.

A concise summary of the central values of Liberalism can be found in John Locke's triad "Life, liberty, and property," which was modified in the American Declaration of Independence to "Life, liberty, and the pursuit of happiness." Locke's concept reveals the complexity of political and economic liberalism. The term "property" here implies that every man has free possession of his own self and labour, as well as the material things incurred thereof. Besides this broad interpretation of "property," Locke also uses the term in the narrow sense of material property, in particular land ownership. Personal freedom and its material basis are seen as the preconditions for the individual pursuit of happiness.[6] Locke claims that human beings constantly strive to improve themselves and that the "desire of happiness" is inherent in the human state. This activity has its source in feelings of pleasure and displeasure, along with a prognostic rationality projecting these feelings into the future. This kind of happiness has nothing to do with moral categories per se, with virtuousness and doing the right thing; rather it arises from passions, interests and the satisfaction of defined and definable needs. Common welfare is seen not as contrary to, but as an unintended side-effect of the individual pursuit of happiness—a concept that has become familiar in the version formulated by Adam Smith. Of course, not everyone can fulfil the "desire of bettering our condition," which seems to be the natural character of (modern) man; nevertheless, according to Smith, it is the very inequality of living conditions that will lead to progress and growth, from which everyone will profit.[7]

Both the idea of private happiness and a modern right to property form the basis of modern urban planning, which emerged as a discipline at the end of the nineteenth century. Not only did the new discipline acknowledge the new social and economic situation, it even integrated the new conditions into its concept of the city. In the following, this development will be discussed on the basis of the writings of three early German theorists: Julius Faucher, Ernst Bruch, and Reinhard Baumeister, all of whom represent liberal modern thinking—albeit to different degrees—either explicitly or in keeping with the common sense of the time. The focus will be on theoretical developments in German-speaking countries which, as Anthony Sutcliffe pointed out, were important for the international planning movement as a whole.[8] The planning theories of that time do not make utopian promises of happiness; neither do they create urban visions detached from reality; nor do they mention "happiness" in a literal sense, but only speak of the requirements which, when fulfilled, generate happiness. The image of the city evoked by these authors is surprising when seen within the context of later developments in modern planning; it is dynamic and centred around the idea of differentiated social needs and attempts to incorporate these differences, step by step, into urban design. In the end, this process is specified in the form of zoning. In spite of certain differences, urban planning in the twentieth century welfare state is based on the image and model of the city developed in the late nineteenth century. In particular, however, there is a striking congruence with the neo-liberal modes of planning found today.

Julius Faucher and the Dynamic Image of the City

Julius Faucher was, unlike Ernst Bruch and Reinhard Baumeister, an important advocate of Liberalism and free trade in Germany. He was a journalist and worked in London for about ten years,[9] where he was able to closely observe the liberal fabric of the city which he admired and propagated as a desirable aim for urban planning in Germany. In a series of essays published in the *Vierteljahrschrift für Volkswirthschaft und Culturgeschichte*, a journal he himself founded, he presented his ideas for a housing reform, thereby outlining his concept for urban development. Between the lines he also provides a new image of the city altogether. As a journalist and economist, Faucher was not a typical exponent of urban planning. The beginnings of the discipline, however, are characterised by a plurality of approaches coming from different fields such as hygiene, economics and statistics. Faucher's ideas were introduced to the inner circle of urban design and planning by Bruch and Baumeister. They also play an important role in Werner Hegemann's classic study, which is considered to be a founding document of the discipline and continues to determine its historiography up until today.[10] Gerhard Fehl in particular pointed out Faucher's importance for the reform of German *Städtebau*.[11]

Faucher's considerations focus on London. There, unlike Berlin, urban boundaries had not been set; the agglomeration grew without a superimposed plan. The capitalisation of real estate was highly developed and large real estate syndicates were responsible for building entire new quarters, thus controlling urban production. Social and functional differentiation was already well advanced, the concentration of city functions as well as the social segregation of residential areas had already taken place. Such a spacious and differentiated structure was only made possible due to the expansion of the transport network, which was unparalleled by that found in any other European city. Although London was much larger than Berlin, it was striking that most of its inhabitants lived in single-family houses, which Faucher considered to be the "normal" way of life. For Berlin, the statistics indicated alarming numbers of people living together in densely built tenement blocks. Since the eighteen-sixties Berlin was growing at an accelerated tempo, land rents were on the rise, and not only the working classes but most of Berlin's population lived in rented flats, faced with oppressive rent charges. The construction of detached houses on the outskirts was only just beginning, reserved for an exclusive clientele. Although the monotony and misery of the English working-class quarters was well known, the fact that it was possible for families to live in a single-family house in a big modern city was esteemed by many planners and for this reason London was considered exemplary. Faucher's explanation is that in London, "where 'competition' and 'the force of capital' have been operative for a long time,"[12] the city was organised in a better and more cost-efficient way, based on the division of labour; here also a new type of modern man was emerging, one who accepted the necessity of commuting daily between his home and workplace and a more structured way of life.[13]

The core of Faucher's theory is the so-called "filter theory"—a term that he did not invent himself, but which is commonly used in the meantime.[14] Faucher notices that the inhabitants of London are more mobile than the inhabitants of other cities. Their choice of residence is not necessarily a permanent one, as they continue looking for the best living conditions according to their social advancement. His description may be based on observation, but it is primarily an abstract model of a dynamic urban organism that carries its inhabitants from the centre to the periphery and transforms itself from its borders. Faucher assumes that new, luxurious residential areas offering the best of living conditions are continually built on the perimeters of the city, unless this is prevented by planning or habits. Faucher's idea of man, which is evident in all his writings and especially here, apparently springs from classical liberal thinking. For Faucher the continual desire to better one's own condition, which appears to be a typical modern characteristic within the context of urban history and the history of housing, is seen as an anthropological constant. The opinion that the private pursuit of happiness will lead to the best for everybody is also a typically liberal view: properties vacated by the wealthy who move to the periphery would in turn be occupied by others seeking a better standard of living, whose houses in turn became vacant, and so on. The working classes should also profit from this continuous migration, although Faucher admits that his concept is not likely to include the very poor. Thus, the houses in London have a "rich and varied history of different uses";[15] on the one hand the old tradition of the single-family household is retained, but on the other the houses are seen as modern facilities, constantly circulating, not closely associated with the lives of their tenants.

What lessons can be learned from this, especially for nineteenth-century Berlin and its dense and crowded tenement blocks? In brief, Faucher believes that the situation in Berlin has arisen due to an imbalance between supply and demand. At the periphery there is a "monopolised ring of building sites," "which constrains new developments in all directions;" this "building site monopoly" causes rent prices to increase and forces the necessity for a high density of building and utilisation.[16] How does this monopoly emerge? One reason is that there is little demand; according to Faucher the long tradition of the walled city and the building style dating back to absolutism have created bad habits that block modern urban development; the natural impulse for improvement has been repressed. The fiscal system is especially to blame, as no fees are charged for public infrastructures—according to Faucher, this ignores the economic law of give and take.[17] Furthermore there was the dominating market position of the established landowners whose estates were kept off the market, resulting in a lack of supply. This is made possible by the fragmented structure of small building companies that are unable to act independently as large real estate and building syndicates could. What is Faucher's response to this? He recommends breaking through the constricting belt around the city and building new suburban quarters beyond the city boundaries; a role model for this could be Carstenn's exclusive residential areas near Hamburg and Berlin. This policy would break the monopoly, create competition and cause prices to fall. This would be feasible only for big building companies, which are in a position to wholly finance such suburban quarters and their infrastructures.[18]

At first sight, this seems to be an appeal against planning and in favour of the construction of the city within a free market system. However, it is not quite as simple as it seems; Liberalism should not be seen as the simple rejection of governmental control. In Faucher's theory, national or municipal authorities do in fact play a role, providing special public infrastructures charged for within an ordered tax structure, ensuring cost transparency[19]—the economic game requires a framework of taxes and laws to enforce and regulate it. Another task of public administration is to educate the population, thus improving the demand within the housing markets, for example by supporting building associations in establishing better models of housing and living.[20] Another important task for public administration in the field of urban development is the planning and maintenance of a public traffic system; the construction of railway lines should not lag behind urban development, but drive it forwards, Faucher claims.[21] Common prosperity based on the division of labour and economic growth, the main concept of Liberalism since Adam Smith, can only evolve if accepted traditions are abandoned and the dynamics of circulation are allowed to develop. Freedom and freedom of movement are not simply given facts, but provisions must be made for them. This means, for example, that a modern traffic system must be made available to ensure an efficient organisation of space.[22] Thus it is an essential task of a liberal planning practice to initiate the freedom of circulation and allow the emergence of a spontaneous order.

Differentiated, Gradual, and Unobtrusive Planning—Ernst Bruch and Reinhard Baumeister

Julius Faucher's perception of the modern city and its spatial organisation enter the discussions on planning via Ernst Bruch and Reinhard Baumeister, who play an important role in planning history;[23] indeed their writings are considered to provide the foundations of modern urban planning. They must be seen as "modern," particularly in connection with the "Hobrechtplan" for Berlin in 1862. This plan is characterised on the one hand by a liberal attitude—urban planning is restricted to differentiating between private and public spaces and to defining the position of streets and alignments, whereas the building development within these alignments is subject to few regulations and open to private speculation. On the other hand, however, the plan follows old urban patterns and traditions. It restricts itself to dictating the layout of the streets; nevertheless this layout is prearranged for the entire future city and set within clearly defined city limits. Therefore it ensures the development of a compact city with uniform façades, producing a city image rooted in the absolutist town planning of the eighteenth century. Of course, the "Hobrechtplan" does not attempt to create urban spaces with a complex geometry or a three-dimensional city fabric—the idea of the city as a work of art is hindered by an economic understanding of the city at the beginning of the nineteenth century.[24] Nevertheless it produces a homogeneous cityscape which corresponds to the eighteenth-century ideal of a rational order dominating over individual preferences as well as to the early liberal opinion that all landowners must be treated equally.

The simplicity and negativity of the "Hobrechtplan" directly opposes the positive approach of the new planning concepts, whose aim is to establish a new image and model of the city.[25]

The Berlin plan is seen by Bruch as a "straight-jacket,"[26] inhibiting the evolvement of the new city. It is not private capital, which the new concepts hold responsible for the densely built Berlin tenement blocks and the housing misery; in their eyes the culprit is the "building site monopoly," resulting from the "disgusting abuse of government."[27] "The police prescribes tenements for four million Berlin people," declares Hegemann, summing up the ideas of Faucher and Bruch.[28] All in all the "artificiality" of the planned cities created by the absolutist planning authorities and their successors in the nineteenth century is contrasted with the "naturalness" of old, "organically" grown towns, upon which the new cities are to be modelled,[29] enabling them to deal with different and changing requirements. At the end of the nineteenth century, social differentiation grows more acute and can no longer be ignored. Whereas James Hobrecht conceives his plan with an early liberal society and an economic system of small ownership in mind—already anachronistic at that time—Bruch, Baumeister, and modern urban planners design their city to cater for the multiple needs of a differentiated class society, and therefore they are interested in the differentiation of urban space.

The new planning concepts do not only criticise the miserable housing situation, but also the monotony of the Berlin tenement blocks and the "levelling" effect on the different uses and social classes caused by this type of building. An enquiring eye is able to discover some kind of urban "division of labour" in this homogenous structure, says Bruch, but it is not reflected in the architectonic form. Thus, all in all Bruch demands a correlation between urban use and building type.[30] Bruch and Baumeister clearly see that the modern city differentiates itself in a self-regulating way; they are aware of the concentration of city functions, the peripheral movement of industry and the mechanisms of land rent distribution. The "natural" form of the city seems to be a "flat cone shape"[31] with high rents and buildings in the centre and spacious low-rise buildings at the periphery. This "structural model," also present in Faucher's theory, can be traced back to economic theories, especially Thünen's model of land rent distribution,[32] which refers to farming practices but can also be applied to urban uses. On the other hand this distribution of building heights and densities can be observed empirically in many cities—although not in Berlin, however, where an outdated planning practice had prevented such a development. Ideal economic models as well as statistical analysis form the basis of the new city visions, which are not utopias, but strive to reproduce reality. It is not architects who design the new city, but economists such as Faucher and statisticians like Bruch, who comments on the Berlin plan with all the background knowledge of an official working in the municipal statistics bureau.[33]

Modern planning follows the creativity of the free market system, which does not produce an entirely chaotic city, but organises urban uses in a self-regulating way. Speculation tends to place like with like, Faucher claims; and this natural process of concentration and separation is useful, because a random mix of uses and social classes would result in trouble and dissonance.[34] So, which components and separations feature in "Bruch's functional city,"[35] which Baumeister adopted and left more or less unchanged? There would be industrial districts situated near railway lines or waterways at the urban periphery, where large pieces of land are available cheaply; then there would be business districts concentrated in the city centre; residential areas should have narrow streets and small blocks to enable the building of small houses and tenement blocks; and finally luxurious residential areas for the wealthier inhabitants situated in scenic areas at the periphery, with easy access to all the amenities of the city centre.[36] The city plan and the layout of streets and blocks should reflect the usage; each quarter should have its own individual character and be bordered off by a green belt. The compact city will be dissolved and a new decentralised agglomeration will emerge, "where the planets will retain their independence, each with its own centre of gravity; with their satellites they will form a large, loosely structured and light whole where everything fits together easily."[37]

This image, which anticipates the central concepts of modern urban planning in the twentieth century decades before they became widely accepted, was not intended to be implemented in an authoritarian way—it was to evolve in a self-regulating fashion with the aid of a certain amount of planning, but not too much. Bruch proposes a happy compromise between planning and laissez-faire; too much extensive planning could not meet the needs of the complex situation; yet the abandonment of planning altogether would cause heavy defects such as, for example, the lack of an overall transport network. His proposal for Berlin therefore is to give up the overall plan, to lay plans only for the most important traffic axes, and to build these using public funds; the planning of the areas in between could then be left to private efforts.[38] Such an arrangement assumes that the different individuals and groups each best know their own needs; the free play of forces seems to be preferable to an overall planning that would not have sufficient knowledge of the "real" interests and conditions. A plan evolving in this way would thus best succeed by coordinating the various interests. Another advantage, as Juan Rodriguez-Lores pointed out, is that unobtrusive planning such as this does not alter the distribution of private property.[39] This is quite an important aspect for modern planning, which has to deal with the new veto and compensation rights of property owners. Last but not least, it allows a new aesthetics to evolve—giving "the physiognomy of the city a pleasant diversity."[40]

These concepts enter the closer circle of German planning in 1876 via Baumeister's handbook, one of the first handbooks on the subject of town planning.[41] Whereas Faucher's and Bruch's theses are fierce and polemic, and clearly represent a specific attitude, Baumeister's *Stadt-Erweiterungen in technischer, baupolizeilicher und wirthschaftlicher Beziehung* is, as the title suggests, a comprehensive handbook, which presents many different aspects with the intention of providing universally valid information. The theses of Faucher and Bruch, which Baumeister quotes and clearly considers fundamental, are naturalised and become a self-evident basis of the new discipline of urban planning. Baumeister offers a historical review, statistical materials, diverse treatises concerning traffic and hygiene problems and other practical advice; he also makes some decisions about the cohabitation of different social groups and the relationship between planning and market forces. Although these have a genuine political character, they are presented as objective solutions. Baumeister clearly opts against a radical liberalism rejecting all state intervention, but also against socialist or communist approaches. "Self-help" and "state help" are for him two extremes that should be combined.[42] The liberal attitude of his sources persists—although governmental or municipal planning starts to play an important role in the free play of forces, it is seen only as one force amongst others. It is exactly this attitude that allows a scientific perception of planning to emerge. Modern planning will be carried out on the basis of statistical records and an analysis of the markets showing the actual requirements and needs.[43]

The coordination of various needs would be a central function of planning: "Only a comprehensive plan will enable the habitation requirements to be brought into relation to one another in an appropriate way. It allows the formation of groups which can develop and strengthen themselves without disturbing one another."[44] The prerequisite for such a plan is the mobility of the city's population; new inhabitants move in constantly and, even more importantly, this induces other movements, causing the whole urban system to be newly arranged: "This dislocation of the population takes place naturally, because people who are not bound to a certain area (customers, proximity to water, public buildings) make way for people who find the adequate conditions for economic progress here. The latter pay more, the first no longer wish to stay and in consequence they move away to another area."[45] Like Bruch, Baumeister proposes the separation of the city into commercial areas, industrial districts and residential quarters and also the division of residential areas according to different social classes. London, where there is already considerable segregation, serves as a model here. The "development of all cities strives towards this goal," according to Baumeister, and for him this is an unavoidable process that suggests "planning any future large city according to these goals from the start."[46] Thereby planning has to deal with the following problem: "Common public interest demands separate individual districts, where neighbours pursue the same objectives in regard to their buildings, where everyone is therefore free from disturbances; building law, however, demands a free choice of building lots and usage for everyone."[47] Thus a major planning task is to implement an order that is considered natural, either in concordance with or against the law.

Baumeister adopts Bruch's model of a self-confined planning, a model combining comprehensive planning and gradual implementation; it constrains planning in order to allow a more comprehensive orderliness to emerge. This model is adopted and confirmed at the general assembly of the Union of German Architects' and Engineers' Associations[48] in 1874. The central theses are: "1. Extension planning mainly consists of the definition of the main features of the transport network: streets, horse-drawn railways, steam trains, and canals, which should be treated systematically and therefore with a great attention to detail. 2. Only the main lines of the street network are to be planned; existing lanes shall be incorporated as well as byways marked out by the local situation. The subordinate detailed street plan is to be planned only for the near future or left to private development. 3. The grouping of different districts is to be governed by the selection of suitable situations and other characteristics, the only compulsory directive will be imposed by sanitary legislations for industry."[49] Zoning shall not be dictated, but motivated by planning. In 1902 Baumeister formulates: "It is also important to choose the future districts according to location, condition of the ground, and means of transport so that the private developers immediately recognise the practicability and order can evolve, in keeping with Schiller's words, in a 'free, light, and joyful' manner."[50]

Private Pursuit of Happiness and Modern Zoning

The early theories that form the basis of modern urban planning have one trait in common: the rejection of the inflexible forms of organisation dating from the eighteenth century and the search for new "organic" structures of order. This order should not take the form of an external structure, which is imposed on existing individual interests, as the ideal plans of absolutist town planning in the eighteenth century did; a planning model which is more or less impracticable at the outset of industrialisation and the implementation of new property legislations.[51] Urban design at the end of the nineteenth century is no longer something that can be determined by a master builder on the basis of aesthetic criteria; it now demands empirical investigations based on existing and anticipated interests. Urban plans and lifestyle can no longer be dictated by higher authorities—on the contrary, market forces are seen as capable of adequately responding to and articulating disparate requirements. "Happiness" in the liberal nineteenth century is no longer something that can be defined by the authorities. The topos of "common felicity," which had been central to the thinking of the governmental sciences and the policing methods of the eighteenth century, is no longer valid. "Felicity" here meant common welfare established and organised by the powers-that-be, a rational and natural "state of order."[52] This static and collective concept of felicity is replaced by the ideal of private "activity" and "freedom."[53] "Felicity" has become an individual matter, dedicated to the private "pursuit of happiness."

This seems to infer some advantages for planning. The main critique of absolutist governance is not necessarily concerned with demanding an all-encompassing personal freedom; rather it is aimed towards the improvement of techniques of power, an effective exercise of power based on an accurate knowledge of social structures. "Society" is discovered as an autonomous organism, separate from the sphere of politics, or it is just emerging as such. Since the seventeenth and eighteenth centuries, the social sciences have been evolving and distancing themselves from moral and legal philosophy, in an attempt to describe man "as he really is."[54] This reality is discovered in his passions and preferences, and even more in his "interests," a concept of passion purified by reason. It is a new reality that develops alongside the genesis of modern mass society and the resulting new idea of man. In contrast to aristocratic behaviour, characterised by a sense of honour as well as impulses, the aims of the average modern person are foreseeable. "Interests" become the new paradigm in social sciences—the advantage here is that interests are assumed to be consistent and predictable, making them a useful instrument of governmental technique.[55] Thus, a new urban order can be predicted based on the free play of interests.

The dynamic planning proposed by Bruch and Baumeister is specified later. Since about 1900, the city layout and its divisions and zones, regulated by market forces in the early theories, is determined by means of zoning ordinances with various building regulations. The aims relating to zoning are quite diverse. On the one hand the planners have specific ideas related to hygiene and welfare, aiming to keep unhealthy industries away from residential areas, to keep rents low, and to make low-rise buildings available for all classes—a concept that is not really effective and would require further regulations in addition to zone planning. On the other hand the planners attempt to protect individual interests and stabilise the various submarkets, which are endangered by the mixing of factories, tenement blocks, and exclusive residential areas—thus zoning is particularly a response to the new economic basis of modern urban development.[56] The socially and functionally differentiated city, an image we are used to today, evolved in a complex process of development—it is marked out by market mechanisms, which are scientifically analysed by the planners and then naturalised and implemented in a validated form. Through this act of naturalisation, which sees the city as an organism, modern urban planning is able to establish itself as a scientific discipline.[57] The paradox of modern planning here lies in the fact that it tries to produce something that is already presumed to exist—this paradox, however, characterises the project of Liberalism as a whole, as Michel Foucault pointed out.[58]

The *studies of governmentality*, which analyse liberal forms of government following on from the work of Foucault, envisage a broad concept of government, of "governmentality," comprising processes of economic and social regulation.[59] A central point in these studies is that they do not see freedom and government as alternative factors. For them, Liberalism is not only the rejection of governmental intervention; indeed, Liberalism emerges as a criticism of traditional forms of government and calls for the restriction of regulations, yet it creates a new rationality of government based on individual freedom. The freedom envisaged here is not something that already exists; it has to be created. Independent and mobile individuals as well as competition cannot be taken for granted; they have to be constructed by introducing an appropriate framework of laws, traffic infrastructures, and education, amongst other things. The safeguarding of a free market is the task of an active government; competition is one of the historical goals of a successful administration and not a natural condition.[60] Once competition is established, the free play of forces and its rules can be explored. A liberal government gains its laws and norms of intervention by observing the market. The market is no longer seen as an institution that must be regulated by a multiplicity of rules in order to achieve fair prices and a just allocation of goods, as it was in the Middle Ages and up until the seventeenth century; on the contrary it has turned into a place where a new order and a new truth will come to light, where economically verified quantities, prices, and distributions prevail.[61] This order, however, can only be achieved if people believe in it and if it is implemented via the interplay of market and planning.

Endnotes

1 Gerd Albers, "Über den Wandel im Planungsverständnis," *RaumPlanung* 61 (1993): 98: "Vorreiter der Ordnung in einer Welt des laissez faire."

2 Albers, (see note 1), 97–98: "Anpassungsplanung."

3 Werner Hegemann, *Der Städtebau, nach den Ergebnissen der Allgemeinen Städtebau-Ausstellung in Berlin nebst einem Anhang: Die Internationale Städtebau-Ausstellung in Düsseldorf. Vol. 1* (Berlin: Verlag Ernst Wasmuth, 1911), 8: "Kampf der Ordnung gegen das Chaos"— "ein unendlich kompliziertes Ringen zwischen … in den neuen Verhältnissen entwurzelter Gestaltungskraft auf der einen Seite gegen formensprengende, aber formdurstige wirtschaftliche Neukraft."

4 See: Hans Medick, *Naturzustand und Naturgeschichte der bürgerlichen Gesellschaft. Die Ursprünge der bürgerlichen Sozialtheorie als Geschichtsphilosophie und Sozialwissenschaft bei Samuel Pufendorf, John Locke und Adam Smith* (Göttingen: Vandenhoeck & Ruprecht, 1973); Albert O. Hirschman, *The Passions and the Interests. Political Arguments for Capitalism before its Triumph* (Princeton/N.J.: Princeton University Press, 1977); Michel Foucault, *Security, Territory, Population. Lectures at the Collège de France 1977–1978*, ed. Michel Senellart, trans. Graham Burchell (Basingstoke/Hampshire u.a.: Palgrave Macmillan, 2007).

5 See e.g.: Patrick Joyce, *The Rule of Freedom. Liberalism and the Modern City* (London, New York: Verso, 2003).

6 Medick, (see note 4), 75–108; Michael P. Zuckert, *Launching liberalism. On Lockean political philosophy* (Lawrence: University Press of Kansas, 2002), 220–34. Political and economic liberalism have the same theoretical basis; until the beginning of the twentieth century, however, the term "liberalism" was only used for the political movement, economic liberalism had a lot of different names, e.g., "free trade." See: Rudolf Walter, "Exkurs: Wirtschaftlicher Liberalismus," in *Geschichtliche Grundbegriffe. Historisches Lexikon zur politisch-sozialen Sprache in Deutschland. Vol. 3*, ed. Otto Brunner, Werner Conze and Reinhart Koselleck (Stuttgart: Klett-Cotta, 1982), 787–815.

7 Medick, (see note 4), 70–75, 231, 254.

8 Anthony Sutcliffe, *Towards the Planned City. Germany, Britain, the United States and France 1780–1914* (Oxford: Basil Blackwell, 1981); see also: Brian Ladd, *Urban Planning and Civic Order in Germany 1860–1914* (Cambridge/Mass., London: Harvard University Press, 1990).

9 Volker Hentschel, *Die deutschen Freihändler und der volkswirtschaftliche Kongress 1858 bis 1885* (Stuttgart: Klett, 1975), 67–69.

10 Hegemann, (see note 3), 18–36.

11 Gerhard Fehl, "Berlin wird Weltstadt: Wohnungsnot und Villenkolonien. Eine Begegnung mit Julius Faucher, seinem Filter-Modell und seiner Wohnungsreformbewegung um 1866," in *Städtebaureform 1865–1900. Von Licht, Luft und Ordnung in der Stadt der Gründerzeit. Vol. 1*, ed. Juan Rodriguez-Lores and Gerhard Fehl (Hamburg: Christians, 1985), 101–52.

12 Julius Faucher, "Die Bewegung für Wohnungsreform," *Vierteljahrschrift für Volkswirthschaft und Kulturgeschichte* 4 (1865): 147: "wo 'Konkurrenz' und 'Kapitalmacht' am längsten gewirtschaftet … haben."

13 Julius Faucher, "Die Bewegung für Wohnungsreform (Zweite Hälfte)," *Vierteljahrschrift für Volkswirthschaft und Kulturgeschichte* 3 (1866): 87.

14 Fehl, (see note 11), 102, 117–119.

15 Faucher, (see note 12), 157: "wandlungsvolle Geschichte verschiedenen Gebrauchs."

16 Julius Faucher, "Ueber Häuserbau-Unternehmung im Geiste der Zeit," *Vierteljahrschrift für Volkswirthschaft und Kulturgeschichte* 2 (1869): 52, 55: "monopolisirte[r] Baustellenring, … der der Bauunternehmung auf allen Seiten einen Riegel vorschiebt"—"Baustellen-Monopol"; see: Fehl, (see note 11), 124–29.

17 Faucher, (see note 12), 186–90.

18 Faucher, (see note 16), 57–59.

19 Julius Faucher, "Staats- und Kommunal-Budgets," *Vierteljahrschrift für Volkswirthschaft und Culturgeschichte* 3 (1863).

20 Faucher, (see note 12), 197.

21 Julius Faucher, "Die zehnte Gruppe auf der internationalen Ausstellung in Paris," *Vierteljahrschrift für Volkswirthschaft und Kulturgeschichte* 2 (1867): 172–73.

22 See: Faucher, (see note 12), 128; Julius Faucher, "Geschichte, Statistik und Volkswirthschaft," *Vierteljahrschrift für Volkswirthschaft und Kulturgeschichte* 4 (1863): 130.

23 See: Gerd Albers, *Zur Entwicklung der Stadtplanung in Europa. Begegnungen, Einflüsse, Verflechtungen* (Braunschweig, Wiesbaden: Vieweg, 1997), 119–21.

24 Gerhard Fehl, "'Stadt als Kunstwerk', 'Stadt als Geschäft'. Der Übergang vom landesfürstlichen zum bürgerlichen Städtebau," in *Stadterweiterungen 1800–1875. Von den Anfängen des modernen Städtebaues in Deutschland*, ed. Gerhard Fehl and Juan Rodriguez-Lores (Hamburg: Christians, 1983), 135–84.

25 Juan Rodriguez-Lores, "Die Grundfrage der Grundrente. Stadtplanung von Ildefonso Cerdá für Barcelona und James Hobrecht für Berlin," *Stadtbauwelt* 65 (1980): 31, 35.

26 Ernst Bruch, *Berlin's bauliche Zukunft und der Bebauungsplan* (Berlin: Kommissions-Verlag von Carl Beelitz, 1870), 24: "Zwangsjacke."

27 Werner Hegemann, *Das steinerne Berlin. Geschichte der grössten Mietskasernenstadt der Welt* (Braunschweig, Wiesbaden: Vieweg, ⁴1988 [1930], 241: "Baustellenmonopol"—"scheussliche Vielregiererei."

28 This is a heading in Werner Hegemann's *Das steinerne Berlin* ("Stone Berlin") from 1930: "Der Strassenplan von 1858 bis 1862. Die Polizei verordnet Mietskasernen für vier Millionen Berliner" ("The street plan from 1858 to 1862. The police prescribes tenements for four million Berlin people"). For how the police did this, see: Hegemann, (see note 3), 14–17.

29 See: Bruch (see note 26), 2; and Reinhard Baumeister, *Stadtbaupläne in alter und neuer Zeit* (Stuttgart: Chr. Belser'sche Verlagshandlung, 1902), 4–5: "Künstlichkeit"—"Natürlichkeit." Bruch and Baumeister are familiar with this differentiation.

30 Bruch, (see note 26), 3, 15.

31 Bruch, (see note 26), 15: "flache Kegelform."

32 Fehl, (see note 11), 102; note 4.

33 Bruch worked in the municipal statistics bureau in Berlin and was then director of a similar institution in Breslau. He was not personally involved in the German planning discussions, his ideas were received via Baumeister; Hegemann, (see note 3), 41.

34 Faucher, (see note 12), 183; Faucher, (see note 13), 97–99.

35 Juan Rodriguez-Lores, "'Gerade oder krumme Strassen?' Von den irrationalen Ursprüngen des modernen Städtebaues," in Gerhard Fehl and Juan Rodriguez-Lores (see note 24), 124–27: "Bruchs funktionale Grossstadt." (Titel verkürzt)

36 Bruch, (see note 26), 31; Reinhard Baumeister, *Stadt-Erweiterungen in technischer, baupolizeilicher und wirthschaftlicher Beziehung* (Berlin: Verlag von Ernst & Korn, 1876), 80–82.

37 Bruch, (see note 26), 54: "in dem die Planeten ihre eigene Existenz bewahren, einen eigenen Gravitationspunkt bilden und sich mit ihren Trabanten dem grossen, lockerer und leichter zusammengefügten Ganzen zwanglos einfügen."

38 Bruch, (see note 26), 97.

39 Rodriguez-Lores, (see note 35).

40 Bruch, (see note 26), 76: wird "der Physiognomie der Stadt die so wohlthuende Mannichfaltigkeit" verschafft.

41 Albers, (see note 23).

42 Baumeister, (see note 36), 50–51: "Selbsthülfe"—"Staatshülfe."

43 Baumeister, (see note 36), 54–55, 73.

44 Baumeister, (see note 36), 79: "Ein umfassender Plan allein ermöglicht nun auch, die Wohnungsbedürfnisse aller Schichten der Bevölkerung in das richtige Verhältniss zu bringen, Gruppen zu bilden, welche sich einzeln ausbauen können, ohne sich gegenseitig zu stören."

45 Baumeister, (see note 36), 79: "Dieses Verschieben der Bevölkerung findet naturgemäss so Statt, dass Leute, welche durch ihren Beruf nicht an eine bestimmte Gegend (Kundschaft, Wassernähe, öffentliche Gebäude) gebunden sind, Platz machen für solche, welche eben hier die Bedingungen ihres wirthschaftlichen Fortkommens finden. Letztere zahlen mehr, erstern wollen nicht mehr, und wechseln demnach die Wohnung."

46 Baumeister, (see note 36), 83: "die Entwickelung aller Städte strebt diesem Ziele zu"—"jede grosse Zukunftstadt von vorn herein darauf einzurichten."

47 Baumeister, (see note 36), 83: "Das allgemeine Interesse fordert abgesonderte charakteristische Bezirke, worin die Nachbarn gleichartige Zwecke mit ihren Bauten verfolgen, und daher Jeder vor Störungen möglichst sichergestellt ist; aber das Baurecht fordert für Jedermann möglichst freie Wahl seines Bauplatzes und seines Bauzweckes."

48 Generalversammlung des Verbandes deutscher Architekten- und Ingenieur-Vereine.

49 Cited in: Baumeister, (see note 36), 91: "1. Die Projectirung von Stadterweiterungen besteht wesentlich in der Feststellung der Grundzüge aller Verkehrsmittel: Strassen, Pferdebahnen, Dampfbahnen, Kanäle, die systematisch und deshalb in einer beträchtlichen Ausdehnung zu behandeln sind. 2. Das Strassennetz soll zunächst nur die Hauptlinien enthalten, wobei vorhandene Wege thunlichst zu berücksichtigen, sowie solche Nebenlinien, welche durch lokale Umstände bestimmt vorgezeichnet sind. Die untergeordnete Theilung ist jeweils nach dem Bedürfnis der näheren Zukunft vorzunehmen, oder der Privatthätigkeit zu überlassen. 3. Die Gruppirung verschiedenartiger Stadttheile soll durch geeignete Wahl der Situation und sonstiger charakteristischer Merkmale herbeigeführt werden, zwangsweise nur durch sanitarische Vorschriften über Gewerbe."

50 Baumeister, (see note 29), 23: "Ebenso wichtig ist es, die projektierten Bezirke in Bezug auf Lage, Bodenbeschaffenheit und Verkehrsmittel so sorgfältig zu wählen, dass die Baulustigen die Zweckmässigkeit sofort

erkennen, und somit die Ordnung nach den Schiller'schen Worten 'frei, leicht und freudig' zu stande kommt."

51 Fehl, (see note 24), 135–84.

52 See: Mascha Bisping's contribution in this volume.

53 Marcus Sandl, *Ökonomie des Raumes. Der kameralwissenschaftliche Entwurf der Staatswirtschaft im 18. Jahrhundert* (Cologne, Weimar, Vienna: Böhlau, 1999), 381: "gemeinschaftliche Glückseligkeit"—"Tätigkeit"—"Freiheit."

54 Hirschman, (see note 4), 12–14.

55 Hirschman, (see note 4), 48; see also: Michel Foucault, *The Birth of Biopolitics. Lectures at the Collège de France 1978–1979*, ed. Michel Senellart, trans. Graham Burchell (Basingstoke/Hampshire et al.: Palgrave Macmillan, 2008).

56 See: Gerhard Fehl and Juan Rodriguez-Lores, "Aufstieg und Fall der Zonenplanung. Städtebauliches Instrumentarium und stadträumliche Ordnungsvorstellungen zwischen 1870 und 1905," *Stadtbauwelt* 73 (1982): 45–52; Andreas Weiland, "Die Frankfurter Zonenbauordnung von 1891—eine 'fortschrittliche' Bauordnung? Versuch einer Entmystifizierung," in *Städtebaureform 1865–1900. Von Licht, Luft und Ordnung in der Stadt der Gründerzeit. Vol. 2*, ed. Juan Rodriguez-Lores and Gerhard Fehl (Hamburg: Christians, 1985), 343–88; Ladd, (see note 8), 234.

57 See: Giorgio Piccinato, *Städtebau in Deutschland 1871–1914: Genese einer wissenschaftlichen Disziplin* (Braunschweig, Wiesbaden: Vieweg, 1983), 29, 35–36.

58 Foucault, (see note 4).

59 See e.g.: Andrew Barry, Thomas Osborn and Nikolas Rose, eds., *Foucault and political reason. Liberalism, neo-liberalism and rationalities of government* (London: UCL Press, 1996); Ulrich Bröckling, Susanne Krasmann and Thomas Lemke, eds., *Gouvernementalität der Gegenwart. Studien zur Ökonomisierung des Sozialen* (Frankfurt a. M.: Suhrkamp, 2000).

60 Foucault, (see note 55); Nikolas Rose, "Governing 'advanced' liberal societies," in *Foucault and political reason*, ed. Barry, Osborne and Rose (see note 59), 43–47.

61 Foucault, (see note 55).

THE ATTRACTION OF HEIMAT

Homeland Protection in Vienna
around 1900, or
The Preservation and
Reform of the City

Sándor Békési

1

"Homeland protection" or *Heimatschutz* emerged as part of a wide-ranging movement of cultural reform around 1900. It can be considered as a possible response to the problems and irritations caused by rapid modernisation and urbanisation. Homeland protection comprised many different issues, from natural conservation to cultural promotion. In retrospect, for a long time the movement was commonly described merely as a form of reactionary anti-modernism or romantic aestheticism. More recent studies have questioned

1 Schönlaterngasse, 1st district Vienna, around 1910. This area was part of the "old" city centre and one of the real "hot spots" in contemporary debates concerning the cityscape, as it was under threat by a project to build an avenue.

this judgement and paid closer attention to the ambiguities of modernisation and the constructive role of Heimatschutz in criticising the effects of industrialisation, particularly in the period before the First World War.[1]

Yet the relationship between homeland protection and urban development itself is an area that has hardly been investigated. Moreover, *Heimat* and metropolis seem to be a contradiction in terms. In this essay, I will examine the history of early Heimatschutz in Vienna with regard to its programme and urban activities. These provide interesting material for a history of the pursuit of public happiness, especially in the city.

Cities as such symbolise the pursuit of public happiness. The process of urbanisation and the growth of cities are usually the result of a migration of population from the countryside in search of a better life.[2] On the other hand, there is a close connection between the elusiveness of happiness in the city and an increasingly fragmented community, as has been explicitly pointed out, for example, with reference to the urban crisis and urban sprawl in the USA of the nineteen-sixties.[3] This finding, however, can also be applied to other times and places.

For these and other reasons, established circles in Vienna around 1900, faced with massive and rapid changes in the cityscape and society, saw an ideal opportunity for introducing a new definition or reinforcement of their local identity. The idea of preserving the city held a promise to fulfil certain of the population's needs (▶ 1). Its attractiveness is derived from the way it addresses people's innermost emotions. Heimatschutz seems to have linked these sentiments with specific cultural and political forces. The movement gained some support and attention around 1900, and this would not have been the case had it not served some clear and distinct purposes. On a more or less abstract level, these might well be characterised as the pursuit of urban happiness.

I am assuming that every kind of planning proposal and urban message implies the promise of a better life and better future to some extent, even if there is rarely an explicit mention of the word happiness. However, the attraction of Heimatschutz and its visions lay in the fact that it provided an emotional component, linked with an element of identity, which was inherent in the concept of Heimat.[4] Thus, my starting point is the assertion that the pursuit of Heimat—which also applies to the big city—is a specific and manifest form of the pursuit of happiness. In this connection, the publications and programme of Heimatschutz in Vienna around 1900 will be examined to investigate what attempts were made to define and realise Heimat in the city, whilst preserving and reshaping it.

Heimat in the City: Myth and Reality

As early as the late nineteenth century, Heimat became the comprehensive vision of a home whose aesthetic, social, and economic dimensions were all integrated in the so-called vernacular. Heimat was—and again became—the German keyword in many discourses about location, belonging, and identity.

The Heimatschützer were driven by a conviction that the cumulative effect derived from the community's surroundings constituted a key element in a person's quality of life. … It was the broad sweep of one's vision that counted most for them, for it alone allowed the synthesis of buildings, roads, billboards, bridges, and other disparate components of the cityscape into that overall physical-aesthetic entity to which they gave the name Heimat.[5]

Heimat is a phenomenon with ambivalent characteristics, resulting in recent re-evaluations. Although in some ways the idea of Heimat contradicts modern developments such as urbanisation or mobility, at the same time we can see that it absorbs modern qualities and joins forces with other modern constructs. The idea of Heimat always had retrogressive aspects, but it could also be turned around to become a reservoir of progressive protest values and emancipatory reforms. It can exclude certain social groups, but it can also create a balance between local affinity and cosmopolitan openness. Heimat unites topographic and imaginary conceptions of space; it is both the longing for a place to shelter and for a sense of belonging. As we can see, Heimat was just as much concerned with a specific physical location as with a place within society.[6] William Rollins, who investigated German Heimatschutz around 1900 in a comprehensive way, saw a striking association between both the political community and the physical surroundings implied in the idea of Heimat.[7]

We could add that Heimat has always been a myth or a utopian vision, but it is also an effect or a reality. In other words, it was both the pursuit of and, in a sense, the fact of happiness relating to the possibility of a community facing fragmentation and alienation in the large city. Of course, in many ways we are dealing with invented traditions here. And these traditions were already the result of broken, reflexive and aesthetical approaches to Heimat.[8]

The most likely context for evoking Heimat was the small town and the countryside. But in the metropolis we also find structures that are able to create feelings of Heimat in its inhabitants: the old city centre, the "unspoiled" former villages in the suburbs, or even the neighbourhoods in the relatively new areas. Moreover, around 1900 there were several efforts to incorporate the mental construct of Heimat into life in the big city. One of them was homeland protection.

Heimatschutz between Tradition and Reform

In considering the Viennese example of early Heimatschutz after the turn of the century, we should firstly distinguish between a reactionary, nationalistic variation on the one hand and a reform-minded liberal conservatism within the Austrian movement on the other—a differentiation that is rarely made in such an explicit way. Indeed, anti-modernism and Heimatschutz were not the same thing, nor were anti-urban attitudes representative for all parts of the Heimat movement in that early period. The offices of diverse Heimat organisa-

UNTER MITWIRKUNG
FÜHRENDER MÄNNER
⊡ HERAUSGEGEBEN ⊡
VON JOSEPH AUG. LUX
R. VOIGTLÄNDER⁹ VER-
LAG-LEIPZIG U. BERLIN

2

tions were situated in Vienna, but only the liberal-conservative homeland protection association was concerned with issues relating to the city itself.[9]

This approach was first represented in Vienna by the cultural magazine *Hohe Warte* (High Point) (▶ 2). It was published in the period 1904–08 and its editor was the well-known Viennese art critic, architectural theorist and writer Joseph August Lux. He was also a co-signatory in the founding act of the German *Werkbund*. His journal dealt with a wide range of matters: architecture and urban development, interior design, arts and crafts, folk art and homeland protection, art education, and many other topics.

Hohe Warte supported the artistic and aesthetic reform of the cities and the provinces. Whilst doing so, the "care and preservation of valuable vernacular [heimatlich] tradition …" played a central role, as well as the explicit consideration of foreign examples. For Lux, the goal was not only preservation, but also the creation of something new. He stressed not "… the contrast between 'modern' and 'un-modern', but between *good and bad*."[10]

However, the position taken by the journal was not limited to the above issues. It did not only promote beautification or a nostalgic approach, but also included the structural criticism of economy and politics.[11]

2   Front page of *Hohe Warte*. Illustrated half-monthly Magazin Supplying Artistic, Intellectual, and Economic Interests of Urban Culture, 1906/07.

In a way that seemed paradoxical, Lux enthused about old Viennese culture and traditions, about "old buildings with their human smell," and disliked "modern urban roads with their stereotypical meaningless façades."[12] At the same time he was not, of course, free from nostalgia for an idealised past. Also, he was enthusiastic about the architecture of Otto Wagner and showed an interest in the artistic possibilities of the new material called reinforced concrete.[13] As William Rollins pointed out: "This was perhaps a form of 'anti-modernism', but it was nevertheless a reflective and reform-minded one that wanted merely to retain the affective diversity of older city settings."[14] When Lux wrote about his "love for the quiet suburban streets" and "for the faded features and late summer shine of these things from yesteryear," he also voiced the opinion that one could be satisfied if they did not vanish forever. Descriptions like this could be very effective in fostering positive sentiments in an old-Viennese setting. But in this connection Lux was sometimes even more explicit: "I love the hidden, strange feelings of happiness which such places, streets, buildings and flats can evoke."[15]

Lux expected the solution to problematic city developments and the improvement of housing conditions—according to artistic and social principles—to arise, amongst other things, from the reform of administration and eligibility within the town council. More specifically, he was referring to a weakening of the rights of house and property owners.[16] Lux considered the actual goal of the garden city movement, which emerged as a new approach to urban planning in the eighteen-nineties, to be the creation of a society without poverty, and for this reason he quoted Oscar Wilde in this connection.[17]

The architectural historian Ákos Moravánszky regards Lux primarily as a proponent of the garden city idea in Austria around 1900.[18] With his arguments (and dreams) for the convergence of architectural beauty and decent affordable housing in the form of garden settlements, he was also highlighting the pursuit of happiness in the urban landscape.[19]

In 1910 the liberal, reform-oriented Heimatschutz in Vienna received institutional status with the founding of the *Association for Protection and Preservation of Art Monuments in Vienna and Lower Austria* (Verein zum Schutze und zur Erhaltung der Kunstdenkmäler Wiens und Niederösterreichs), which placed greater emphasis on the issue of homeland protection. A few years later, the term Heimatschutz was even incorporated in its official name. The aim of the association was to protect Heimat, whose essence their general secretary defined as "the very specific features of everything in which and how our life takes place." The real beauty and "best substance" of Heimat was seen as a place's image and physiognomy, respectively.[20]

From the beginning, the society's membership included prominent local figures or important representatives of the city and the academic world. In its executive committee we find leading archivists and representatives of the preservation authority, well-established university professors (sometimes including the rector of the University of Vienna) or even the mayor of Vienna.[21] Obviously, this fact contradicts the widespread opinion that

Heimatschutz should have been a merely provincial movement. Instead, we are concerned here with an urban elite. Representatives from the Viennese Association also played an important part in founding the *Austrian Association of Homeland Protection* (Verband österreichischer Heimatschutz-Vereine) in 1912.

Unlike their social backgrounds, some of the contents and values conveyed by the members of the association were of a popular nature. For instance, one of the volumes published by the Association was entitled *The Rescue of Old Vienna* (Zur Rettung Alt-Wiens), and contained a collection of articles which had been published in several Viennese daily newspapers and journals. As we learn in the introduction, all these authors were unified in their "love for Heimat" and their attempt to sustain "the image of Heimat sanctified by art and history."[22] Indeed, the vanishing of Old Vienna was a widespread topos in the popular contemporary perception of urban change.[23] In a more general view, we can agree with Gerhard Vinken and see the "Old Town" around 1900 as an object of the imagination, whose very label contained the assertion of being something historic, original, and authentic.[24] In reality, it should not only have been the result of preservation but also of modern urban experience and modern construction, integrated both in the practice and in the discourse of modern city planning in manifold ways. Vinken perceives 'New-Town' and 'Old-Town' as counter-images and at the same time as related to one another in a modern setting—like two mutually dependent opposites. By definition, this interpretation supports the concept of a dialectical modernity, which can include even its counterpart.[25]

In compliance with Lux, the main goals of the Association included the following: communalising urban land, curbing speculation, the reform of housing, either through rented apartment blocks or detached houses, the reform of building regulations, the separation of traffic roads and residential streets, the decentralisation of administration, the founding of garden cities and the participation of artists and preservationists in the planning process. In particular, the association worked towards the realisation of a preservation law and an advice bureau for construction matters (Bauberatung).[26] Whereas the former was not passed until after the First World War, the latter was introduced sooner. Advice centres for construction matters were one of the key practices of homeland protection in many places and were established in Vienna in 1911. The Association considered them to be the "most energetic means for the realisation of the Heimatschutz way of thinking" and by its own account it was able to win over many of the "most important architects in Vienna." Above all, the goal was to provide the assessment and revision of construction schemes for communities, clients or master builders.[27] However, the group's archive material tells us almost nothing about the way this instrument was actually used. Perhaps a more public form of promotion was invented with the new permanent exhibition *Heimatschutz und Bauberatung* in the Technisches Museum Wien 1914–16, in which the Association was greatly involved.[28] Although the publishing of an official journal had not been very successful for the moment, the protagonists of the association made a name for themselves by holding public lectures, writing publications and petitions to public bodies and also by participating in the consultations for a new building regulation law and the preparations for a preservation law (▶ 3). Furthermore, the Viennese homeland protection also arranged a cooperation with the *Central Office of Housing Reform in Austria* (Zentralstelle für Wohnungsreform in Österreich), with mutual representation in the respective committees. This institution was considered to be the Austrian equivalent of the *Deutsche Gartenstadt-Gesellschaft* and the assembly point for middle-class housing policies. Amongst its members we find many well-known personalities from various professional groups and political orientations such as Richard Weiskirchner, who was later to become the Christian Social mayor of Vienna, or the socially engaged reporter and social democratic politician Max Winter.[29] Indeed, pragmatic concentration and non-partisan practices were characteristic for this area of homeland protection in general. Its outlook had little in common with any of the three dominant political fractions or their "big issues" of the time, whether these were concerned with revolution, Christianity or

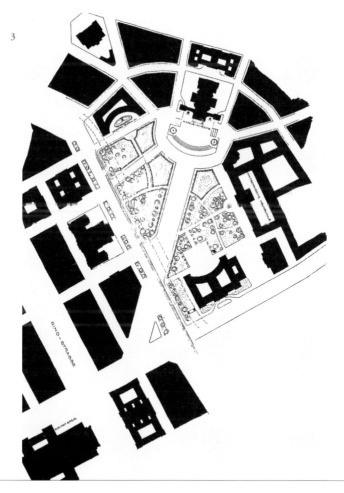

3

3   Proposal of the „Heimatschutz" Association for reshaping the central square Karlsplatz by means of constructing a new avenue between Karlskirche and State Opera, which would have required the demolition of some buildings from the period 1860–70.

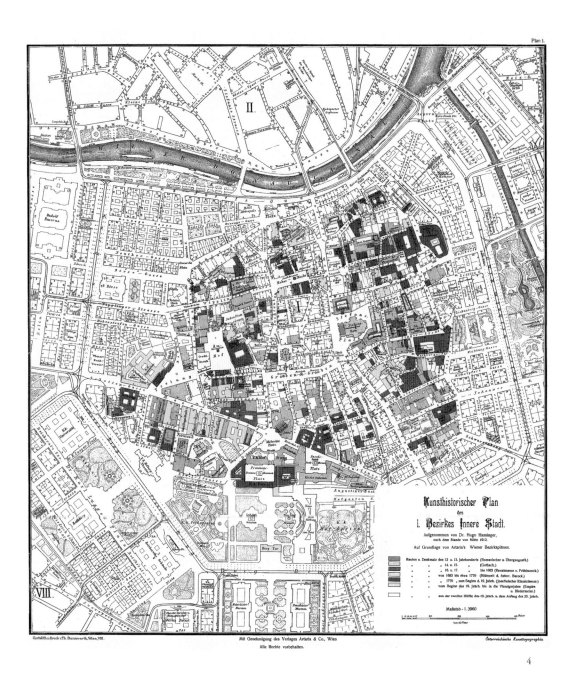

Plan 1.

4 Plan of the 1ˢᵗ district relating to art history, 1912/16 by Hugo Hassinger. Hassinger was an early urban geographer and a leading member of the Viennese Heimatschutz Association. He published the Viennese section of the Austrian Topography for Arts (founded by Max Dvořák) and thus created the first cartographic documentation of vernacular architecture worthy of protection, systematically represented in chronological order.

Volk.[30] In order to understand this movement, it is necessary to distinguish between the different directions of conservatism, depending on whether their main focus is on maintaining the status quo, introducing reforms or returning to former conditions.[31]

Both in their criticism of the big city and in their demands, these types of Heimatschutz virtually agreed with the mainstream or even with the avant-garde approach towards city planning and historic preservation of the time.[32] But until today they have also proved to have much in common with modern urban planning, architecture and new approaches to the protection of cityscapes. It is a remarkable fact that both forms of Viennese Heimatschutz portrayed here always propagated the idea of garden cities based on the more liberal Howard's Plan from Britain, whilst they did not support the nationalistic and racist (völkisch) version by the German Theodor Fritsch at all.

Many of the standpoints of the reform-oriented, liberal Heimatschutz had their precedents in older traditions such as the Arts and Crafts Movement in England, or the aesthetic environmentalism of John Ruskin and William Morris. Others were derived from the participation in contemporary developments such as the idea of garden cities, new preservation standards or the criticism of housing property speculation. However, the greatest innovative achievement of this movement can be seen as the deliberate convergence of manifold approaches in a holistic view, represented by a more or less effective pressure group. In this way, Heimatschutz managed to integrate aesthetical, conservational, hygienic and socio-economic as well as political aspects of the growing city.

With these proposals, amongst others, Heimatschutz was able to react to current urban changes in the city. The turnover of building stock was relatively high in Vienna at the turn of the century. Between 1899 and 1903, an average of 235 buildings were demolished each year and 661 new ones erected. So compared with Berlin and Paris, Vienna should have had the greatest percentage of new and rebuilt building stock in this period. The rate of urban transition is obvious if we consider that only 31.6 per cent of the total building stock in 1900 originated from the period prior to 1861. Interestingly, this rate was even slightly higher in the city centre.[33] This means that in some respects "Old Vienna" was an illusion or a figment of the imagination, and if it was real in a physical sense, it had been confined to small areas (▸ 4). Compared with Berlin and Paris, Vienna also had a high number of large rented apartment blocks. Statistically speaking, an average of fifty-one people occupied one building.[34] Thus, overcrowded and unhealthy housing was widespread in Vienna at that time.

In some ways, contemporary building regulations were seen as insufficient and antiquated. They allowed neither expropriation for the purposes of city intervention nor the effective prevention of too narrow courtyards. Nevertheless, Vienna showed a rapid growth in population. From the period from 1860 to 1900 the city showed the second highest increase in comparison with Berlin, Budapest, London, and Paris, not least due to the immigration and incorporation of former suburbs into the city. By 1905, the metropolis had 1.9 million inhabitants and was the fourth largest city in Europe.[35] The experience of the big city following the extension of the city's boundaries in 1890 and the creation of a Greater Vienna could evoke very different feelings and reactions, ranging from admiration to rejection, from fascination to fear. "Clearly, many of the valorisations of Old and New Vienna do indeed seek to set and maintain boundaries, both real and imaginary."[36] However, in the case of homeland protection, this demarcation did not proceed along an inside/outside dialectic, as described by David Frisby in *Cityscapes of Modernity*: "… the old city as museum is located inside, and the city as modern metropolis is located outside."[37] In theory, Heimatschutz divided the city into three normative zones. These were: 1. the city core with the old areas, constructed before 1850, which still stood and were considered worthy of protection; 2. the belt of former inner suburbs and nearby parts of outer suburbs, with its "amorphous mass" of rented apartment blocks, built mainly after 1850; and 3. the peripheral outer suburbs, which were able to retain many of their rustic features despite being incorporated into the city (▶ 5). Thereby, outer Vienna was indeed able to serve as a showplace for both the protection of the old winegrowing villages and the construction of new garden cities.

Conclusions

As I have attempted to show, parts of the homeland movement around 1900 can be seen more as a moderate version of modernity than as an opponent to it. This was indeed the case in Vienna at that time. The distinguishing feature of the movement was a mixture of pragmatism and idealism or even sentimentality. Its utopia represented not just an impossible idyllic scheme or wishful thinking, but also the definite will to change. The reform-minded, liberal-conservative Heimatschutz emphasised (or even created) the connection between the old and the new city, between tradition and reform, between large-scale structures and small-scale places, and not least between aesthetic and socio-economic reforms.[38] Its aim was to preserve the old city, mainly from the time before 1850, and at the same time to reshape the recently built city structures. Heimatschutz took up a kind of middle position between applied urban planning and the imagination of city dwellers, interpreting in both directions. With regard to "happiness," it should be pointed out that Heimat as the imagination of the city was a value that could be successfully communicated to the general public. It embraced certain deeply-rooted longings and fantasies of bourgeois society. Rather than being escapist illusions, these visions and practices mediated between people's dreams and the realistic possibilities of making these dreams come true. The imagery of Old Vienna and Heimat were vehicles that connected innermost emotions and wishes with their outward manifestation in the city.

In the end, the Heimatschutz movement questioned the seemingly inevitable results and the common values of the classic progress paradigm and underlined the fundamental role of social developments. In this way, it promised the possibility of a happy life in the big city, based on both the Old and the New.

5

5   Heiligenstädter Straße 157, 19th district Vienna, around 1900. The professional photographer August Stauda recorded old buildings throughout the whole city that were threatened by demolition, by order of the later Heimatschutz Association president Count Karl Lanckoronski, as characteristic examples of "The Disappearance of Old Vienna."

Endnotes

1 Andreas Knaut, "Ernst Rudorff und die Anfänge der deutschen Heimatbewegung," in *Antimodernismus und Reform. Zur Geschichte der deutschen Heimatbewegung*, ed. Edeltraud Klueting (Darmstadt: Wissenschaftliche Buchgesellschaft, 1991), 20–49; Vittorio Magnago Lampugnani and Romana Schneider, eds., *Moderne Architektur in Deutschland 1900 bis 1950: vol. 2: Reform und Tradition* (Stuttgart: Hatje, 1992); Winfried Speitkamp, *Die Verwaltung der Geschichte: Denkmalpflege und Staat in Deutschland 1871–1933* (Göttingen: Vandenhoeck & Ruprecht, 1996); William H. Rollins, *A greener vision of home: Cultural politics and environmental reform in the German Heimatschutz Movement 1904–18* (Ann Arbor/Mich.: University of Michigan Press, 1997); Diethart Kerbs and Jürgen Reulecke, eds., *Handbuch der deutschen Reformbewegungen 1880–1933* (Wuppertal: Hammer, 1998); Thomas Rohkrämer, *Eine andere Moderne? Zivilisationskritik, Natur und Technik in Deutschland 1880–1933* (Paderborn et al: Schöningh, 1999); Kevin Repp, *Reformers, Critics, and the Paths of German Modernity: Anti-Politics and the Search for Alternatives 1890–1914* (Cambridge/Mass., London: Harvard University Press, 2000); Antje Senarclens de Grancy, *"Moderner Stil" und "Heimisches Bauen": Architekturreform in Graz um 1900* (Cologne, Weimar, Vienna: Böhlau, 2001); Maiken Umbach and Bernd Hüppauf, eds., *Vernacular Modernism: Heimat, Globalization, and the Built Environment* (Stanford/Cal.: Stanford University Press, 2005).

2 Cor Wagenaar, "Cities and the Pursuit of Public Happiness. An Introduction," in *Happy: Cities and Public Happiness in Post-War Europe*, ed. Cor Wagenaar (Rotterdam: NAi Publ., 2004), 12–21; Eric E. Lampard, "The Pursuit of Happiness in the City: Changing Opportunities and Options in America," in *Transactions of the Royal Historical Society, Fifth Series* 23 (1973): 175–220.

3 Lampard, (see note 2), 218–19.

4 English has no equivalent for "Heimat." If we consider the various translations of Heimat into English, we find such diverse results as "home," "homeland," "native region," "birthplace" or "homestead." *Heimat* is a rather vague term and to a non-German speaker it often has a peculiar and slippery quality. But it seems that the variety of meanings is in no way unsettling to German speakers. For more see Peter Blickle, *Heimat: A critical theory of the German idea of homeland* (Rochester/NY et al.: Camden House, 2002), 1–6.

5 Rollins, (see note 1), 3.

6 Celia Applegate, *A nation of provincials: The German idea of Heimat* (Berkeley/Ca. et al: University of California Press, 1990), 19; Katharina Weigand, ed., *Heimat: Konstanten und Wandel im 19./20. Jahrhundert* (Ottobrunn: Bergverlag Rother, 1997); Blickle, (see note 4), 28, 31; Umbach and Hüppauf, (see note 1), 113, 116; Gunther Gebhard, Oliver Geisler, Steffen Schröter, "Heimatdenken: Konjunkturen und Konturen. Statt einer Einleitung," in *Heimat: Konturen und Konjunkturen eines umstrittenen Konzepts*, ed. Gunther Gebhard, Oliver Geisler and Steffen Schröter (Bielefeld: transcript, 2007) 10, 22, 44.

7 Rollins, (see note 1), 9.

8 Eric J. Hobsbawm, "Introduction: Inventing Traditions," in *The Invention of Tradition* ed. Eric J. Hobsbawm and Terence Ranger (Cambridge et al: Cambridge University Press, 1989), 1; Wolfgang Lipp, "Heimat in der Moderne. Quelle, Kampfplatz und Bühne von Identität," in Weigand, (see note 6), 51–72, 57.

9 See also: Sándor Békési, "Heimatschutz und die Großstadt. Zur Tradition und Moderne in Wien um 1900," *Österreichische Zeitschrift für Geschichtswissenschaften* 20 (2009:1): 95–130.

10 "… betont nicht den Gegensatz zwischen 'modern' und 'unmodern', sondern zwischen GUT UND SCHLECHT" Joseph August Lux, "Vorwort des Herausgebers," *Hohe Warte* 1 (1904/05): 1 (emphasis in orig., transl. by S. B.).

11 At the same time we should not underestimate the importance of the aesthetic approach, because "aestheticism formed a tremendously important avenue for the popular articulation of environmental concern in England … In Germany a very similar set of material and cultural factors soon helped give rise to the Heimatschutz." Rollins, (see note 1), 69.

12 Joseph August Lux, *'Wenn du vom Kahlenberg…': Das künstlerische Stadtbild Wiens, wie es war und wird* (Vienna et al.: Akademischer Verlag, 1907), 5–6.

13 Joseph August Lux, *Ingenieur-Aesthetik* (Munich: Lammers, 1910), 48–49.

14 Rollins, (see note 1), 72.

15 "Ich liebe die heimlichen, seltsamen Glücksgefühle, die solche Orte, Straßen, Häuser und Wohnungen gewähren." Lux, (see note 12), 6.

16 Joseph August Lux, "Mißstände der gegenwärtigen Großstadtanlagen. Das Wohnungselend im Zusammenhang mit unserer wirtschaftlichen Verfassung," *Hohe Warte* 1 (1904/05): 49–55.

17 Joseph August Lux, "Neuland im Nordosten Wiens," in Lux, (see note

12), 105–111, 110; Lux, "Eine Gartenstadtbewegung im Nordosten Wiens," *Der Architekt* 11 (1905): 46–48.

18 Ákos Moravánszky, *Competing Visions. Aesthetic Invention and Social Imagination in Central European Architecture, 1867–1918* (Cambridge/Mass. et al: MIT Press, 1998), 58.

19 Lux, (see note 12), 110–11.

20 "Das Wesen und der Zauber der Heimat liegt also in der Besonderheit und Eigenart alles dessen, worin und wie sich unser Leben abspielt." Karl Giannoni, *Heimatschutz*, vol. 6 of *Flugschriften des Vereins zum Schutze und zur Erhaltung der Kunstdenkmäler Wiens und Niederösterreichs* (Vienna: Gerlach & Wiedling, 1911), 5 and 7.

21 *Jahresbericht für 1914* (Bundesdenkmalamt, Archiv, Heimatschutz 2, Fasz. 1), see also Heimatschutz 3, Fasz. 1, Z. 22.

22 *Zur Rettung Alt-Wiens*, vol. 2 of *Flugschriften des Vereins zum Schutze und zur Erhaltung der Kunstdenkmäler Wiens und Niederösterreichs* (Vienna, Leipzig: Hof-Verlags-Buchhandlung Carl Fromme, 1910).

23 Wolfgang Kos and Christian Rapp, *Alt-Wien: Die Stadt, die niemals war*, exhibition catalogue of Wien Museum (Vienna: Czernin,[2] 2005 [2004]).

24 Gerhard Vinken, "Die neuen Ränder der alten Stadt. Modernisierung und ‚Altstadt-Konstruktion' im gründerzeitlichen Basel," in *Stadtformen. Die Architektur der Stadt zwischen Imagination und Konstruktion*, ed. Vittorio Magnago Lampugnani and Matthias Noell (Zurich: gta-Verlag, 2005), 130–41.

25 Cornelia Klinger, *Flucht, Trost, Revolte. Die Moderne und ihre ästhetischen Gegenwelten* (Munich, Vienna: Hanser, 1995), 10, 16, 23 and 31; Karl Heinz Bohrer, "Nach der Natur. Ansicht einer Moderne jenseits der Utopie," Merkur 41 (1987:7): 631–45, 631–32; Peter L. Berger, Brigitte Berger and Hansfried Kellner, *Das Unbehagen in der Modernität* (Frankfurt a. M. et al.: Campus, 1987 [1973]), 153; Shmuel N. Eisenstadt, *Tradition, Wandel und Modernität* (Frankfurt a. M.: Suhrkamp, 1979), 227–29.

26 Hans Tietze, *Das Wiener Stadtbild*, vol. 4 of *Flugschriften des Vereins zum Schutze und zur Erhaltung der Kunstdenkmäler Wiens und Niederösterreichs* (Vienna, Leipzig: Hof-Verlags-Buchhandlung Carl Fromme, 1910) 43; Giannoni, Heimatschutz, 44, 55–59; Karl Giannoni, "Heimatschutz und Städtebau," *Zeitschrift des Österreichischen Ingenieur- und Architekten-Vereines* 65 (1913): 745–48.

27 *Rechenschaftsbericht für 1913* (Bundesdenkmalamt, Archiv, Heimatschutz 2, Fasz. 1); unmarked information sheet (Bundesdenkmalamt,

Archiv, Heimatschutz 6, Fasz. 2 Bauberatung).

28 Bernhard Tschofen, "'Heimatschutz und Bauberatung.' Ein museales Zeugnis: Österreich-Ideologie im Technischen Museum Wien (1914–1916)," in *Politik der Präsentation. Museum und Ausstellung in Österreich 1918–1945*, ed. Herbert Posch and Gottfried Fliedl (Vienna: Turia + Kant, 1996), 319–30; *Schönes Österreich: Heimatschutz zwischen Ästhetik und Ideologie*, exhibition catalogue (Vienna: Selbstverlag Österr. Museum für Volkskunde, 1995), 70–77.

29 "Mitteilungen," *Der Städtebau* (1912): 108; Wilfried Posch, *Die Wiener Gartenstadtbewegung. Reformversuch zwischen erster und zweiter Gründerzeit* (Vienna: Edition Tusch, 1981), 32.

30 Werner Suppanz, "'… stets im Zusammenhang des Ganzen…' Metaerzählungen der politischen Lager Österreichs um 1900," *newsletter MODERNE*: Zeitschrift des SFB *Moderne—Wien und Zentraleuropa um 1900* 6 (2003:1) 19–24.

31 Martin Greiffenhagen, *Das Dilemma des Konservatismus in Deutschland* (Munich: Piper, 1971), 32ff. See also: Rolf Peter Sieferle, *Fortschrittsfeinde? Opposition gegen Technik und Industrie von der Romantik bis zur Gegenwart* (Munich: Beck, 1984) 157, 170.

32 Hermann Josef Stübben, "Stadtbauplan und Bauordnung im Hinblicke auf Kleinwohnungen," *Zeitschrift des Österr. Ingenieur- und Architekten-Vereines* 16 (1910), 249–55; Rudolf Eberstadt, "Wiener Wohnverhältnisse," in Rudolf Eberstadt, *Neue Studien über Städtebau und Wohnungswesen* (Jena: Fischer 1912), 157–204; Werner Hegemann, ed., *Der Städtebau: Nach den Ergebnissen der Allgemeinen Städtebau-Ausstellung in Berlin* vol. 2: *Verkehrswesen, Freiflächen: Paris, Wien, Budapest …* (Berlin: Verlag Ernst Wasmuth, 1913), 276–77.

33 Reinhard E. Petermann, *Wien im Zeitalter Kaiser Franz Josephs I.: Schilderungen* (Vienna: Lechner, 1908) 4, 132, 141. However, the last figure does not reveal whether remodeled buildings are also included or not.

34 Petermann, (see note 33).

35 Petermann, (see note 33), 130, 144.

36 David Frisby, *Cityscapes of Modernity. Critical Explorations* (Cambridge: Polity Press, 2001) 218.

37 Frisby, (see note 36).

38 The example of Bologna in the 1970s shows the possibility of an ambitious program of socially responsible urban preservation shows. See Filippo de Pieri and Paolo Scrivano, "The revitalization of historical Bologna," in *Happy: Cities and Public Happiness in Post-War Europe*, (see note 2), 452–59.

HAPPINESS THROUGH DISCIPLINE

Soviet Cities in the Travelogues of Foreign Visitors in the Nineteen-twenties and Nineteen-thirties*

Marina Dmitrieva

"Good to be alive! … Look at us, we are driving, we are satisfied! Perhaps happiness is expecting us…"
Ilya Il'f and Evgenii Petrov, *The Golden Calf, 1931*[1]

"My image of the city and the people is the same as that of the intellectual climate: obtaining a new optic for these things is the doubtless fruit of a stay in Russia."
Walter Benjamin, *Moskauer Tagebuch, 1926–27*[2]

Happiness was an important component of the Soviet utopia. Slogans such as "Man is born to be happy just as the bird is born to fly"[3] or well-known song lines proclaiming that "we are forgers, and our spirit is young / we are forging the keys to happiness"[4] expressed clichés of the Soviet era that were repeated again and again. According to these, the people of the Soviet Union inhabited the happiest country in the world. Such optimism and the belief in a bright future distinguished Soviet society as a "place of cheerfulness."[5] Posters, exhibitions and films were expected to represent a constant state of happiness. An atmosphere of good cheer was also invoked at workers' assemblies and mass demonstrations. These forms of representation insinuated, however, that happiness would not come by itself. In order to attain it, the Soviet citizen had to be educated in discipline and self-motivation, if necessary by force and through deprivation. This educational process was mainly targeted at the Soviet youth. The notorious slogan, "We thank Comrade Stalin for our happy childhood!" (▸ 1), emerged at the time of the Great Terror, a time characterised by fear and mutual mistrust, feelings that came to dominate the everyday lives of many Soviet people.[6]

The greater the discrepancy between utopia and everyday life, the greater the necessity became to express this collective euphoria coherently. In the course of the industrialisation associated with the first and second five-year plans (1928–1932; 1933–1937), Soviet propaganda focused on the new economic order that was being constructed in the Soviet state. This was evident in the propaganda journal, *The USSR in Construction*, which was published in several languages. It was designed to demonstrate a new social order and a new view of life, replacing a capitalist society that was associated with chaos and lack of progress. Urbanisation was a strong focus of this image. As a paradigm, it meant not only that new cities and modern factories were being constructed. It also involved the design of public spaces, staged as settings for new forms of collective happiness. Such promises of new happiness were extremely suggestive and even seemed credible to Western European intellectuals, successfully blurring their view of Soviet realities. Many of them pictured Soviet Russia as an ideal country. Most of them had a preconceived image of Russia, long before setting foot in the Soviet Union. André Gide recalled his expectations in the famous book *Retour de l'U.R.S.S.* (which ultimately concluded with a damning judgment of the Soviet system): "Who can say now what the Soviet Union used to mean for us? It was more than the motherland of our choice: it was an example for us, a glaring idol … There was, then,

СПАСИБІ ПАРТІЇ,
СПАСИБІ РІДНОМУ СТАЛІНУ
ЗА ЩАСЛИВЕ, ВЕСЕЛЕ
ДИТИНСТВО.

1

we thought, a country where utopia had been given the chance of realisation."[7] Gide spoke for many left-wing intellectuals who shared his expectations.

In what way did foreign travellers describe the Soviet Union as a blessed land? What role did Soviet propaganda play in shaping their views, and how did the reality they saw correspond to their ideal? In addressing these questions, I shall look in particular at Soviet urban designs, one of the dimensions of the bright future on which Soviet propaganda placed great emphasis, as well as at the image of the everyday life of Soviet citizens, as seen through the eyes of foreign visitors. Michel Foucault described buildings such as prisons, schools, barracks, and factory workshops as "spaces of discipline."[8] Applying this notion to the Soviet case, we could extend this list to include communal houses, labour clubs, pioneer and labour camps, recreational parks, and organised mass formations accompanying official festivities, i.e., spaces in which human existence was instrumentalised by allocating it to prescribed settings. All of these "ideal places" were displayed to foreign voyagers. For many of them, they exemplified how the Soviet person was kept under surveillance, formed, subjected to normalisation, and educated to happiness. The individual and the mass, personal freedom and its curtailment in the collective, such were the central questions with which

1   Poster with slogan in Ukrainian: "We thank the Party, Comrade Stalin for our happy childhood," 1937.

visitors concerned themselves regarding the new social experiments, which most of them measured against their personal experience.

On the Question of Genre

Accounts of journeys to the Soviet Union are a particular and distinctive category of travel literature.[9] In most cases, travellers who undertook such a journey were seeking to redefine themselves. Russia was no ordinary tourist destination. In many cases, it was associated with hopes and illusions, such as the desire to be cured from the wounds of capitalist isolation, the hope of a happy future for humanity and the wish to witness a realised utopia of a better human order. Such expectations became particularly high as the Nazi regime established itself in Germany. Soviet propaganda made skilful use of these circumstances. Often travellers departed in a highly distressed frame of mind, as in the case of Walter Benjamin, and hoped to be saved by their journey. This was particularly true for those Western intellectuals who sympathised with socialism. Some of them, like the artists Herwarth Walden and Heinrich Vogeler, even chose to settle in the Soviet Union after their trip and became victims of Stalinist oppression in subsequent years. Thus, for many intellectuals, trips to the Soviet Union were a sort of pilgrimage. One did not simply travel to the Soviet Union; one undertook a pilgrimage to the altar of communism, with the sense of devotion and expectation fitting to such an enterprise.[10] The young social democrat Herbert Weichmann, who was to become the mayor of Hamburg after the Second World War, described his anticipation of a journey across the Soviet Union with his wife in 1931 in the following terms: "This is what … emanates from Russia: not only constructivism,[11] but also the promise that in this country the implementation of paradise on earth is on the march towards realisation."[12] Given such expectations, the impressions of such travellers were on the whole very emotional, ranging from uncritical enthusiasm to a rejection that was almost as radical. For many of them, there is an evident lack of objective distance to their object of analysis. Even André Gide, for instance, could not evade remarking on the sense of warmth, the "brotherly spirit" he felt when meeting young people or factory workers.[13] Nearly all the foreign visitors proved Benjamin's assessment to be right. He argued that a stay in Russia was "a very precise testing stone:" "It will force everyone to choose their standpoint and to specify it precisely."[14]

The Itinerary and Organisation of the Trip

In most cases, a trip to the Soviet Union was an organised undertaking. It was very rare for foreigners to make individual plans. Independent travellers were still required to use the services of special organisations in Russia. From the mid-nineteen-twenties onwards, the Soviet foreign trade department opened several travel agencies in Germany and other Western European states. In 1925, the "All Union Society for Cultural Links Abroad" (known under the abbreviation VOKS in Russian) was founded. Many tourists called it the "Kameneva" Institute, after its director Ol'ga Kameneva. No foreigner travelling to the Soviet Union could bypass this organisation. It facilitated and controlled access to institutions, accommodation, and other formalities. In 1929, its function was taken over by Intourist, the Soviet foreign travel board. It made sure that travellers made the "right" contacts, protected them from the wrong ones, and controlled the itinerary of the trip. VOKS also published *Guide to the Soviet Union*, written by Alexander Radó and modelled after German Baedeker. The first edition, printed in 1925, comprised Moscow, Leningrad, Odessa, Kiev and Char'kov; the 1928 edition also explored the Asian parts of Russia. This guide was a useful companion for many travellers. But from the nineteen-thirties onwards, individual tourism became increasingly difficult.[15] Many travellers complained about poor quality and overpriced accommodation.

Apart from general tourism, some Soviet organisations such as the Writers' Union organised their own trips. Their programme was even more regimented, with even greater limitations on individual freedom. Tourists travelling with such programmes experienced their reception in the Soviet Union as a "sumptuous affair" and thought of the Soviet Union as a "writers' paradise."[16] Among the Western authors who travelled in such a context were André Gide, Lion Feuchtwanger, Romain Rolland, Arthur Hollitscher, Henri Barbusse, as well as other more or less well-known authors. As Gide recalled, he and his companions received generous royalties for translations of their works and publications in newspapers (with circulations of up to 400,000!). Thanks to the generosity of their hosts, who met their every wish on the thoroughly planned trips, they did not even need touch their fees on their journey. One such trip was organised by the Soviet journal *Sovremennaia Architektura* (Contemporary Architecture) in 1932. Its guests were a group of French and Belgian architects connected with the French journal *Architecture d'aujourd'hui,* who wished to study constructivist architecture.[17] Another series of trips was related to the tenth anniversary of the October Revolution in November 1927, when the Soviet government issued invitations to a number of prominent personalities from abroad. There were also specialised trips in connection with the annual revolutionary festivities of 1 May and 7 November. Tourists had very few options when it came to changing the prescribed routes. Nearly all of them describe the same cities and places. This context made it even more difficult for them to make independent judgements. In addition, most of the tourists did not speak Russian and thus had to rely on the translators allocated to them. Gide, who was accompanied by two friends who spoke some Russian, could screen the information he received to some extent. By contrast, Feuchtwanger was entirely reliant upon it.

Tourists would typically arrive by train from Germany via Poland. Some, like Herbert and Elisabeth Weichmann, came by boat from Stettin to Leningrad. From there, they travelled onwards to Moscow and further south, to the Ukraine and the Caucasian Federation. Gide chose an extravagant variation, arriving by plane in Leningrad from Le Bourget airport in Paris.

In the Russian media and fictional literature, this tourism boom was reflected in diverse ways. The theme of the foreign visitor was interpreted in grotesque comedies such as *The wondrous adventures of Mr West in the land of the Bolsheviks* by Lev Kuleshov (1924), or the children's poem *Mister Twister* by Samuil Marshak (early nineteen-thirties) and Andrei Platonov's drama *Fourteen Little Red Huts* on the subject of collectivisation (1932), to name but a few. In all of them, the Soviet Union is depicted as a mine of happiness. In a certain sense the satirical gangster novel *The Golden Calf*, by Ilya Il'f and Evgeny Petrov, also belongs in this category. Its main character Ostap Bender, a chevalier of fortune, travels through Russia in search of good luck. He, too, is in some ways a tourist, a foreigner who looks at everyday life under socialism from a distance. He thus obtains a different, critical perspective of his own country. The novel's leitmotif is the quest for happiness, which turns out to be a difficult undertaking. Implicitly, the novel suggests that it could only succeed if the hero became integrated in the collective socialist undertaking, although this path remains closed to him. Bender makes his voyage through Russia by car as an "individual tourist," or occasionally in a special tourist train as a false member of an official delegation, seeking to celebrate the opening of the Eastern railway branch in Central Asia and meeting several foreign sightseers along the way. Travellers are contrasted with Soviet citizens. They are portrayed as naive, often stupid, and their appearance and behaviour is quite different to that of the Soviet people. Bender's perspective is a satirical perversion of the image of the foreigner visiting the land of the Soviets.

First Impressions

Egon Erwin Kisch, the "flying reporter," allowed the fleeting nature of a traveller's impressions to shape the entire form of his account. He went on his first trip to the Soviet Union in 1925, during the time of the New Economic Policy (NEP). The train in which the reporter travelled from Moscow to Erevan becomes a fixed point, while the country and life observed from the window are described as passing, fragmentary impressions. As the train approaches Moscow, the capital "turns around the train …"[18] In the window, a landscape of steppes and forests stretches out, only rarely interspersed with urban elements, and the variety and changeability of ethnographic types form a colourful image of the long journey. But even where Kisch stops to gain a closer look at the city, he remains a fleeting observer, cutting out some details in passing and recomposing them later in the form of a collage. "Moscow crawls by," he writes, "an orgy of contrasts, an Asian village with houses built in the style of American skyscrapers, cardboard sledge and omnibus, baroque palace and wooden hut, Stanislavsky and Meyerhold, the booming of the press and dictatorship, the court opera ballet and 'blue blouses', street bazaar and department store."[19]

Despite these "American" houses, which many tourists perceived as signs of modernity but also as something alien to Russia, the village character of Moscow is one of its striking features for many of its visitors in the nineteen-twenties. Ella Maillart, a young tourist from

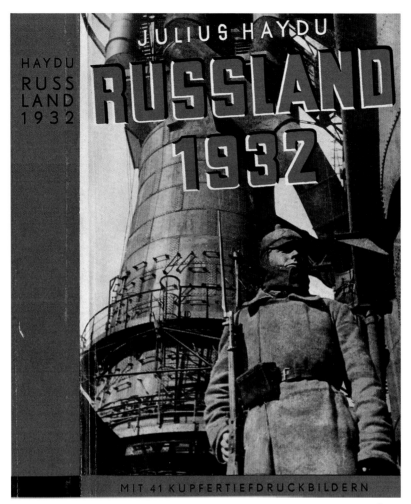

JULIUS HAYDU

HAYDU
RUSS
LAND
1932

RUSSLAND

1932

MIT 41 KUPFERTIEFDRUCKBILDERN

Switzerland travelling to Russia in 1930, perceived the city with both candour and curiosity. She witnessed the erection of the new "House of the Soviets" by Le Corbusier.[20] Ella Maillart remarked on the peculiarity of Russian, particularly Muscovite, urbanity: "With its low-storey wooden houses, surrounded by fenced gardens, occasionally interrupted by the stone walls of a luxury house or a picturesque Church, Moscow has nothing of a Western metropolis."[21]

The philosopher of urban life, Walter Benjamin, felt that the Russian capital was not just "Asiatic," but a "non-city" altogether. In his view Moscow, which he visited in the snowy and cold winter of 1926/27, was the "quietest metropolis." In its streets, the "Russian village" was "playing hide and seek." Indeed, he concluded, wherever y ou look, Moscow "does not look like the city itself but rather like its faint counter-image."[22] In contrast to many other visitors, Benjamin travelled alone, and thus had to rely on the help of some friends

2   Book cover, Julius Haydu, *Russland 1932*.

and institutions such as VOKS. Moreover, his was a journey undertaken under exceptional personal circumstances. Benjamin was seeking the love of Asia Lacis. At the same time, he was also contemplating whether or not to join the KPD. Thus, the trip was accompanied by considerable emotional tension. In the end, Benjamin decided not to live in the Soviet Union but to return to Berlin.

Benjamin perceived the rhythm of the city both optically and haptically. He travelled by tram, fighting his way on board through the vast crowds of fellow passengers. He explored the new city "on strolling serpentine paths,"[23] and had to learn how to walk on the icy roads. He sought refuge in places that seemed more familiar, like cafés, but these places turned out, at best, to be basic canteens. He also fled from the streets to find himself in overcrowded apartments or "caves," as he described them, or in overheated hotel rooms. In these places, Benjamin found no refuge, no sense of personal freedom.

Despite his ignorance of the Russian language, Benjamin was sensitive enough to perceive that the country was in a brink situation. "Schematically abbreviated," he wrote to Martin Buber, for whose journal he had promised to write his impressions: "Moscow shows signs

3

3   Book cover, Herbert und Elisabeth Weichmann, *Alltag im Sowjetstaat*, 1931.

4

of all possible future outcomes: the possible failure of the revolution and its success. In both cases, however, there will be something unpredictable, something far removed from all the programmatic visions of the future. This leaves its mark, hard and clear, on the people and their environment today."[24]

Benjamin remained quite indifferent to the radical new art emerging in Russia. Instead, he developed a real passion for popular toys and icons. By contrast, the American Alfred Barr, Jr. (who became the first director of the Museum of Modern Art in New York), also travelling to Moscow and Leningrad via Berlin with his wife Gene in the winter of 1926/27, was predominantly interested in modern art. While he considered Leningrad to be one of the most beautiful cities of the eighteenth century, he described Moscow's architecture as "unpicturesque disorder" and remarked on its "lack of consistent style."[25] Such dismissive remarks notwithstanding, Moscow's new buildings, designed in the style of "Gropius,"

5

"Corbusier" or "Bauhaus," as he put it, with their rational structure, clear lines and in stark contrast to the "chaotic" construction of old Moscow, caught his eye.

While most people travelling to the Soviet Union in the nineteen-twenties focused on the old historical architecture and marvelled at the exotic diversity of the NEP bazaars, their common reaction at the beginning of the nineteen-thirties was: Russia was being rebuilt from scratch. In 1932, a book containing positive propaganda for Moscow was published by the Hungarian writer Julius Haydu, who lived in Vienna. In the book, which featured photographs from the official Russian press agency (▶ 2), he argued that Russia was a "construction site."[26] He believed that this atmosphere, signifying a new beginning and the belief in a bright future, was also discernible in the faces of the people he encountered: "People in Russia feel like the first fighters for a great idea. It fills them with hope and they are certain of its victory."[27] The British couple W.P. and Zelda K. Coates shared this impres-

5   Narkomfin House in Moscow, 1928–29, communal center, Photograph by Charles Dedoyard, 1932.

sion on their journey in 1935: "We sauntered through many streets; there was scarcely one in which several high and extensive buildings were not in the course of erection."[28]

In contrast the Weichmanns, a couple who made one of the most detailed accounts of everyday life in the Soviet Union in this period, remarked on how the new buildings—such as Moscow's recently built main postal station—stood out against the general state of devastation, the lack of provision and infrastructure which they encountered everywhere in Russian cities. The photomontage on the cover particularly illustrates the difficulties of everyday Russian life, showing queues in front of food stores and homeless children (▶ 3). Reflecting on this contrast, they asked the question: "Is this decline in life's external appearance juxtaposed here with a new, internal life form, richer and happier than the appearance reveals?"[29] With these words they voiced a question that was fundamental for all foreign visitors to Soviet Russia: how did this vision of happiness correspond with the realities with which they were confronted on their trip? And did the ideal exist at all?

From the Komunalka to the House Commune: Private Spaces

The extreme shortage of space that arose from the enforced accommodation of several families in one apartment, resulting from a general lack of housing, dominated everyday life in the Soviet Union. Benjamin perceived these overcrowded apartments, often occupied by up to eight families, as "small cities" or "field camps." People did not live there, but "camped out." In his view, Bolshevism had "abolished private life."[30] Ilf's and Petrov's novel *The Golden Calf* coined the term "raven settlement" (voronya slobodka) for such communal flats, defined by a lack of space and particularly rough manners. By contrast, the official trips through the Soviet Union presented everyday life in Russia under the paradigm of New Living. The first example realised was the House for the Staff of Narkomfin, the employees of the Soviet finance ministry. This large complex on Novisnky Bul'var dates back to 1928/29 and was designed by Moissei Ginzburg and Ignatii Milinis as a house commune. It consisted of a long horizontal building containing a living block (▶ 4), a communal centre (▶ 5) and a laundry. The fourth planned unit, a crèche in a circular form, was never built. This architectural project was to embody the constructivist ideas of the rational organisation of life. In order to educate people, step by step, towards the consciousness of a socialist way of life, the house commune comprised three types of residential quarters, reflecting the transition from the "petit bourgeois" family to the collective socialist reality. Type A consisted of small apartments on two levels with foldable beds, built-in furniture, a kitchen unit (the "Frankfurt Kitchen" type) and sanitary facilities. Types B and C were being gradually reduced to sleeping units. Collective washing facilities for several persons were available in the corridors. The communal block, connected to the living block by a covered walkway, accommodated a kitchen, a dining room, sport facilities, club rooms and a library. The crèche was to free the parents of the care of their children. In summer, the flat roof was to serve as a dormitory for children. This residential complex was located in a park and designed to reflect a new form of human order in harmony with nature.[31] Alfred Barr visited the family of the writer Sergei Tretyakov, who was allocated a "bourgeois" apartment in this building. Barr was taken aback by the discrepancy between the concept of New Living and the exceptionally inadequate way in which it was executed, which failed to live up to American standards. "In fact, only the superficial things are modern," he wrote, for "the plumbing, heating, etc., are technically very crude and cheap, a parody of an exceptionally modern idea without any of the technical traditions required to carry it out."[32] Members of the delegation of French and Belgian architects who visited the Ginzburg house had similar impressions. Charles Dedoyard, who took the photos of the building (▶ 4, 5), deplored the "exécution lamentable" of many of the objects of the new architecture.[33]

Visitors who commented on the extravagance of the communal house found the small scale of the sleeping rooms as well as the small number of bathrooms inadequate. Nonetheless, all of them registered the enthusiasm with which residents took part in this experiment. Dedoyard summed up his impressions in the following words: "La personnalité de l'individu doit s'effacer devant la collectivité."[34] All the same, visitors noted a mixture of the old and the new in the design of the rooms, which was not consistent with the style of the architecture: "The walls are adorned with portraits of Lenin and icons in a curious state of harmony, the old religion alongside the new."[35] As the Weichmanns remarked, the possibility of individual privacy was purposefully undermined by the organisation of living space in this house. "In this way, it was intended to educate people in the spirit of collectivism."[36] But where was the boundary, travellers asked, "between free will and servile regimentation, between apartment and barracks?"[37]

Public Spaces

The density, overcrowding and shabbiness of the private spaces, which could only serve as sleeping quarters, stood in stark contrast to the light, spacious and modern public spaces in which the "actual" life of the Soviet person took place: for instance in the labour clubs, in which the Soviet person was to become a "collective human" and which was designed to fulfil his or her needs. Here, modern constructivist architecture offered a setting for theatre performances, lectures, chess games (but no card games), or a venue for ceremonies such as "red christenings" or marriages (▶ 6).

A place of great importance and, according to Karl Schlögel, a "central topos of Soviet culture,"[38] was the Central Park for Culture and Recreation in Moscow, which was named after Gorki following his death. Situated on the banks of the Moskva River, the park was planned in 1928 according to the designs of the avant-garde architect Konstantin Mel'nikov. The park did not obtain its final shape until 1937. With its regular structure, its classicist park pavilions, its ornamental flower beds and its granite embankments, this park embodied the Stalinist architectural ideal along with its retrospective monumental spirit (▶ 7). Almost

6   Zuev Labour Club, Architect Ilja Golosov, 1927–30, Photograph from Julius Haydu, *Russland, 1932*.
7   Central Park of Rest and Culture, riverside, designed by Alexandr Vlasov, 1936.
8   Children's corner in the Moscow Central Park of Rest and Culture, Photograph from W.P. and Zelda K. Coates, *Scenes from Soviet Life*, 1936.
9   Water sport at Central Park for Culture and Recreation, Photograph from W.P. and Zelda K. Coates, *Scenes from Soviet Life*, 1936.

10

all foreign visitors gave a description of the park in the accounts of their journeys. André Gide visited this *hortus conclusus* again and again. "As soon as you pass through the gate, you feel as though you are in a different world," he marvelled.[39] This Soviet Arcadia was separated from the outside by a monumental fence made of cast iron, designed on classicist examples. Visitors were led through the majestic gate to a socialist paradise, providing a completely new recreational facility whose aim was to combine educational projects with sports for the workers. Although the Central Park in Moscow, like many others like it that were subsequently built in other cities, had historical precedents—most notably Central Park in New York and the summer estates of the eighteenth century Russian nobility—it still made a great impression on its foreign visitors. The Coates couple found "two immense artistically shaded portraits of Lenin and Stalin worked in flowers" near the entrance. "At a distance of a few hundred yards some artists-gardeners touching up the portraits looked like Lilliputians."[40] In 1935 on the main promenade, Ervin Sinkó saw "an endless row of larger-than-life, painfully amateurish portraits of martyrs of the international revolution. Beneath each portrait, the martyr's name and the date and details of his murderers were inscribed."[41] The park also had several tribunes for speakers who would inform the public of the political situation or explain scientific problems, as well as numerous pavilions for playing chess, theatre or sports. At the end of the nineteen-thirties, a German military attaché saw speakers explaining the Molotov Ribbentrop pact to the public. (As he recalled it,

10   Central Park for Culture and Recreation with parachute-jumping platform, Photograph by the architect Hannes Meyer, 1932.

this found support among the population.)[42] Visitors also remarked on the dance halls with loud jazz music which, towards the end of the nineteen-thirties, was increasingly replaced by Russian folk dancing with instructors. Part of this construction of a socialist utopia was dedicated to a "Children's City," which attracted the attention of many visitors (▶ 8). Smaller children played or slept here while their parents entertained themselves in the park. The older children could acquire skills in small purpose-built saw mill, for instance, or take some exercise (▶ 9). Near the main gate, a long queue marked the entrance to a tower for parachute jumping (▶ 10).

"What happens if a parachute does not open?" asked one of the visitors. "Oh," replied the attendant, "the jumper gets his money back if he applies for it personally."[43]

Although the Central Park was one of the main attractions of the city, it did not have the atmosphere of a fun-fair. In the first instance, the park was there for the purposes of public agitation and political education. The acquisition of good manners was part of this package. Many foreign visitors pointed out the notably good manners of people promenading in the park, regardless of whether they took part in the entertainment programme or just sat around as romantic couples on the park benches. Special rules of behaviour were to be adhered to in this special place. Behind these cast iron gates, the disposition of the people who were crammed into the trams or communal apartments, so characteristic of Soviet everyday life, was forgotten. Ervin Sinkó did not meet a single "frivolous person" in the park.[44] The Weichmanns marvelled at the sedate manners of people who walked "with gravitas and stiffness" through the gardens.[45]

The Happy City

Whether it was used euphorically or with question marks, "happiness" was the word that occurred most frequently in accounts of journeys to the Soviet Union. "Russian people seem happy," remarked André Gide.[46] Kurt Kläber enjoyed watching the Moscow crowds:

> Many people are having a day off today. They are enjoying themselves. They are laughing. There are young workers wrapped up in thick shirts. A cheeky face protruding from under a cap. Girls, round, red-cheeked, their firm legs in crude boots. Older ones, slow, portly. Old people. Children. The laughter is getting louder …
>
> Cheers! Yes, it is a city that is enjoying itself, this Moscow, a happy city. A city of pleasure and of work.[47]

Lion Feuchtwanger also saw Moscow as the city of happiness: "This entire, large city of Moscow was breathing contentedness and harmony, more than that: happiness itself."[48] His visit, between November 1936 and February 1937, was particularly celebrated in the media, and served to cover up the devastating effect of Gide's book. Upon his return, Feuchtwanger wrote the report, *Moskau 1937. Ein Reisebericht für meine Freunde*, in which he even justified the show trials; this publication met with extremely negative reactions in the West.[49] The Russian translation, which appeared in the same year, was published with a circulation of 200,000; however it was withdrawn from bookstores and libraries after just one year.[50]

For Feuchtwanger, the reconstruction of the new Moscow according to Stalin's "general plan" of 1935 became a metaphor for the construction of a new world, in which "rational planning" was juxtaposed with the "individual's will for profit." This necessitated, as he put it "deprivations in private life."[51] The general plan dated 1935 realised the slogan of the "transformation of Moscow into an exemplary socialist city, capital of the world's proletariat," first formulated in 1931, in a new form that was no longer constructivist. Though the 1935 plan did leave out some radical concepts for spatial solutions formulated in the avant-garde, it was also combined with Renaissance models of an ideal city. More specifically, Stalin's general plan was to return to the older "feudal" ring structure of the city, dismissing new avant-garde plans in favour of a hierarchical ordering of space that rested on the traditions of pre-revolutionary Russian architecture.[52] The straight thoroughfares traversing the body of the medieval city structure were superimposed onto the ring structure of Moscow. Radial roads led to the city centre, which was no longer to be marked by the Kremlin. Instead, the plan envisaged a giant building, with a huge Lenin statue on top, to be known as the Palace of the Soviets. This was to replace the Cathedral of Christ the Saviour on the bank of the Moskva, not far from the Kremlin.

Feuchtwanger learned all the details of the plan from a huge electrically-powered model that was shown to him on his trip. He enthused about the size and beauty of the project of a metropolis "built up from the ground according to the rules of reason."[53] Many other travellers, by contrast, were struck by the discrepancy between the large "models" of reconstruction in propaganda literature and their own visual impressions. Weichmann's impression of the people in Russia was that they appeared depressed, tired, faint, and grey. According to him, only the Russian propaganda was colourful and seductive.

Antoine de Saint-Exupéry, who spent some time in Moscow in 1937 and witnessed the 1 May demonstrations as an insider and not, like most foreigners, from the tribune, made notes on the disciplined march of mass configurations accompanied by aeroplanes flying in formation. What he saw here was "Stalin's promised land, according to his orders."[54] The exemplary prison colony at Bolshevo near Moscow, with its "happy inmates," signified for him a form of "collective enslavement" and exemplified the state of surveillance and patronage that, in his view, prevailed everywhere.[55]

Happiness?

"'Good to be alive!'—said Balaganov. 'Look at us, we are driving, we are satisfied! Perhaps happiness is expecting us …'" Ostap Bender counters his travel companion's naïve expectation of finding happiness on his journey with the image of a surrealist Fata Morgana:

'Are you sure?'—asked Ostap.—'Happiness is awaiting us on the road? Perhaps it is even fluttering its wings with impatience? Where is Admiral Balaganov,'—it said. 'Why have we been waiting for him so long? You are a psycho, Balaganov! Happiness is not waiting for anyone. It is wandering around the country in long white garments, singing a children's song: 'Oh, America—that's a country! Here people are promenading and drinking without *zakuski*.' But this naïve chick has to be caught, you need it to like you, you have to court it. As for you, Balaganov, you will never make it with this chick.'[56]

For many foreign pilgrims to Soviet Russia, the search for happiness also turned out to be illusory, disappointing, or even dramatic. In particular, many found that their idea of happiness differed from that of the people they met. These people were happy because, like Shura Balaganov, they found themselves in a state of a permanent expectation of happiness. As Saint Exupéry aptly remarked, they were "at home in the dream."[57] They were also happy and proud to serve as the harbingers of happiness for the whole of humanity, and to this end they were prepared to accept severe deprivation in their own personal situation. Their diffuse ideas on the private and the public, widespread in the Soviet Union of the nineteen-twenties and nineteen-thirties which celebrated the growing "collectivisation of the private," were characterised by a dramatic lack of living space. Accordingly, official Soviet ideology shifted the prime locus of human life towards public areas.

One important result of a visit to the Soviet Union was, as Benjamin put it, the prospect of obtaining a new perspective both on its intellectual atmosphere and on one's own values and norms. In the end, for many Western tourists it meant having to say good-bye to the idea that people could be educated in a new form of happiness. "Happiness demands," as Gide wrote, "that each individual be robbed of their individuality. The happiness of all can only be attained at the cost of the individual."[58] His conclusions on Russia are damning: "And I doubt that in any country today, be it Hitler's Germany, the spirit is less free, more subjugated, more frightened, more terrorised and yoked."[59]

Endnotes

* Translated from German by Dina Gusejnova.

1 "Khorosho zhyt' na svete!—skazal Balaganov.—Vot my yedem, my syty! Mozhet byt', nas ozhidaet schastye…" Ilya Il'f and Evgenii Petrov, *Zolotoy telyonok* [The Golden Calf] (Moscow: Panorama, 1995), 66.

2 "Es ist mir mit dem Bilde der Stadt und der Menschen dasselbe wie mit dem Bilde der geistigen Zustände: die neue Optik, die man auf sie gewinnt, ist der unzweifelhafte Ertrag eines russischen Aufenthaltes." Walter Benjamin, *Moskauer Tagebuch. Mit einem Vorwort von Gershom Scholem* (Hamburg: Edition Suhrkamp, 1980), 163.

3 This slogan is taken from the short story *A Paradox* (1894) by Vladimir Korolenko.

4 "My kuznezy, i dukh nash molod//kuyem my k schastiyu klyuchi."

5 Mickhail Rykhlin, *Räume des Jubels* (Frankfurt a. M.: Suhrkamp, 2003).

6 Karl Schlögel, *Terror und Traum: Moskau 1937* (Munich: Carl Hanser Verlag, 2008).

7 "Qui dira ce que l'U.R.S.S. a été pour nous? Plus qu'une patrie d'élection : un exemple, un guide. Ce que nous rêvions, que nous osi-

ons à peine espérer mais à quoi tendaient nos volontés, nos forces, avait eu lieu là-bas." André Gide, *Retour de l'U.R.S.S.* (Paris: Editions Gallimard, 1978 [1936]), 18; André Gide, *Retouches à mon Retour de l'U.R.S.S.* (Paris: Editions Gallimard, 1937). Gide's journey in 1936 took nearly two months—from 17 June to 22 August. Besides Moscow and Leningrad, he also visited the Caucasian Federation and holiday resorts at the Black Sea.

8 Michel Foucault, *Surveiller et punir: Naissance de la prison* (Paris: Gallimard, 1975).

9 Sylvia R. Margulies, *The Pilgrimage to Russia. The Soviet Union and the Treatment of Foreigners, 1924–1937* (Madison/Milwaukee, London: University of Wisconsin Press, 1968); Christiane Uhlig, *Utopie oder Alptraum? Schweizer Reiseberichte über die Sowjetunion (1917–1941)* (Zurich: Rohr, 1992); Paul Hollander, *Political Pilgrims, Travels of Western Intellectuals to the Soviet Union, China, and Cuba, 1928–1978* (New York: Oxford University Press, 1981); especially see: Matthias Heeke, *Reisen zu den Sowjets. Der ausländische Tourismus in Russland 192—1941* (Münster, Hamburg, London: LIT, 2003).

10 Michail Ryklin, *Kommunismus als Religion* (Frankfurt a. M.: Verlag der Weltreligionen, 2008).

11 "Constructivism" refers to building here and not to an artistic movement.

12 "Das ist … das aus Russland ruft: nicht nur der Konstruktivismus sondern die Verheißung, dass in diesem Lande die Verwirklichung des Paradieses auf Erden schon auf dem Marsche ist." Herbert and Elisabeth Weichmann, *Alltag im Sowjetstaat. Macht und Mensch. Wollen und Wirklichkeit in Sowjet-Rußland* (Berlin: Brückenverlag, 1931), 6.

13 "J'ai senti parmi les camerades nouveaux une fraternité subite s'établir …" Gide, *Retour de l'U.R.S.S.*, (see note 7), 21.

14 "Es wird jeden nötigen, seinen Standpunkt zu wählen und genau zu präzisieren" Benjamin, (see note 2), 163.

15 Heeke, (see note 9), 25–97.

16 Margulies, (see note 9), 89.

17 See anonymous report in: *Sovremennaja architektura* (1933:2): 59. Records by French and Belgian architects published in *Architecture d'aujourd'hui* 8 (November 1932). Photos of this trip are preserved at the Canadian Centre of Architecture, Montreal. Many thanks to the Center, and especially to Anne-Marie Sigouin, for giving me the opportunity to study this valuable collection of photos.

18 Egon Erwin Kisch, *Zaren, Popen, Bolschewiken* (Berlin, Weimar: Aufbau Verlag, 1977) (first published in 1927 by Erich Reiß Verlag, Berlin), 9–10.

19 "Moskau kriecht vorbei, Orgie der Kontraste, asiatisches Dorf mit Häusern in amerikanischem Wolkenkratzerstil, Kistenschlitten und Autobus, Barockpalast und Holzhütte, Stanislawski und Meyerhold, Presseaufschwung und Diktatur, Hofopernballett und 'Blaue Blusen', Straßenbasar und Warenhaus …" Kisch, (see note 18), 9.

20 Ella Maillart, *Ausser Kurs. Eine junge Schweizerin in der revolutionären Sowjetunion* (Zurich: eFeF-Verlag, 1989), 21. She meant the Zentrosoyuz Building, erected between 1928 and 1936.

21 Maillart, (see note 20), 11.

22 Benjamin, (see note 2), 99.

23 Walter Benjamin, "Moskau," in Benjamin, *Ges. Schriften*, ed. Rolf Tiedemann und Hermann Schweppenhäuser, vol. IV (Frankfurt a. M.: Suhrkamp, 1991), 316–48, here 317.

24 "Moskau lässt schematisch verkürzt alle Möglichkeiten erkennen: vor allem die des Scheiterns und des Gelingens der Revolution. In beiden Fällen aber wird es etwas Unabsehbares geben, dessen Bild von aller programmatischen Zukunftsmalerei weit unterschieden sein wird und das zeichnet sich heute in den Menschen und ihrer Umwelt hart und deutlich ab." Benjamin, (see note 2), 12.

25 Alfred Barr Jr., "Russian Diary 1927–1928," *October 7* (Soviet Revolutionary Culture) (1978): 10–57, 11.

26 Julius Haydu, *Russland 1932* (Vienna, Leipzig: Phaidon-Verlag, 1932).

27 "Russlands Menschen fühlen sich als Vorkämpfer eines großen Gedankens. Sie sind davon erfüllt und ihres Sieges sicher." Haydu, (see note 26), 179.

28 W.P. Coates and Zelda K. Coates, *Scenes from Soviet Life* (London: Lawrence and Wishart, 1936), 49.

29 Weichmann, (see note 12), 18.

30 Benjamin, (see note 2), 327.

31 Victor Büchli, "Moisei Ginzburg's Narkomfin Communal House in Moscow: Contesting the Social and Modernist World," *Journal of the Society of Architectural Historians 57* (1998:2): 160–81, 174.

32 Barr, (see note 25), 13.

33 Charles Dedoyard, "Sur le chantier soviétique," *Architecture d'aujourd'hui 8* (November 1932), 70–71, 71.

34 Dedoyard, (see note 33), 70.

35 "An den Wänden hängen in erstaunlicher Eintracht Lenin-Bilder und Heiligenbilder, die alte und neue Religion." Weichmann, (see note 12), 48.

36 "Die Menschen sollen auf diese Weise zum Kollektivismus erzogen werden." Weichmann, (see note 12), 44.

37 Weichmann, (see note 12), 45.

38 Karl Schlögel, "Der Zentrale Gor'kij—Kultur- und Erholungspark (CPKiO) in Moskau," in *Stalinismus vor dem Zweiten Weltkrieg: neue Wege der Forschung*, ed. Manfred Hildermeier et al. (Munich: Oldenbourg, 1998), 255–274, 264; Schlögel (see note 6), 522–30. See also: Katharina Kucher, *Der Gorki-Park. Freizeitkultur des Stalinismus, 1928–1941* (Cologne, Weimar, Vienna: Böhlau, 2007).

39 "Aussitôt la porte franchie on se sent tout dépaysé." Gide, *Retour de l'U.R.S.S.*, (see note 7), 23.

40 Coates, (see note 28), 61.

41 "… eine endlose Reihe überlebensgroßer, mit peinlichem Dilettantismus gemalter Porträts von Märtyrern der internationalen Revolution. Unter jedem Porträt der Name und die Angabe, wann und durch wen der Betroffene getötet wurde." Ervin Sinkó, *Roman eines Romans. Moskauer Tagebuch* (Berlin: Das Arsenal, 1990), 174.

42 Schlögel, (see note 38), 255–56 (cit. from: Hermann Teske, ed., Ernst Köstring, *der militärische Mittler zwischen dem Deutschen Reich und der Sowjetunion 1921–1941* (Frankfurt a. M.: Mittler 1965), 124–25).

43 Coates, (see note 28), 63.

44 Sinkó, (see note 41), 139.

45 Weichmann, (see note 12), 82.

46 "Ceci reste pourtant : le peuple russe paraît heureux." Gide, *Retouches à mon Retour de l'U.R.S.S.*, (see note 7), 63.

47 "Viele haben heute ihren freien Tag. Sie sind fröhlich. Sie lachen. In dicke Blusen gehüllte junge Arbeiter. Unter den vorgeschobenen Mützen das kecke Gesicht. Mädchen, rund, rotwangig, die festen Beine in derben Stiefeln. Ältere, langsam, behäbig. Alte. Kinder. Das Lachen verstärkt sich…Jubel! Ja, es ist eine frohe Stadt, dieses Moskau, eine glückliche Stadt. Eine Stadt der Freude und der Arbeit." Kurt Kläber, "Fahrt nach Moskau, 1931," in *Unterwegs nach Eriwan. Reisen in die Sowjetunion 1918 bis 1934*, ed. Manfred Jendryschik (Halle, Leipzig: Mitteldeutscher Verlag, 1988), 423–27, 426.

48 "Die ganze, große Stadt Moskau atmete Zufriedenheit und Einverständnis, mehr als das: Glück." Cit. After: Lion Feuchtwanger, *Moskau 1937. Reisebericht für meine Freunde* (Berlin, Weimar: Aufbau Verlag, 1993), 12.

49 First published by Querido-Verlag Amsterdam in 1937.

50 Feuchtwanger, *Moskva 1937* (Moscow: Goslitizdat, 1937). The book was withdrawn from book stores and libraries a year later.

51 Feuchtwanger, (see note 48), 22–31.

52 From 1931–32, an international competition for the project of the Palace of The Soviets took place; many famous foreign architects took part, among them Le Corbusier. The decision of the jury signalled a digression from the ideas of New Constructivism and the Functional City.

53 Feuchtwanger, (see note 48), 26–27.

54 Antoine de Saint-Exupéry, "Reportagen. Moskau," in Exupéry, *Dem Leben einen Sinn geben* (Düsseldorf: dtv, 1964), 23.

55 Exupéry, (see note 54), 41.

56 "… 'Vy v etom tverdo uvereny?'—prosil Ostap.—'Schastye ozhidaet nas na doroge? Mozhet byt', eshche mashet krylyshkami ot neterpenia? Gde,'—govorit ono,—'admiral Balaganov? Pochemu ego tak dolgo net? Vy psikh, Balaganov! Schastye nikogo ne podzhidaet. Ono brodit po strane v dlinnych belych odezhdakh, raspevaya detskuyu pesenku: "Akh, Amerika—eto strana, tam gulayut i pyut bez zakuski." No etu naivnuyu detku nado lovit', ey nuzhno ponravitsa, za ney nuzhno ukhazhivat'. A u vas, Balaganov, s etoy detkoy romana ne vyydet.'" Il'f and Petrov, (see note 1), 66.

57 Exupéry, (see note 54), 43.

58 "Le bonheur de tous ne s'obtient qu'en désindividualisant chacun. Le bonheur de tous ne s'obtient qu'aux dépens de chacun." Gide, *Retour de l'U.R.S.S.*, (see note 7), 41.

59 "Et je doute qu'en aucun pays aujourd'hui, fût-ce dans l'Allemagne de Hitler, l'esprit soit moins libre, plus courbé, plus craintif (terrorisé), plus vassalisé." Gide, *Retour de l'U.R.S.S.*, (see note 7), 55.

"… A BETTER, HAPPIER WORLD"

Visions of a New Warsaw after World War Two

Jacek Friedrich

1

In a Poland destroyed by the Second World War, the question of how a city should look, which functions it should have, and the ends it should serve became a highly relevant and topical matter. In 1947, in the introduction to his urban planning textbook, Tadeusz Tołwiński observed that an unsatisfactory city environment contributed to "the degeneration of the leading European nations."[1] Not surprisingly, Tołwiński identified the main goal of the modern urban designer as being "to provide good quality living space and a convenient workplace for the widest social stratum."[2]

In face of the tremendous destruction of the majority of the largest cities in Poland, the matter of rebuilding cities became a key economic, political and social issue. The first task at hand was the rebuilding of Warsaw.[3] Poland's largest city had been so utterly demolished in the war (▶ 1) that town planners even considered whether it might be more advisable to rebuild a small administrative capital in place of the former metropolis, or to "shift" the position of the city to land that had not been destroyed by the ravages of war.[4]

There is no doubt that the rebuilding of Warsaw was among the central tasks with which the Polish state—indeed the whole nation—was faced. The slogan "The Whole Nation is Building its Capital," so ubiquitous in the following years, had extensive psychological origins. Tołwiński, the planner quoted above, believed that the rebuilding of Warsaw was the key issue for "the further development of Polish culture."

The matter of rebuilding Warsaw—and more importantly of remodelling it—took place under exceptional circumstances, in that the existing cityscape played only a minor role for urban planners. Paradoxically, the destruction of the city engendered the hope of a great revival. Pre-war Warsaw was known as a city with certain flaws. This opinion persisted even

---

1 The historical centre of Warsaw in 1945.

after the city was destroyed; the following words were published in the inaugural edition of a periodical devoted to the problems of post-war Warsaw: "Before the occupation, the shape of Warsaw was the antithesis of a rational layout. A mixing of all city functions … and elements in an unplanned and cramped development created a situation of urban chaos in which it was impossible to work, live, or relax in a satisfactory way."[5]

Even before 1939, efforts had been made to rectify this situation. In 1934, the milieu surrounding the architectural avant-garde produced and publicised a developmental plan for the capital entitled "functional Warsaw"[6], whilst around the same time the city authorities began to approach the task of modernising the urban structure of the city.[7] Stanisław Ossowski aptly noted in 1945: "The brave urban planner from 1938, who sketched a model for the future Warsaw, realised that … his plans … would be spread out over a hundred years."[8] After the war, however, the destruction of the city opened up the possibility of realising these utopian visions within the span of one generation.

The enthusiasm and conviction expressed here may be difficult for today's reader to grasp. It is captured, however, in a statement published at the beginning of 1946 by Wacław Ostrowski, soon to be one of the creators of the *Biuro Odbudowy Stolicy* (Office for the Rebuilding of the Capital, or BOS), which determined the spatial development of Warsaw in the years immediately following the war. Ostrowski recalls how difficult it had been before the war to develop any serious concept of urban design, and then goes on to observe: "As a result of the destruction of Warsaw, the situation has changed fundamentally. The developments that paralysed the work of urban planners and inhibited the healthy development of the city now lie under heaps of rubble." Ostrowski continues: "… Of course the matter is not quite as simple as that. Warsaw was not entirely demolished. The Germans did not destroy every building completely."[9] The tone of this statement is exceptional, but it demonstrates the conviction of the majority of circles concerning architecture and urban design, not only in Poland.[10]

It comes as little surprise, then, that plans for the future of Warsaw were even conceived during the war. Shortly before the final destruction of the old town in the Warsaw Uprising of 1944, Stanisław Dziewulski and Zygmunt Skibniewski developed visions of a new and better capital.[11] Interestingly, the wartime destruction even served to inspire historical preservationists, who drew up spirited visions of a romantic reconstruction of the medieval walls surrounding Warsaw.[12]

It is worth adding here that, while the Polish people were envisioning a rebuilt Warsaw as the heart of a Poland, which was to be reborn after the war, the Germans were developing entirely different plans for the city. At the beginning of 1944, the German governor of the District of Warsaw, Ludwig Fischer, described the city's post-war future as follows:

> The city of Warsaw must undergo fundamental changes regarding the composition of
> its present population. In the long term, we cannot permit Warsaw to house nearly a

million people of foreign nationality, as must continue to be the case for the time being. … In the long term, this agglomeration of such a large number of Poles will be a dangerous focal point that must be removed. … When the great evolution expands over the Eastern terrain after the war, Warsaw … again will fill its natural role as a location with a great power of attraction. Thus it will not be difficult in the course of a few years to increase the population of Warsaw by hundreds of thousands of Germans.[13]

The defeat of the Third Reich made the realisation of these plans impossible. However, the two-month battle during the Warsaw Uprising, followed by the systematic destruction of the city by the special *Vernichtungskommando* after the uprising was crushed, ensured that little of Warsaw's pre-war form remained. Nonetheless, this did not mean that Polish architecture gave up on thoughts of rebuilding. The first full-scale vision for rebuilding Warsaw was developed by a team led by Maciej Nowicki shortly after the uprising, when the left bank of the city lay in ruins. It was a modern vision, so vivacious that one of Nowicki's co-workers called it "an idea of a Warsaw so beautiful and stirring that it would require several generations to realise."[14]

2

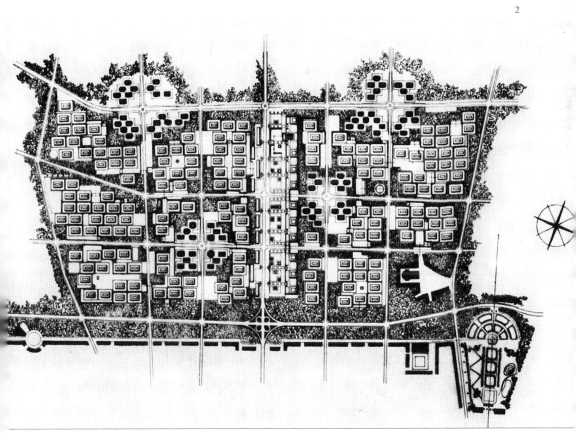

2   Maciej Nowicki: Design for rebuilding downtown Warsaw, 1945. Fragment showing the changing rhythm of low and high buildings.

3   Maciej Nowicki: Design for rebuilding downtown Warsaw, 1945. Fragment showing the Parliament Building.
4   Maciej Nowicki: Design for rebuilding downtown Warsaw, 1945. Group of buildings.

Nowicki foresaw the creation in its complex entirety (▶ 2, 3, 4); the relics that had been saved from destruction by the war would be spliced with entirely new portions of the city. The transportation system was especially modern; pedestrian and vehicular traffic were to be kept separate, and a part of the pedestrian traffic was to be routed on a second, higher level. For the realisation of this progressive idea, Nowicki decided to exploit the city's rubble. This unique building material, which was an inexhaustible resource in a demolished city, was to be used for the construction of certain office buildings, whose assets would be affordability as well as a visual features resulting from the special nature of their components. The practical side of this project was no less relevant in this case.[15]

Still more interesting is that the architect saw the city centre of this organism as the "theatre" of "city centre"[16] or "big city"[17] life. At the heart of this "theatre," Nowicki envisioned an extensive terrace, elevated above street level. All around there were to be stores and cafés, as well as high-rise buildings of a "varied profile." Characteristically, Nowicki called this urban composition the "tribune of the city centre's theatre," whose stage was to be the extensive *Aleje Jerozolimskie* (Jerusalem Avenue), along with its buildings. It is worth citing a poetic description of this urban composition: "At night the terrace-tribune would gleam softly, at the level of café lighting, and the dark wall opposite the office buildings, deserted by that time, would become the stage of a mechanical neon review."[18]

The metaphor of the theatre highlights Nowicki's specific approach towards architecture. Although he was educated at Warsaw Polytechnic University in the spirit of functionalism, he nonetheless maintained a certain distance from the doctrine.[19] Without disregarding pragmatics, he moved in architectural directions with farther-reaching ideas. His view, namely, was that the functionality of architecture was connected with forms of life, which unceasingly changed and in turn inspired changes in architecture. As a result, he believed that all good architecture, including historical architecture, was functional, and ceased to be functional as a result of the flow of time.[20]

From our perspective, another aspect of Nowicki's polemics with functionalism is still more interesting, that in which he evokes Frank Lloyd Wright's ideas of organic architecture. Because Nowicki closely connects this architect's vocation with the idea of happiness, it is worth addressing the argumentation it contains more broadly:

> The epoch of machinism created the concept of machines for living, giving the maximum amount of life comfort, and even the least partial and most practical followers of that doctrine believed that the main objective of architecture—on the scale of a city, home, or interior—should be to create the conditions necessary for the happiness of man. The project of defining this happiness, outlined either in personal or group terms and often subconsciously applying the slogan of enlightened absolutism, 'for you, but without you;' became the most important element of professional work and brought differences in life views to the precipice between the creator and audience of art. The

'functionalist' architects did not understand that the platform between their art and man, whose eyes and intellect it is to delight, must be built with these unchanging values, without which art becomes only fashion.[21]

Although Nowicki did not disregard pragmatic matters, this decidedly humanistic understanding of architecture ensured that his work advanced postulates far beyond the technocratic horizons of functionalism. Perhaps the following words, written in 1945, best illustrate his position:

> In harmony between the social climate and acts resulting from it, lies the socialisation of architecture. We are pondering … why it is necessary to take up labour to create such a climate, and what is required for its creation. If the result of labour is good architecture, there are of course aesthetic benefits. Aesthetic benefits heighten the joy of life. But in the course of reality, joy of life is not the primary necessity; first it is necessary to have something to eat and somewhere to live in order to evaluate what joy is. We are indeed trying to demonstrate that good architecture is indispensable to proper social development, and why it should be one of the first human needs.[22]

Nowicki did not stop at propagating that architecture could fulfil an especially important social role. He observed that "education through architecture is the most constant and also the most effective of all modes of education that social structures can provide," indicating that the "joy that beauty gives" could be felt "through contact with good architecture."[23]
As a consequence of such an outlook, Nowicki aspired to the vision of a Warsaw with a deeply aesthetic influence, which was to intensify the "joy" to which he so willingly refers in his texts. As one of the means that was to be employed, a two-fold mode of architectural narration was introduced into the project. One mode was oriented towards the traditional method of perception of architecture, i.e., from the position of the pedestrian passer-by, while the second mode was concerned with the perception of the city from the perspective of a car passenger. In this respect, Nowicki strived to incorporate a changing rhythm of high and low buildings[24] (▶ 2).
While Nowicki began his work with the BOS by deciding which direction rebuilding would take, the vision he presented never came to fruition. His position, which we might call organic, or even to a certain degree philosophical, was defeated in a conflict with the technocratic position, which dominated in the later activities of the BOS.[25] "Technocrats can only be philosophers in rare circumstances" noted Lech Niemojewski, standing against architectural progressivism in his criticism of the BOS.[26] Paradoxically, the multifaceted and far-reaching qualities of Nowicki's vision were disadvantageous to its advancement: in the prevailing conditions of the immediate post-war period, it was more technocratic and more temporary propositions that were expected.[27]

Under the changing conditions of the social and political regime in post-war Poland, it was realistic to propose a series of housing settlements which continued on from projects begun before the war by the *Warszawska Spółdzielnia Mieszkaniowa* (Warsaw Housing Cooperative, or WSM), although these also rested on an ideological foundation to a certain degree. Based on communal and socialist ideas, these projects were connected with left-wing principles, as were the architects who proposed them. Amongst these, an especially important position was held by Helena and Szymon Syrkus, both before and after the war.[28] In 1946, they published a programme for building new communal settlements, as well as for expanding existing ones. The projects for which they were responsible before the war demanded an arduous procedure of land reclamation, along with adaptations to existing urban design and transportation conditions. With the communalisation of Warsaw's ground, accompanied by the new social conditions, the settlements could be built in a much more rational manner. It was possible to realise the extensive plans due to the development of modern technological solutions (especially standardisation and prefabrication), along with the belief that there was a greater possibility of bringing to life a programme of a society based on the communal ideal than before the war. In their expansive programme, Syrkus and Syrkus were aware that, while the development of urban planning and technology allowed them to think about the realisation of these goals, they would disturb the conservative habits of the majority of society. "Therefore the educational role of already operating communal settlements is crucial," they wrote, "That is why it is such an urgent matter to add the elements that are lacking in dwarfish settlements. This is the only way in which domestic communalism can defeat resistance and lead the way to the gradual transformation of society."[29] In order to speed up the process of transformation, they were convinced "that it was necessary … to use a few working examples to show the working class the advantages of a communal settlement over the antisocial alternative of tenement housing."[30]

The settlement in the programme designed by Syrkus and Syrkus was intended not only to serve a practical goal, but also to encourage a new mentality to emerge, perhaps even a "new man." This new man would find satisfaction not only in realising private goals within the egoistic sphere of family life, as reflected in the saying "my home is my castle" (which they rejected), but also in the building of social relations and community. Urban planners and architects were to stimulate this process as far as it was in their power to do so. "The spatial arrangement of the settlement," they wrote "is thus not mere decoration, designed to cover over an internal emptiness, but a living form, reflecting real social contents. This form will be enriched by the development and broadening of interpersonal connections in their various manifestations."[31]

Thus the settlement was to be equipped with diverse structures facilitating community life, including nurseries, a pre-school, schools, playgrounds, cultural parks, sports fields, and co-operative inns and stores. In order to fulfil various types of practical needs, facilities would be provided for the benefit of the entire commune: a communal laundry and baths, shared

5

6

5, 6   Helena and Szymon Syrkus and team: Koło housing estate, 1947–1950.

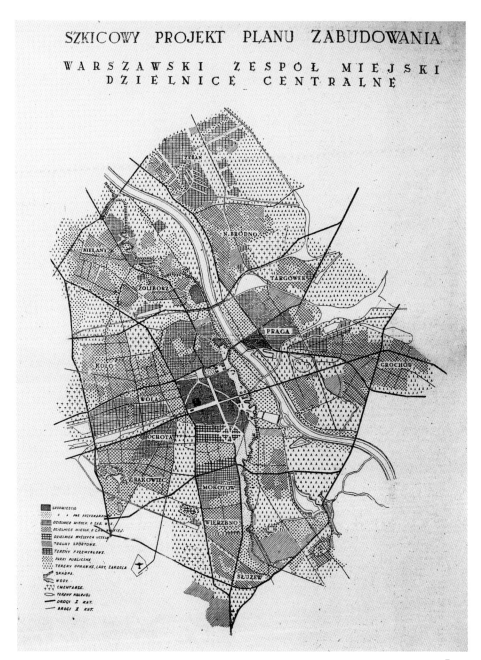

7   Zygmunt Skibniewski and Stanisław Dziewulski: General plan for rebuilding Warsaw, 1946.

refrigerators, vacuum cleaners, and mechanical dishwashers in individual buildings. At the very heart of the settlement was a meeting place called the "modern agora." All of these elements were to be the "urban manifestations of the democratic aspiration for social interaction, for seeking contact with other people as a 'source of knowledge and truth, a source of a norm of fairness and effectiveness of activity.'"[32]

In the first years after the war, a few settlements of this sort were realised in accordance with the programme, among which the most interesting was the settlement of Koło (▸ 5, 6).

The milieu which had been associated with the architectural (and often the political) left-wing before the war not only tried to continue realising co-operative housing projects, but also gained considerable influence as far as the plans for the rebuilding of the whole of Warsaw were concerned. Many of the architects connected with the Warsaw Housing Cooperative joined the roster of the BOS when it was commissioned on 14 February 1945.[33] The director of the BOS, Roman Piotrowski, explained the dominant role of this particular milieu:

> These people became the conceptual core of the BOS. And this is not just in connection with their skills and qualifications. They were people from the circles closest to the radical left, and even belonged to it before the liberation of the city. And thus, as regards politics, they occupied a key place in the BOS.[34]

Lech Niemojewski voiced a similar opinion a few years later, criticising the group and drawing attention to its leftist roots both on ideological and architectural grounds. Looking back on the pre-war endeavours of representatives of the milieu, he noted ironically:

> The destruction of just eighty-five per cent of Warsaw inspired in them tasks of still greater dimensions. No wonder, then, that necessity, ambition and a complete lack of practical experience aroused in them a desire to carry out Corbusierian experiments on Warsaw that was almost dead on its feet.[35]

Around the same time, in June 1949, Stefan Tworkowski criticised the BOS from the position of socialist realism. He also recognised the influences of Le Corbusier,[36] calling the BOS project "typical formalism, raised up on the basis of technocracy and social and urban utopias."[37]

These related ideological positions of the front representatives of the BOS were at that time distinct: essentially they were connected with ideas of architectural and social progressivism.

Not surprisingly, then, during the development of the BOS's concept of rebuilding in 1945, its main goal was still described by Tworkowski (although in a different political situation) as "an idea realised through urban planning based on social justice."[38] In 1945, this idea was still coloured with leftist humanism, as another fragment of the text demonstrates: "The city does not lend itself to creation as a mere monument, complete and uniform; rather, on its old skeleton, it must develop in the likeness of the man that inhabits it, who was and is the motor of its development and of its subsequent triumphs and falls."[39] As a consequence of these thoughts on urban space, Tworkowski confronted architects with an unusually difficult task with the following words: "We need ideas that have imaginativeness and courage, industriousness and dedication, light-heartedness and humour, as well as Polishness and cosmopolitism—all captured and translated into the language of drawing, and then into a palpable, living city."[40] His own opinion on the matter of the work of the Office for the Rebuilding the Capital was: "This is a game with the highest stakes of all—the future of Warsaw. ... Man awaits."[41]

These words are not devoid of pathos. This is indeed rare among texts related to the activities of the BOS. It is worth noting that the phraseology applied in its publications is generally far removed from the affected, intense formulations found in Nowicki's texts; the technocratic inclinations of the BOS's employees manifested themselves not only on the drafting board, but also in the statements made by the "Bosiaks," as they were called at the time.[42]

It was precisely this technocratic trait that prevented the leadership of the BOS, convinced of the soundness of its views, from attaching more importance to the consideration of a wider range of opinions. The architects assembled in the BOS were fully aware of the weight of responsibility and social expectation that had fallen upon them.[43] A programme of urban structuring for Warsaw published at the beginning of 1946 (▶ 7) indicated the wide range of problems that would have to be resolved in the course of the project.[44] Especially important among these was the matter of providing the residents of the capital with the best conditions "in the time when they are working and the time when they are at home."[45] The project members identified with ideas that were deemed "progressive" at the time. They contrasted the vision of the city of the future sketched on their drawing boards with the city of old, whose spatial structure, in their opinion, had prevented the proper development of man.

Writing about a new Warsaw, they noted that there would be "every facility necessary in the life of a large city that has always been lacking in the chaotically built cities of the last century."[46] This typical contrast between old and new is again underlined by the words of Adam Kotarbiński, in his vision of a new city district to be founded on principles different from those that had come before: "It is necessary ... to assure residents of the natural neighbourliness that has been neglected in the past century: next to the house there must be an open space, covered in vegetation. Houses will be surrounded by greenery, and not by pavements."[47]

A higher quality of life and sense of fulfilment and happiness in the new city was to be enhanced by creating an abundance of green open spaces. The composition of city districts

was also to serve this purpose, providing the supply of consumer products and a general access to cultural institutions and goods. The aim of this type of composition of districts was identified as "creating the possibility of encouraging the initiatives of human individuals, allowing them to meet and pursue activities leading to creative and useful achievements."[48] When these words were written in 1946, the buildings that were to achieve these aims were not only "community centres, large libraries, concert halls and theatres," but also churches.[49]

This was soon to change. In the late nineteen-forties, when the communist party seized complete control over the whole of social life in Poland, this of course encompassed architecture and urban planning. Within the stringent framework of the new programme there was certainly no place for the religious pursuits of mankind, which the BOS architects had still taken into consideration in 1945–1946; the humanist perspective evident in the publications from this time faded into memory.

During the course of their wholesale seizure of control, the communists moulded architectural projects in the direction of ideological homogeneity. This tendency is illustrated in the vision for the rebuilding of the capital presented in July 1949 as part of the Six Year Plan for Rebuilding Warsaw (▶ 8, 9). This plan was presented by the Polish communist leader

8   Six-Year Plan for Rebuilding Warsaw, Centralny Dom Kultury (Central House of Culture), 1949–1950.

Bolesław Bierut in the form of an exceptionally richly illustrated book, which became the printed monument of totalitarian urban planning.

The text and the images were to demonstrate the legitimacy of the road taken by the new government. It started out from the position that pre-war Warsaw had been "a city in which the natural rights of man to space, light and green spaces were not made available to the working class"[50] and that "the working class suburb lacked fundamental communal facilities, was devoid of green, and was built in the style of a barracks, in mud and filth."[51]

In contrast the text noted that, thanks to communist party policy as defined in the Six-Year Plan, "for the first time in the history of Warsaw, the working population is to receive its rightful comforts, light, dryness, aesthetic surroundings and appropriately heated living spaces, including every convenience that a modern civilisation can put to man's disposal."[52]

Not only were the living conditions to serve the development of man in this system. Monumental buildings in the city centre were to be given an architecturally "beautiful expression, characterising the new epoch of genuine humanism—an epoch defending the rights of the working man."[53] To illustrate these words, the plans called for unusually wide

9 Six-Year Plan for Rebuilding Warsaw, Marszałkowska Street, 1949–1950.

streets and squares, along which would stand powerful monuments and buildings in the forms of socialist realism. These streets and squares were to be constantly filled with parading crowds, with flags and banners in their hands. This image left no doubt as to the clear propagandistic character of the projected rebuilding of Warsaw.[54]

The architectural vision presented at that time was also accompanied by a literary vision predicting the happy, bright future of the city. One example of this style is embodied in a fragment of a 1950 poem by Mieczysław Jastrun entitled "Warsaw":

> The broad perspective of the avenue opens
> To the future, which waits a street further
> For the edifice of light.[55]

The words chosen by Bierut to conclude one of his speeches are characteristic. After unfurling a vision of rebuilding the Polish capital, he declared, "This will be our great contribution towards the building of a better tomorrow; a better, happier world."[56]

The promise of a better, happier world was inscribed in the propaganda of the Stalinist era. Here, it is clear that the ecstatic rhetoric departed from reality. Around 1956, at the time of the political thaw, it became necessary to settle accounts with the practices of the Stalin era, in which megalomaniac projects had concealed the difficulties of the everyday existence of city residents. This kind of criticism was even expressed by representatives of the architectural establishment at the time—such as Adolf Ciborowski in a report from the summer of 1956. Holding the position of Head Architect of the Capital City of Warsaw, Ciborowski declared that due to the investment politics conducted in the previous years, the real improvement in living conditions in the capital had not been as substantial as planned; indeed in some areas there had even been "a worsening of life difficulties for residents."[57] Not surprisingly, then, a pragmatic propaganda of modernity dominated in post-thaw rhetoric.

To people indoctrinated by the power and monumentality of the Stalinist era, the years after 1956 offered a more modest vision of individual happiness, in a small but private and practically appointed apartment in a modern building. This type of "cameralistic" propaganda even found its way into children's books. An unusually interesting example is a richly illustrated, poetic history of architecture for children, in which modern architecture is described as follows:

> Reinforced concrete, glass and plastic,
> wide rectangular windows
> apartment number one hundred and twelve
> block number five
> …

A pleasant apartment, though modest
air conditioning, a wardrobe in the wall ...
In the kitchen a refrigerator, a television
close to the couch.[58]

It is no coincidence that the period under the government of Władysław Gomułka was described as an era of 'small stabilisation.' However, this does not mean that architecture generally became resigned to the abandonment of a certain vision of happiness. Rather, happiness had to be given a less collective, more private character.[59] The paradox here is that this was to be accomplished mainly by the construction of apartment blocks (▶ 10), which earned the scornful name "blokowisko" and became a synonym for the degradation and homogenisation of the individual in the communist system.

In the Gomułka era the question of the construction of housing again became a key issue in Warsaw, returning in subsequent versions of urban plans for Warsaw in 1956, 1961, and 1964. It is thus characteristic that urban planners, who envisioned that the population of Warsaw would grow from just above one million in 1964 to three million in 2000, en-

10

10   Halina Skibniewska: Sady Żoliborskie housing estate, 1958–1963.

countered the resistance of the state authorities, who decided to limit the rate of population growth in the city. The main reason for this seems to have been the fear that living conditions for the residents of Warsaw would deteriorate.[60] Thus we can see how the momentous utopian ideas that flourished in the years immediately following the war gave way to the pragmatic, perhaps even restricted, vision of happiness characteristic of an era of 'small stabilisation.'

Endnotes

1 Tadeusz Tołwiński, *Urbanistyka* [Urban Planning] vol. 1: *Budowa miasta w przeszłości* [Building the Town in the Past] (Warsaw: Trzaska, Evert i Michalski, 1947), 5.

2 Tołwiński, (see note 1), 6.

3 It is not, of course, my purpose here to cover in detail the discussion of the matter of the rebuilding of Warsaw after the War. For an extensive treatment of the first phase of this discussion, see: Jan Górski, "Dyskusje o odbudowie Warszawy w latach 1945–1946. Charakterystyka okresu i dyskusji, ich zakres, kontrowersje, związek z przeszłością [Discussion on the Rebuilding of Warsaw, 1945–1946. The Character of the Period and of the Discussions, the Range of the Discussions, Controversies, Associations with the Past]," in *Warszawa stolica Polski Ludowej* [Warsaw, the Capital of People's Poland], vol. 1 (Warsaw: Państwowe Wydawnictwo Naukowe, 1970), 75–140.

4 Stanisław Ossowski, "Odbudowa stolicy w świetle zagadnień społecznych [The Rebuilding of a Capital in the Light of Social Issues]," originally published in 1945, reprinted in: Stanisław Ossowski, *Dzieła* [Works] vol. 3: *Z zagadnień psychologii społecznej* [On the Problems of Social Psychology] (Warsaw: Państwowe Wydawnictwo Naukowe, 1967), 396.

5 Grażyna Terlikowska-Wojsznis, "O Warszawie, która będzie [On the Warsaw to Come]," *Skarpa Warszawska*, October 21, 1945, 2.

6 See for example: Bolesław Malisz, "W poszukiwaniu przyszłego kształtu Warszawy. Wizja Warszawy funkcjonalnej [In Quest of the Future Shape of Warsaw. A Vision of a Functional Warsaw]," in *Początki planowania przestrzennego w Polsce* [The Beginnings of Urban Planning in Poland] (Warsaw: Państwowe Wydawnictwo Naukowe, 1979), 93–110; Helena Syrkus, "Warszawa funkcjonalna (1934) [A Functional Warsaw: 1934]," in Helena Syrkus, *Ku idei osiedla społecznego. 1925–1975* [On the Way to the Idea of a Social Housing Estate. 1925–1975] (Warsaw: Państwowe Wydawnictwo Naukowe, 1976), 149–59; Helena Syrkus, *Społeczne cele urbanizacji* [The Social Goals of Urbanization] (Warsaw: Państwowe Wydawnictwo Naukowe, 1984), 248–57.

7 See for example: Stanisław Różański, "Planowanie przestrzenne Warszawy [Urban Planning in Warsaw]," in *Warszawa II Rzeczypospolitej* [Warsaw at the Time of the Second Republic] vol. 1 (Warsaw: Państwowe Wydawnictwo Naukowe, 1968), 321–46; Jan Zachwatowicz, "Rozwój przestrzenny, urbanistyczny i architektoniczny Warszawy międzywojennej [The Spatial, Urban and Architectural Development of Interwar Warsaw] *Warszawa II Rzeczypospolitej. 1918–1939* [Warsaw at the Time of the Second Republic. 1918–1939]," vol. 3 (Warsaw: Państwowe Wydawnictwo Naukowe, 1971), 275–89.

8 Ossowski, (see note 4), 394.

9 Wacław Ostrowski, "Założenia podstawowe projektu [The Fundamental Assumption of a Project]," *Skarpa Warszawska*, February 17, 1946, 2.

10 For example, see the words of Lewis Mumford: "the horrendous destruction that befell Warsaw, had the single positive outcome, that it cleared the way for bold creative efforts." Lewis Mumford, "Warszawa żyje [Warsaw Lives]," in *Warszawa stolica Polski Ludowej* [Warsaw, the Capital of People's Poland], vol. 2 (Warsaw: Państwowe Wydawnictwo Naukowe, 1972), 333. This originally appeared in the preface of the brochure, Stanisław Albrecht, *Warsaw Lives Again* published in 1946.

11 On the topic of the conspiratorial activities of Polish architects in the war years, see: Helena Syrkus, *Społeczne cele* (see note 6), 351–79.

12 Reconstructive sketches for Warsaw's Barbican and New City Gate were made by Jan Zachwatowicz, who was inclined to reconstruct monuments even before the Warsaw uprising. Reproduced in: *Architektura* 7/8 (1950): 229.

13 "Die Stadt Warschau muss eine grundlegende Änderung hinsichtlich der Zusammensetzung ihrer jetzigen Bevölkerung erfahren. Es geht nicht an, dass auf die Dauer in Warschau fast eine Million Fremdvölkische leben, wie es z. Zt. noch der Fall ist. … In dieser Zusammenballung einer derartig grossen Menge von Polen ist auf weite Sicht ein Gefahrenherd zu erblicken, der beseitigt werden muss. … Wenn nach dem Kriege die grosse Entwicklung zum weiteren Osten einsetzt, wird Warschau … erneut zwangsläufig ein derartiger Anziehungspunkt werden. Es wird deshalb ohne Schwierigkeiten möglich sein, im Zeitraum weniger Jahre die Bevölkerung Warschaus um Hunderttausende von Deutschen zu vermehren." "Memoriał Ludwika Fischera z początku 1944 r. w sprawie Warszawy [Ludwig Fischer's Memorandum on Warsaw from the Beginning of 1944] ed. by Józef Kazimierski," *Rocznik Warszawski* 1 (1960): 312–13; 323–24.

14 Report of Stefan Hołówko. Quoted after: Tadeusz Barucki, *Maciej Nowicki* (Warsaw: Arkady, 1986), 12.

15 The general founding of Nowicki's project was related by the anonymous author of the publication "Praca architektoniczna–śródmieście Warszawy. Pracownia Dyskusji Architektonicznej pod kierownictwem inż. arch. Macieja Nowickiego [Architectural Work–Downtown Warsaw. The Studio for Architectural Discussions, Lead by the Architect Maciej Nowicki]," *Skarpa Warszawska*, October 28, 1945, 2. See also: Barucki, (see note 14), 10–13; Jerzy Hryniewiecki, "Maciej Nowicki 1910–1951," *Projekt* 1 (1957): 3–8.

16 Praca architektoniczna, (see note 15), 2.

17 Hryniewiecki, (see note 15), 7; Barucki, (see note 14), 21.

18 Praca architektoniczna, (see note 15), 2.

19 On the topic of the penetration of modernist ideas into the academic development of architects at Warsaw Polytechnic in the interwar years, see: "Rozmowy z profesorem Włodzimierzem Padlewskim. Młoda architektura [Conversations with Professor Włodzimierz Padlewski. Young Architecture]," in *Włodzimierz Padlewski: architektura i sztuka. W roku jubileuszu stulecia urodzin* [Włodzimierz Padlewski: Architecture and Art. In Commemoration of the Centenary of his Birth], ed. Hubert Bilewicz (Gdańsk: Akademia Sztuk Pięknych w Gdańsku, 2008), 2–47. Padlewski studied with Maciej Nowicki.

20 Nowicki continued his criticism of functionalism and International Style after his departure from Poland. For example, see: Harry Francis

115

Mallgrave, *Modern Architectural Theory. A Historical Survey, 1673–1968* (Cambridge/Mass.: Cambridge University Press, 2005), 339–40.

21 Maciej Nowicki, "W poszukiwaniu nowego funkcjonalizmu [In Quest of a New Functionalism]," *Skarpa Warszawska*, November 4, 1945, 1–2.

22 Maciej Nowicki, "Uspołecznienie architektury [Socializing Architecture]," *Skarpa Warszawska*, December 16, 1945, 2.

23 Nowicki, (see note 22).

24 Barucki, (see note 14), 21.

25 Jan Górski wrote about the conflict between the organic and technocratic concepts for rebuilding Warsaw: Górski, (see note 3), 80, 106.

26 Lech Niemojewski, "Bilans pięciolecia odbudowy Warszawy [Five Years of Rebuilding Warsaw. The Outcome]," in *Warszawa stolica Polski Ludowej*, (see note 10), 268.

27 Report of Zbigniew Gąsior. Quoted after Barucki, (see note 14), 12.

28 They also played an important role in the activity of the CIAM. See for example: Eric Mumford, *The CIAM Discourse on Urbanism, 1928–1960* (Cambridge/Mass., London: The MIT Press, 2000). Helena Syrkus was vice-president of CIAM from 1948 to 1954.

29 Helena i Szymon Syrkus, "Udział spółdzielczości mieszkaniowej w realizacji pierwszego trzyletniego Narodowego Planu Gospodarczego dla Warszawy," [The Contribution of Housing Cooperatives towards the Realization of the First Three-year National Economic Plan for Warsaw] originally published in 1946, reprinted in: Helena Syrkus, *Ku idei osiedla społecznego*, (see note 6).

30 Helena Syrkus, *Ku idei osiedla społecznego*, (see note 6), 395.

31 Helena Syrkus, *Ku idei osiedla społecznego*, (see note 6), 398.

32 Helena Syrkus, *Ku idei osiedla społecznego*, (see note 6), 399. This statement was made by Stefan Żółkiewski, who was one of the foremost propagators of Marxism in culture in postwar Poland.

33 On the topic of BOS, see for example: Alicja Kączkowska, "Biuro Odbudowy Stolicy. Historia i struktura organizacyjna [Office for the Rebuilding of the Capital. Its History and Structure]," in *Warszawa stolica Polski Ludowej*, (see note 3), 341–65 and Roman Piotrowski, "BOS. Wspomnienia kierownika Biura Odbudowy Stolicy [BOS. Memories of one of the Heads of the Office for the Rebuilding of the Capital]," *Rocznik Warszawski* 1 (1960): 256–73.

34 Piotrowski, (see note 33), 261.

35 Niemojewski, (see note 26), 268.

36 Stefan Tworkowski, "Kształtowanie przestrzenne Warszawy socjalistycznej [Urban Planning in Socialist Warsaw]," in *O polską architekturę socjalistyczną. Materiały z Krajowej Partyjnej Narady Architektów od bytej w dniu 20-21.VI.1949 roku w Warszawie* [In Favour of Polish Socialist Architecture. Documentation of the National Party Meeting of Architects in Warsaw. 20–21 June 1949] (Warsaw: Państwowe Wydawnictwo Techniczne, 1950), 99.

37 *O polską architekturę*, (see note 36), 100.

38 "O kompozycji urbanistycznej Warszawy; uwagi inż. arch. Stefana Tworkowskiego w związku ze szkicowym projektem ogólnego planu zabudowania miasta, opracowanym przez Wydział Urbanistyki Biura Odbudowy Stolicy, z dnia 4 X 1945 r. [On the Urban Composition of Warsaw. Comments Made by the Architect Stefan Tworkowski on the Preliminary Town Project Designed at the Urban Planning Department of the Office for the Rebuilding of the Capital. 4 October 1945]," in Jan Górski, ed., *Odbudowa Warszawy w latach 1944–1949. Wybór dokumentów i materiałów* [The Rebuilding of Warsaw. 1944–1949. A selection of Documents and Materials] vol. 1 (Warsaw: Państwowe Wydawnictwo Naukowe, 1977), 320.

39 Górski, (see note 38), 321.

40 Górski, (see note 38), 314–15.

41 Górski, (see note 38), 325.

42 Piotrowski, (see note 33), 257.

43 The BOS also came under fire in public opinion and the press (at that time still operating with relative freedom). For more on this, see: Piotrowski, (see note 33), 265–66.

44 Jan Górski, *Warszawa w latach 1944–1949. Odbudowa* [Warsaw in the Years 1944–1949. Rebuilding] (Warsaw: Państwowe Wydawnictwo Naukowe, 1988), 308–10.

45 Zygmunt Skibniewski and Stanisław Dziewulski, "Program urbanistyczny Warszawy [Urban Programme for Warsaw]," *Skarpa Warszawska*, March 10, 1946, 2.

46 Skibniewski/Dziewulski, (see note 45).

47 Zygmunt Skibniewski and Stanisław Dziewulski, "Program urbanistyczny Warszawy (dokończenie) [Urban Programme for Warsaw. Conclusion]," *Skarpa Warszawska*, March 17, 1946, 2 (the section regarding housing districts was developed by Adam Kotarbiński).

48 Skibniewski/Dziewulski, (see note 47).

49 Skibniewski/Dziewulski, (see note 47).

50 Bolesław Bierut, *Sześcioletni plan odbudowy Warszawy* [Six-year Plan for the Rebuilding of Warsaw] (Warsaw: Książka i Wiedza, 1950), 77.

51 Bierut, (see note 50), 78.

52 Bierut, (see note 50), 181.

53 Bierut, (see note 50), 265.

54 For the propagandist character of the rebuilding of Warsaw, see: Arnold Bartetzky, "Stadtplanung als Glücksverheißung. Die Propaganda für den Wiederaufbau Warschaus und Ost-Berlins nach dem Zweiten Weltkrieg," in *Imaginationen des Urbanen. Konzeption, Reflexion und Fiktion von Stadt in Mittel- und Osteuropa*, ed. Arnold Bartetzky, Marina Dmitrieva, Alfrun Kliems (Berlin: Lukas Verlag, 2009), 51–80.

55 Mieczysław Jastrun, *Warszawa* cited from: Wojciech Tomasik, *Inżynieria dusz. Literatura realizmu socjalistycznego w planie propagandy monumentalnej* [The Engineering of Souls. Socialist Realist Literature as a part of the plan for 'Monumental Propaganda'] (Wrocław: Fundacja na Rzecz Nauki Polskiej, 1999), 89.

56 Bierut, (see note 50), 361.

57 [Adolf Ciborowski], "Referat Naczelnego Architekta M. St. Warszawy [Report by the Chief Architect of the Capital City of Warsaw]," *Miasto* 9 (1956). 3

58 Roman Pisarski, *Domy, zamki, pałace* [Houses, Castles, Palaces] ill. by Czesław Wielhorski (Warsaw: Biuro Wydawnicze "Ruch", 1963), 32.

59 See for example: Jacek Friedrich, "'Dziś kupuje się mebelek funkcjonalny'. Kilka słów na marginesie jednej sceny z filmu Stanisława Barei 'Małżeństwo z rozsądku' ['Nowadays one buys functional furniture.' Some remarks in the margin of a scene in Stanisław Bareja's movie 'A marriage of Convenience']," in *Dom—spotkanie przestrzeni prywatnej i publicznej na tle przemian cywilizacyjnych XIX i XX w.* [Home—the Meeting of Private and Public Space in the Context of Cultural Transformations in the Nineteenth and Twentieth Centuries], ed. Zbigniew Opacki and Dagmara Płaza-Opacka (Gdańsk: Wydawnictwo Uniwersytetu Gdańskiego, 2008), 301–14.

60 *Informacja o Planie Warszawskiego Zespołu Miejskiego i Planie Ogólnym Warszawy do 1985 roku* [Information on the Plan for a Larger Warsaw and the General Plan for Warsaw up to 1985] (Warsaw: Prezydium Rady Narodowej m. st. Warszawy, 1969), 3.

HAPPY LIVING IN A NEW SOCIALIST TOWN

The Construction, Distribution, Management, and Inhabitation of Apartments in Post-War Yugoslavia and Czechoslovakia*

Ana Kladnik

Since the Renaissance, the planning and building of towns has been more or less explicitly connected with the idea and the promise of happiness, be it in a political, social, or artistic sense.[1] It is not the intention of this article to trace the entire history of utopian or ideal cities created by architects, philosophers, and rulers. Following on from the definition that cities are the result of collective efforts, which rely on the general support of society for their success,[2] I shall concentrate on the endeavours of architects, authorities, and city inhabitants to generate happy cities in European socialist countries after the Second World War. This subject will be approached by examining the construction, distribution, management, and inhabitation of apartments in socialist countries in a case analysis of two towns, Havířov and Velenje, which were built on green open spaces in socialist Czechoslovakia and Yugoslavia in the nineteen-fifties. On the one hand, focus will be placed upon the relationships between architects and planning authorities, the mechanisms related with the distribution of the apartments and the function of the new towns for the self-legitimisation of socialist power, and on the other hand, on the question of how inhabitants living in these new apartments reacted on a daily basis.

Urban Planning, Happiness, and Socialism

To understand the ideological roots and historical premises of urban planning in the socialist period, it is useful to trace back the ideas of happiness in new cities to the so called Utopian Socialists[3] in the first half of the nineteenth century, for whom architecture was one of the tools for the socialist transformation of society. In 1842, Étienne Cabet published his utopian novel *Voyage en Icarie*, presenting a vision of "fraternity" and "mutual happiness."[4] A few years later, several hundreds socialists calling themselves "New Icarians" arrived in Nauvoo, Illinois, intent upon building a city of joy, based on the idea of an egalitarian communism in which private property would be abolished and everyone would work in harmonious fellowship towards the common good.[5] Like Cabet's Icarians, the followers of early socialists such as Robert Owen, Charles Fourier, and Henri de Saint-Simon gave "a new impetus to the dream of happiness in all its contradictions, promising perpetual felicity in this life to many who had never dared consider the thought".[6] Like Cabet's *Voyage en Icarie*, their writings were treated "not simply as experiments of thought, models to be contemplated, but as blueprints to be put into effect". Some sixteen model communities modelled on Owen's textile factory in New Lanark were launched between 1825 and 1830, the most famous of which was "New Harmony" in Indiana (1825–27). The adepts of Fourier followed suit and the *Phalanstères* became established in Romania, France, Russia, Great Britain, Brazil, and other parts of the New World.[7]

The early socialists paved the way for far more ambitious undertakings such as Ebenezer Howard's Garden City or the urban visions of twentieth century modernists like Le Corbusier and other avant-gardists, all of whom wished to make their contributions towards creating better, happier societies. Inter-war modernism was very critical of the political establishment, and its critical attitude partly coincided with the leftist political views of many of its protagonists.

By the early nineteen-fifties, the modernist-inspired "International Style" became the household style of the capitalist establishment. Meanwhile, in the socialist European countries, Socialist Realism was imposed by the Soviet Union, until it gave way to a rather basic form of modernism. In his highly eloquent report as chief urban planner of the new socialist town Nová Dubnica in Slovakia, Jiři Kroha, the inter-war avant-gardist and politically engaged architect of the post-war era, enthusiastically described how a whole new cultural, artistic and political life emerged from the Soviet model of Socialist Realism in those days. He claimed to link the present with tradition, whilst gradually eliminating old and outlived prejudices in architecture and town planning. He finished his report by suggesting that a large amount of greenery should be present in the town centre, giving a picturesque and joyful character to the town.[8] As Henriett Szabo pointed out in her article on *Stalintown* (Sztálinváros) in Hungary, it was not so easy for Hungarian architects to adopt the new style of Socialist Realism dictated by Moscow. Many of them had their roots in inter-war modernism, which was now heavily criticised as capitalist and formalist, whereas Socialist Realism was promoted as being vital and close to the people. The new ideology claimed to combine socialist contents with national forms, the ideas of the international proletariat and patriotism, modernity, and tradition.[9] Nevertheless, in the view of many contemporaries, Socialist Realism was something appealing; a style which gave the people the impression that they were the new kings, that they represented the power that determined history.[10]

1

1 Building project for the new town Velenje by chief architect Janez Trenz, around 1960.

"I Did not Fight with the Partisans so that New Houses Could be Built that Look Exactly Like the Old Ones"[11]
The Newly Planned Towns of Velenje and Havířov

The towns built in socialist European countries were mostly the result of the economic policy's focus on the development of heavy industry. Typical representatives of the new towns, which grew up as settlements for workers in a nearby industry, are Nowa Huta in Poland, Havířov, Poruba and Nová Dubnica in Czechoslovakia, Sztálinváros in Hungary, Stalinstadt in the GDR, Dimitrovgrad in Bulgaria, and Velenje in Yugoslavia. Concentrating on two of these towns, Velenje and Havířov, it is important to provide a description of the general background behind their planning.

INVESTORS AND CONTRACTORS OF THE APARTMENTS

In the nineteen-fifties, heavy industry was the most promising branch of Yugoslavia's economy. Nevertheless, the planning of the new town Velenje in Slovenia—not just as a mining colony as it was conceived at state level—was more or less a local matter under the management of the *Coal Mine Company Velenje* (CMCV). The director of CMCV was drawn into many conflicts with members of the party elite because he did not agree with the plans to develop Velenje merely as a mining colony. Additionally, he had some disagreements with the architects of the town. Primarily, he was impressed by the settlement of the Siemens Company in Germany,[12] admiring its building arrangement, its square-shaped market, and its abundance of green areas. He did everything in his power to design a new town plan for Velenje. From an architectural point of view, there was nothing wrong with the miners' houses that were planned by the first town architect. Living spaces were oriented towards the south, whereas additional facilities and all the stairways faced north. The shape of the houses was very close to the common notions of miners found in the visual arts at the time. But the CMCV director compared the aesthetics of New Velenje with that of pre-war buildings in mining colonies, especially the mining areas in the river Sava region. Although New Velenje had entirely different, new architecture, he was convinced that the architects had not been ambitious enough.[13]

The CMCV director also found no common language with a new architect, coming from the Slovenian Republic's design institute, who in fact became the chief urban planner of Velenje (▶ 1); again, the ambitions of the director went beyond the acceptance levels of the architect.

The planning of and investment in the construction of the town of Havířov in Czechoslovakia was a central priority of the state. Great economic importance was placed on the building of new socialist towns in the Ostrava-Karviná region in the Eastern Czechia in the five-year-plan (1949–1953).[14] The design and construction of projects in Havířov were mostly carried out by *Stavoprojekt Ostrava* (reorganised in 1954), which was one of the state design institutes in a new regional system established by the Ministry of

Chcete stavět rodinný domek?

2

Se zájmem jsme v minulých dnech četli usnesení ÚV KSČ k řešení bytové otázky. Mezi jiným se zde hovoří o tom, že v zájmu zamezení dlouhodobé rozestavěnosti je nutné, aby si budoucí družstevníci a individuální stavebníci opatřili včas potřebné finanční prostředky dlouhodobým pravidelným spořením. K tomu účelu budou finanční ústavy organizovat prostřednictvím státních spořitelen účelové stavební spoření.

Rada KNV v Ostravě přijala usnesení, jímž se upravují platné směrnice státního výboru pro výstavbu rodinných domků a ostatních staveb soukromým stavebníkům.

... nebude stavebník proplácet v penězích, neboť faktury za materiál bude prodejna zasílat

Local Enterprise. Nevertheless, employees of the Stavoprojekt Ostrava came from all parts of Czechoslovakia.[15]

In order to provide better living conditions for their increasing number of workers in Velenje, CMCV took out a loan from the investment sources of the Yugoslavian Federation and the Slovenian Republic to finance the building of the apartments.[16] But since building a new mining town was not the republic's priority, most of the investment funds were engendered by the increasing production activities of CMCV itself. In order to keep the company's records straight, the costs for the building of apartments were categorised as CMCV material costs.[17] After the apartments had been built, the company sold them to other enterprises in the town.[18] In 1960, CMCV began selling the apartments to individuals[19] on thirty years' credit at an interest rate of one per cent.[20] The company's income from these sales was intended to be invested in the building of further apartments, but as the local newspaper pointed out, the apartment sales progressed very slowly.[21] Even though it was a priority to build the apartments, it was not possible to meet the needs of the increasing number of new workers.[22] For that matter, CMCV helped individuals build their own family houses by providing them with construction materials or funds.[23] At the same time, in the Ostrava-Karviná region, the District National Committee decided to give priority for building family houses to those who had a guarantee of private savings, confirmed by the state savings bank[24] (▶ 2). Nevertheless, rumours were beginning to spread regarding the family house built by the director of CMCV himself. He built his house at the foot of the hill, in a solitary position with a beautiful view of the newly-erected town, above the main road. The house was white and square-shaped and, as the priest of Velenje remembers, people used to call it a petrol station.[25]

---

2   The article "Do you want to build a family house?" addresses all members of the family, encouraging them to save money in their savings books, 1959.

As CMCV was the chief investor in the apartments, its management structure incorporated a special apartment commission. An apartment could only be provided to a person who fulfilled certain conditions, for example he must be an employee of CMCV (or other public services important for the town's development) and have a family. Other criteria for the priority list were commitment at the workplace, years of employment, and activities in political organisations, especially participation in the National Liberty Movement, or internment during the Second World War.[26] Although the majority of the inhabitants of Velenje were happy or even enthusiastic participants in voluntary work, this work was not voluntary in the true sense of the word, since a specific number of hours of voluntary work was one of the conditions for gaining the right to housing[27] (▶ 3).

In August 1963, the presidents Josip Broz Tito and Nikita Khrushchev visited Velenje (▶ 4). Khrushchev's wife Nina had a special visiting programme. She took a look at some of the new apartments for miners, which she found very pleasant. She asserted that she was convinced that these could not really be miner's apartments, they must be apartments allocated to engineers and leading employees of CMCV, and so the director proposed that she choose any apartment she wished to see. After an hour, the first lady of the Soviet Union concluded: "Comrades, now I believe that miners and their families in Velenje live in really beautiful and modern apartments."[28] But in spite of the omnipresent idea of equality, a certain degree of social stratification was recognised and privileges were enjoyed by the technical and humanistic intelligentsia in the strata of the social elite. An examination and comparison of the distribution lists of the first inhabitants of three blocks situated in the town centre, with their social status, revealed the following: for the first building, the skyscraper, seven apartments were distributed to engineers, two to technicians, and one each

3

3   From 1947 to 1959, people from Velenje had done 558,000 hours of voluntary work and from 1960 to 1964 an additional 450,000 hours. In 1961 the local newspaper published a heading with the slogan "We are building a new world and a new spring."

4

to a teacher, waiter, worker, and miner. Additionally, one apartment was occupied by the vice-director of ČMCV. In the second building, most of the apartments (forty-six in all) were distributed to the miners, and in the third, most of the apartments were distributed to engineers, doctors, and managers.[29] The Apartment Committee was criticised and accused of granting better apartments to certain individuals, but the committee mostly defended itself by stating that these were simply rumours spread by envious wives.[30]

The giant *Ostrava-Karviná Coal Mine Company* had a special National Office for the Management of Apartments (*OKR Správa sídlišť n.p.*). The company had about 26,000 apartments for their workers in eleven towns in the region. Each town had a central office and additional offices responsible for the distribution and maintenance of the apartments. One such office was the Local Apartment Commission in Havířov (*Středisko Havířov*). The decision concerning who was allocated a certain apartment was made on the basis of where the person worked, and whether he or she was single or had a family. Nevertheless, in 1960, the National Office found that there was an enormous number of one and two-room apartments, and that this was not good for future families, so they needed to plan more apartments with three and four rooms.[31]

4   Celebrations make people happy. Apartments with balconies situated around Velenje main square were ideal for watching parades, festivals, and visits of political delegations. Josip Broz Tito's and Nikita Khrushchev's visit on 30 August 1963. From the left: director of the Velenje Coal Mine Company, Nestl Žgank, Khrushchev and Tito; behind: Nina Khrushcheva.

On the level of the People's Republic of Slovenia there was an Apartment Administration (*Stanovanjska uprava*) with a branch office in Velenje. This office had to co-operate closely with CMCV to ensure that the rent from the apartments was collected and paid into the republic's apartment fund according to the regulations.[32] On a local level, the apartments were managed by the Residence Community (*stanovanjska skupnost*). Each apartment house had an Assembly of Tenants (*svet stanovalcev*) which acted as a kind of parliament, and an Apartment Council (*hišni svet*) serving as an operative and executive organ. Immediately after thirty-eight families had moved into an apartment house in the centre of Velenje, the assembly of tenants had voted for its Apartment Council and named the housekeeper.[33] Despite the extensive advertising of services organised by the Residence Community, such as dry cleaner's shops or laundry services,[34] people preferred to wash and dry their clothes at home, especially since nasty incidents tended to happen, such as laundry being stolen.[35] Many suggestions were made to the people living in Velenje on the subject of how to take care of the town's image; they were encouraged to plant flower decorations on the balconies, greenery around the houses, etc. The authorities even went so far as to prohibit drying laundry on the balconies as this was not considered aesthetically pleasing,[36] or to ban children from playing on the green areas around the houses. Initiatives by the Socialistic Union of the Working People of Slovenia (*SZDLS—Socialistična zveza delovnega ljudstva Slovenije*)[37] were founded to organise voluntary work for cleaning up green areas, parks, paths and playgrounds. But the goal was to engage all the inhabitants of Velenje in voluntary work, including all political and social organisations.[38] The "aesthetic propaganda" in the local newspaper even went so far as to claim that inhabitants were now accusing themselves of being the cause of dissatisfaction: "We succeeded in mobilising people, day after day, to voluntarily dig, level, and plant, but now we are not able to sustain and take care of what we have done. We are responsible for the causes, why are we not satisfied with the appearance of our Velenje!"[39]

In the new apartments in Havířov, most of the problems encountered by the inhabitants had to do with the inappropriate heating system or fungus in the apartments and with the mud on the streets outside the apartments. The inhabitants reported these problems to the housekeeper of the apartment building, who was also a member of the local apartment commission in Havířov. When the housekeeper did not react to their complaints, they took the matter further, either to the Town Committee of Havířov or directly to the National Office for the Management of Apartments.[40] But when even this had no effect, in 1960 they wrote a letter to the Czechoslovakian State President Antonín Novotný to explain the problems arising from the inadequately heated apartments.[41] In this petition, three Street Committees (*Uliční výbor*) in Havířov, with altogether fourteen lists of signatures from the inhabitants of apartments, explain to the president that they indeed live in modern apartments, but that the heating system is unsatisfactory. They also complain about the fact that they are paying for hot water which they do not get. Finally, they appeal to the president to provide a quick solution, now that winter is here, for the sake of their children's health and so that the Christmas holidays could be joyful.

"We Could be Really Content, Happy, and Proud of our Town." Descriptions of Happiness

In 1960, the newspaper of one of the branch mines of the coal mine company in the Ostrava-Karviná region published an article entitled, *An apartment or a car?*[42] Its author argues that, because of the influences from the West, families in Czechoslovakia measure the meaning of their lives in terms of Spartak cars.[43] He explains that up until 1958, the difficulties encountered when it came to building a family house caused more and more families to spend their quickly increasing family budgets on cars. Furthermore, a certain kind of arrogance appeared in society; that is to say, a person with a car was seen to be "better" than others. But, as the author claims, this is a false interpretation.

> In the United States, it is necessary to have a car to get to work. We do not need that, because we have a very well developed public transport system. Nevertheless, it is true that having a car is a nice thing, as it brings you certain moments of joy. For a peaceful, fruitful and happy life we firstly need a good and comfortable apartment. This apartment should have as many rooms as the number of members in the family. It is an apartment with a bathroom and other modern facilities; an apartment with a library,

5

> radio, television and other equipment that we need to lead a cultural life. A man who lives in bad conditions but buys himself a car is like one who buys himself cigarettes but does not have clothes.[44]

In the nineteen-sixties, the number of automobiles grew and in Havířov some families could afford to buy a car thanks to higher salaries. The first car a family had was not just a car; it was a little short of a revolution. It was a symbol of progress, of emancipation and of freedom; moreover, it was privately owned.[45]

Philosophers and religious thinkers have often defined happiness in terms of living a good life, or flourishing; some authors emphasise that, by nature, it is a purely individual emo-

5 An attempt to bring a "picturesque" and "joyful" character to the town: house decorations from the late nineteen-fifties, showing a mother with her children on a sunny day in the Czechoslovakian industrial town of Nová Dubnica.

tion. In the sources related to socialist town planning, the term *happy* or *happiness* is rarely used explicitly. For the architect Kroha, as already mentioned, it was necessary to plan the town with a picturesque (*malebný*) and joyful (*radostný*) character (▶ 5). However, his report on building the new town Nová Dubnica was rather an exception. In the general urban plans for the building of new towns in the Ostrava-Karviná region or in Velenje in Slovenia, no mention of any such emotional terms is made. But this does not mean that the happiness of the inhabitants living in the town was not taken into consideration by architects or the authorities.

One of the first architects in Velenje took into account almost all of the trends in building at the time to ensure that the flats for the coal miners were healthy and well-equipped, thereby offering a high contemporary standard. The very shape of the houses was designed to appear familiar to the miners; the architects adapted the new buildings to the customary form of traditional mining colonies. They tried not only to create contemporary flats in a functional sense, but also to bring the aesthetics of the new houses as close as possible to the social status and culture of the coal miners. But what the first architects of New Velenje saw as an appropriate architectural form, was perceived by the director of CMCV in an entirely different way. Their intention to make the coal miners feel at home when they arrived in their new houses was understood by the director as reactionary and contrary to the new progressive socialist times. In his opinion, the desire for a more advanced statement signalising a new era, visible from afar, remained unfulfilled. However, the miners probably felt quite content in their newly built houses, as they were familiar with hipped roofs, and there was also enough space around the houses to accommodate small gardens.[46]

Implicitly or explicitly, the mention of happiness can be found in local newspapers owned by the coal mine companies in Havířov and Velenje, as for example in the article "An apartment or a Car?" quoted above, in which a car is considered to give us joy (*radost*), and an apartment is necessary for a happy life (*šťastný život*). Among the archive materials there are many eloquent letters of complaint written by the new inhabitants of Havířov,[47] in which terms such as happiness (*štěstí*), or satisfaction (*spokojenost*) are used.

Conclusion

The task of implementing happiness for the majority in town development was a modern idea within the context of the democratisation of social housing. In the West as in the East, the provision of healthy and comfortable apartments with functional public facilities for the inhabitants was a central concern of urban planning. Prosperity as a public aim and happiness for workers had become a justification for state intervention. The heart of prosperity was seen to lie in sunny and airy apartments with bathrooms and central heating, with green spaces in front of the building where children could play safely, and with kindergartens, schools, shopping centres, and services available within a short walking distance. In this concept, the door to happiness was seen as the entrance to the hallway of an apartment, as a set of keys given out to the inhabitants by the housing administration. It is likely that a young couple indeed felt very happy in this situation.[48] In the years immediately following 1945, socialism was immensely popular, not only within the socialist countries but all over Europe. It promised a one-way street to a better future, and was powered by a very seductive political philosophy that, by then, had developed an effective iconography of symbols, colours, visual performances and not least architecture.[49] Another name given to new towns was "town of youth," since the inhabitants were mostly young people in their twenties who came to new towns where they were needed to work in the coal mines and were thus guaranteed jobs. They either came with their families or alone, starting a family once they had settled in the town. For the authorities it was a crucial matter—whether on a local or a state level—to provide good quality living conditions for the workers. At a time when there were apartment shortages all over Czechoslovakia or Yugoslavia, beautiful apartments were built in new towns. Paraphrasing Alain de Botton, new towns were intended not to symbolise an existing social reality, but rather to bring a new reality into being.[50] The decision concerning which apartment was allocated to which family was made by a special commission on the basis of stipulations for a priority list; the personal data of the candidates was also taken into consideration. The administration for the management of the apartments was constituted in close cooperation with the investors. On the one hand, the administration office tried to organise people's everyday life in the town, and on the other, the commission was the first instance should the inhabitants wish to register complaints about problems in their apartments. Political delegations made ostentatious displays of their interest in the construction of towns and the living conditions of the town's inhabitants. It may be assumed that, after their official visits to the town, they left with the impression that the miners' apartments were not a Potemkin village. Looking closely at the archive materials or interviews with the first inhabitants,[51] it seems that no matter what problems they may have encountered in getting an apartment, or what condition the apartments were in, the inhabitants' enthusiasm and happiness at having an apartment, as well as their hope and belief in a better future, were indeed real and are sure to have influenced life in the newly erected towns in a positive way.

Endnotes

* I would like to thank the project team of "Socialist Dictatorship as a World of Meaning", and in particular Pavel Kolář, Michal Kopeček, and Michal Pullmann.

1 Rudolf Stegers, "Kein Aus für das Glück in der Stadt," in *Glück, Stadt, Raum in Europa 1945 bis 2000*, ed. Romana Schneider and Rudolf Stegers (Berlin: Akademie der Künste/Birkhäuser, 2002), 16.

2 Cor Wagenaar, "Cities and the Pursuit of Public Happiness," in *Happy: Cities and Public Happiness in Post-War Europe*, ed. Cor Wagenaar (Rotterdam: NAi Publishers, 2004), 17.

3 The name "utopian socialism" was introduced by Marx and Engels to distinguish it from their own "scientific socialism." Darrin M.

McMahon, *Happiness: a history* (New York: Grove Press, 2006).

4 McMahon, (see note 3), 374

5 McMahon, (see note 3), 373.

6 McMahon, (see note 3), 375.
The utopian socialists followed Enlightenment assumptions, "which tended to present happiness as a natural condition and course. Happiness, in the Enlightenment view, was impeded only by pain-inducing prejudice, practice, and false belief." If those obstacles were removed, "individuals would be free to follow their natural trajectory." The utopian socialists were heirs to this aspect of the Enlightenment tradition. McMahon, (see note 3), 381.

7   McMahon, (see note 3), 386–87.

8   Appending note on the new socialist town in Slovakia. See: Archív mesta Nová Dubnica [Archive of the Municipality of Nova Dubnica]; box Atelier národneho umělec Jiřího Krohy Praha: Průvodní zpráva nového socialistického města na Slovensku [Studio of the national artist Jiri Kroha, Prague: Primary Report on a New Socialist Town in Slovakia].

9   Henriett Szabo, "Stalintown," in *Happy: Cities and Public Happiness in Post-War Europe*, (see note 2), 185.

10 "Socialist-realist Palaces for the Common Man," in *Happy: Cities and Public Happiness in Post-War Europe*, (see note 2), 50.

11 Famous dictum of the director of the Coal Mine Company at Velenje, a decisive and authoritative rejection of the architect's design concept.

12 Nestl Žgank, *Spomini 'rdečega kralja'* [Memories of 'the red king'], ed. Damijan Kljajič and Vlado Vrbič (Ljubljana: Karantanija, 1999), 130.

13 Nande Korpnik, "Arhitekturna privoved Velenja," [Architectural Narrative of Velenje] *Oris* 53 (2008): 166.

14 Zemský archiv v Opavě [Regional Archive, Opava], fond: SMKNV, box 3575; Sig.: 715.
    For further information on the organisations responsible for investment, design, and construction, as well as on the changing system of investment, see: K. Elman Zarecor, "Manufacturing a Socialist Modernity: The Architecture of Industrialised Housing in Czechoslovakia, 1945–56" (PhD diss., Columbia University, 2008), especially 460–64 and 503–09.

15 Green town. Film by David Vigner, Davis Film Studio, 2006.

16 Arhiv Premogovnika Velenje [Archive of the Coal Mine Company Velenje], box U 10.

17 Žgank, (see note 12), 141.

18 For example, in 1961 the Coal Mine Company Velenje sold two three-bedroom apartments, and in 1960 a family house, to the company Gorenje. Arhiv Premogovnika Velenje, box U 10.

19 Arhiv Premogovnika Velenje, box U 14.

20 Arhiv Premogovnika Velenje, box U 10.

21 *Rudar* [Miner], November 6, 1960, 2.

22 In the years when the need for apartments was at its greatest, the Coal Mine Company Velenje built wooden houses (barracks), or so-called provisories, for miners and their families. These houses were supposed to serve only until families moved in to the real apartments (in fact, the provisories remained in use until the nineteen-eighties). In 1953, the author of an article in a local newspaper argued that they were only quite good places to live in if the housewife took good care of them (rather than going to work for a priest and thus neglecting husband, children, and the house). *Velenjski rudar* [Velenje's Miner], May 1, 1953, 3.

23 *Rudar*, March 10, 1953, 4.

24 "The savings book is the key to a house with a garden!" *Dukla*, April 10, 1959, 1.
    The possibility of building an individual family house was provided at state level in Yugoslavia and Czechoslovakia in order to resolve the apartment problems.

25 Interview with Msgr. Marjan Kuk, February 16, 2008, unpublished.

26 Regulations on the leasing of the apartments belonging to the Coal Mine Company Velenje. See: Arhiv Premogovnika Velenje, box U 14.

27 In 1960 the Management Committee of CMCV decided that each worker who had received an apartment, but not yet fulfilled the conditions relating to voluntary hours, was required to pay 55 dinars for each unfulfilled voluntary hour. Arhiv Premogovnika Velenje, box U 14.

28 Žgank, (see note 12), 241.
    One year before, in October 1962, the President of the Presidium of the Supreme Soviet at the time, Leonid Brezhnev, visited Velenje. His wife, along with their daughter and President Khrushchev's daughter, took a look at some apartments in the centre of Velenje and asserted that they

had been very pleasantly surprised. *Rudar*, October 27, 1962, 2.
    The representatives of the American Embassy or French parliamentary delegation focused on town construction and the living standards of the town inhabitants. *Rudar*, June 22, 1963, 3.

29 Arhiv Premogovnika Velenje, boxes U 14 and U 19.
    There were various categories of apartment available, for which different rents were paid. In Velenje, for example, there were seven apartment categories. For a monthly rent of twenty-five dinars per square metre, there was a first category apartment, which was to be healthy, airy and dry, with a bathroom, English toilet, the right to use the laundry room and the basement, and electrical and water drainage installations, situated near the town centre. On the other hand, apartments in the seventh category were offered for three dinars per square metre; these were very unhealthy and dangerous apartments, which could better be described as barracks. *Rudar*, April 3, 1954, 2.

30 *Velenjski rudar*, November 15, 1953, 6.

31 Archív Ostravsko-karvinské doly [Archive of the Ostrava-Karviná Mining Company], box Dukla, Havířov Dolní Suchá, II./14.

32 Zgodovinski arhiv Celje [The Celje history archive], box OBLO Šoštanj-Velenje 7.

33 The housekeeper was a miner with a salary of around 30,000 dinars; as housekeeper, he earned an extra 5,000 dinars per month. His wife was a cleaning lady, who received 200 dinars per family each month for cleaning the corridors and stairs. *Rudar*, April 17, 1963, 12.

34 For example see: *Rudar*, October 14, 1961, 12.

35 *Rudar*, April 17, 1963, 12.

36 An unsuccessful campaign against hanging laundry out to dry between the balconies and windows of the apartment blocks (which were provided with drying rooms!) was started by the Municipality of Dimitrovgrad in Bulgaria. Ulf Brunnbauer, *"Die sozialistische Lebensweise" Ideologie, Gesellschaft, Familie und Politik in Bulgarien (1944–1989)* (Cologne, Weimar, Vienna: Böhlau, 2007), 160–61.

37 The Socialistic Union of the Working People of Slovenia was founded in 1953 from the Liberation front. It was the most widespread mass organisation under the control of the Communist Party.

38 *Rudar*, April 29, 1961, 7.

39 *Rudar*, April 17, 1965, 5.

40 Archív Ostravsko-karvinské doly, Administration of the housing estate, no. 16–26 or Státní okresní *archiv* Karviná [State Regional Archive, Karviná], MěstNV Havířov (1954) 1955–1980, no. 14.

41 Complaint made by the workers about the heating system and distribution of hot water in a letter to the President of Czechoslovakia Antonín Novotný on 8 January 1960. Státní okresní *archiv Karviná*, (see note 40).

42 *Dukla*, December 22, 1960, 2.

43 A Spartak is a Škoda 450 which was designed in 1953 and later renamed Felicia. The name Spartak was commonly also used to refer to other types of Škoda cars, such as the Škoda 440, which was also named Orlik or Rival.

44 *Dukla*, December 22, 1960, 2.

45 "A Car for Everyone," in *Happy: Cities and Public Happiness in Post-War Europe*, (see note 2), 218.

46 Korpnik, (see note 13), 166–67.

47 Státní okresní *archiv Karviná*, (see note 40).

48 György Konrád, "Rückblick auf die Beglückung," in *Glück, Stadt, Raum in Europa 1945 bis 2000*, (see note 1), 8.

49 Wagenaar, (see note 2), 18.

50 Alain de Botton, *The Architecture of Happiness* (London: Penguin Group, 2006), 142.

51 Interviews with the first town inhabitants of Velenje and Havířov, unpublished; interviews with inhabitants of Havířov in Green town (see note 15) and J. Jílková, "Každodenní život obyvatel města Havířova od jeho počátků do poloviny šedesátých let 20. století [The everyday life of the people from Havířov town from the beginning until the mid-nineteen-sixties]," (MA thesis: Ostrava University, 2007).

DOES URBAN LIFE MAKE FARMERS HAPPY?

The Central Settlements of
Collective Farms in the
Estonian SSR*

Mart Kalm

1

In post-industrial society, the polarity of country and city life is no longer important, but this used to be a source of considerable concern in industrial societies. The process of industrialisation in major parts of Europe resulted in people moving away from the country-side; agricultural production became concentrated in fewer, larger farms, so that traditional villages and their infrastructure almost completely vanished during the second half of the twentieth century. However in the Soviet Union, where the people had been experiencing problems ensuring food supplies ever since collectivisation, the authorities tried to improve the production of food products not only by industrialising agriculture but also by introducing an urban lifestyle in the countryside. An apartment building with all modern conveniences was supposed to make country people happy. But in spite of the fact that apartment buildings sprang up in villages and facing out onto open fields, it was the muddy roads, poverty, alcoholism, and a sense of hopelessness that continued to characterise country life in the Soviet Union. This situation could also be found in Estonian villages, but agriculturalists in the Estonian SSR (Soviet Socialist Republic) cleverly managed to take advantage of the bottomless character of the Russian market and to survive as best they could by testing the limits of the economic model forced upon them. As a result, by the nineteen-seventies, living conditions in the countryside were already generally much better than in the city. Little by little small, well-structured centres developed all around the country, sometimes called agro-towns. Throughout the entire USSR the architecture of these central settlements in Estonian collectives was considered to be outstanding.[1] This was a new pattern of settlement in Estonia and it is interesting to see how the characteristics of urban and rural life increasingly began to merge. But to what extent did the people who had moved from the farmhouses to the apartment buildings of these new settlements consider themselves to be the fortunate beneficiaries of progress, and to what extent did they feel like

1   The despised post-communist environment: abandoned housing in Lõõla, Paide region. Built by the "9 May" collective farm in the early nineteen-eighties for farm workers in a village which was first mentioned in 1564.

victims of the extermination process that was so characteristic of the occupying Soviet regime? This paper will approach these questions, combining aspects relating to architectural, social, and cultural history.

Collective farming and the story of the kolkhozes is a chapter in history that Estonians today are not particularly interested in, because Estonian society is now dominated by neo-liberalism and national discourse.[2] Even though a nostalgic discourse does exist, propagated and defended by former agricultural figures,[3] there is a lack of in-depth fundamental research that would facilitate an impartial overview.[4] In 2006, Rein Lang, the Minister for Justice, called for the demolition of ugly abandoned kolkhoz buildings[5] (▶ 1). In the ongoing process of washing away all remnants of Soviet occupation, the desire to erase this unpleasant memory is understandable, even though thousands of people still live in the environment that the kolkhozes created. It is also impossible to read the Estonian landscape without understanding this part of its history.

The Idea of Eliminating the Polarity of City and Countryside

In the *Manifesto of the Communist Party* (1848), Karl Marx and Friedrich Engels prescribed "the unification of agriculture and industry, thus helping to eliminate the polarity of city and country life"[6] as one of the means of building a class-free society. Elsewhere, Friedrich Engels expresses the idea as follows: "The only thing that can tear village society out of its isolation and monotony where it has been vegetating for thousands of years without change, is the equal and balanced distribution of the population around the country and a tight relationship between industrial and agricultural production along with the necessary enlargement of the available means of transportation. This, of course, assumes the abolition of capitalist production."[7] While Charles Fourier's housing unit *phalanstère* tried to create a synthesis of the virtues of country and city life, the great ideas of urban development usually focused on the problem of over-population in the cities with garden cities and ribbon cities, or on approaches such as Bruno Taut's *Die Auflösung der Städte* (The Dissolution of Cities, 1920) and Frank Lloyd Wright's *Broadacre City* (1932). When Le Corbusier approached the French regionalist trade unions in 1930 and designed a modernist farmhouse, he too found that country life had become underdeveloped and social factors that had been formerly used to entice people to the cities now also had to be employed here.[8] Such a disparaging attitude towards country life with its continual dependency on the eternal cycle of nature was very common, even after the Second World War, as can be seen in the works of Henri Lefebvre, who wrote: "Rural society was (and remains) one of a lack of abundance, of scarcity and deprivation accepted or rejected, and of prohibitions that developed and normalized those deprivations."[9]

Thanks to collectivisation, capitalist production disappeared from agriculture in the Soviet Union. When speaking about collective farming, the Russian abbreviation kolkhoz, based on the first syllables of *kollektivnoye khozyaistvo* (collective household) is often used. In

Estonian it was adopted as *kolhoos*. The new, third programme of the Communist Party of the Soviet Union, which was adopted in 1961 and in use in the period of Khrushchev's leadership, stipulated that:

> Kolkhoz settlements will gradually develop into large city-like settlements, with residential houses in good condition, public buildings, services and cultural as well as health facilities. … Erasing the socioeconomic, cultural and vernacular differences between city and country will become one of the most important results of advancing communism.[10]

Such utopian enthusiasm existed even among otherwise rational Estonian architects during the days when the "material and technical basis of communism," as it was called then, was being established. For example, Ants Mellik wrote:

> This metropolis of communism—a huge industrial-agrarian-cultural concentration—consists of powerful automated factories situated either underground or covered with terraces of greenery; sufficient wooded areas alternating with territories of intensive agriculture and horticulture that give several harvests a year thanks to the conditions of an artificial climate; cattle farms; natural and artificial bodies of water; beaches and recreation grounds. Numerous cultural establishments are concentrated in primary and secondary centres. Although the material assets per person would be much greater in such an environment than now, there is no excessive concentration, compression or congestion.[11]

Communism, which was supposed to be the bright future of all humanity, was not achieved within the twenty years that the party's programme had prescribed for it—indeed, nor was it achieved later. However, these city-like settlements actually were developed. This was made possible thanks to reforms that favoured agriculture, put into motion in the Khrushchev era because starvation forced the country to re-evaluate its dominant opinion that considered the proletariat to be important, but not farmers. In the study of Soviet society, the reassessment and methods of normalisation generally prove more interesting than the official doctrine;[12] therefore it makes more sense to look at the real changes that took place in the countryside.

Collective Farms

THE STALIN ERA—COLLECTIVISATION

In Russia, a certain line of development can be seen leading from the traditional village to collective farms. Capitalist relations were underdeveloped and the more wealthy farmers—"*kulaks*"—who stood slightly apart from the rest of the village community at the beginning of the twentieth century, were destroyed at the beginning of the nineteen-thirties when their lands were confiscated and they were sent off to Siberia. In terms of the form of settlement, it was the linear village that dominated in Russia, and it was not an overly dramatic task to transform this into the centre of a kolkhoz. Of course, moving from a private farmhouse into an apartment building was a complete break from tradition, but at least the compact settlement was natural and traditional for these people.[13]

Estonia, with a little more than one million inhabitants, remained something of an exception in every respect, and it did not really represent the common paradigm of the USSR. Before Estonia was annexed by the Soviet Union in 1940, it already had a completely developed and functioning system of capitalist farms (more than 140,000). Though there were indeed some compact villages with a spatial structure going back to the middle ages, most of the land had already been divided up in the nineteenth century.[14] Starting in the eighteen-sixties, when farms were being bought *en masse*, new buildings were constructed outside the villages and the settlements became increasingly dispersed. After Estonia became independent, the eternal dream of its farmers finally came true—with the land reform in 1920, all land was taken away from the Baltic German landlords and given out as smallholdings. This also meant that a scattered pattern of settlement completely dominated. Not all the smallholdings proved viable and stronger farmers took these over, but this did not change the fact that, by the end of the nineteen-thirties, the dominant pattern in the Estonian landscape was that of fields, dotted with interspersed independent farms.

In an attempt to create equality the Soviet occupation, which came with the Second World War, first dealt primarily with the redistribution of nationalised land, favouring farmers with small farms and new settlers (the maximum size of farms was to be thirty hectares). The leaders of the Estonian SSR naively hoped to avoid collectivisation—they remembered reading in the pre-war media about the prevalence of imposed collectivisation in Russia, which they now greatly feared. However in 1947, the Communist Party issued a regulation—the "Formation of Collective Farms in the Lithuanian, Latvian and Estonian SSRs"—which bore witness to the fact that the USSR, victorious in the war, was asserting its international standing, the impetus for the Cold War being firmly in place. The authorities only managed to get Estonian countrymen to consider collective farms after deporting 29,000 people to Siberia on 25 March 1949.[15] Following this, more than one hundred collective farms were created per day; and by mid-April there were 2,500 of them. From then on collective farms were amalgamated, so that by 1975 there were only 188.[16]

People who joined these collective farms, established in such an atmosphere of terror, did not know how to manage them properly; nor did they wish to. Agricultural production in the early nineteen-fifties dropped noticeably and at the same time 57,000 people—most of them young—escaped from collective farms to the cities.[17] Collective herds were placed in the barns of former larger farms because, as yet, they had no buildings of their own. In the nineteen-fifties, it was not customary for collective farm workers to receive any payment, or if so it was only paid in kind.[18] Food for the family was obtained from small, regulated households, where it was only permitted to keep one cow, two pigs, etc.

State farms (*Sovkhoz, sovetskoye khozyaistvo* = Soviet household) were also established alongside the collective farms, but to a lesser extent. These were mostly created on the grounds of former town and state manors—for example, seed-growing or stud farms and former schools of agriculture became *Sovkhoz* technical schools (*sovhoostehnikum*). In the nineteen-fifties, the state poured enormous funds into state farms—new buildings were erected and the workers were paid wages—all for the purposes of demonstrating that collective farming could be successful.

Immediately after the kolkhozes were established, the state commenced work on the designing of the spatial planning of the kolkhoz.[19] An individual farm was proclaimed to be a hotbed of ideologically harmful individualism and an economic obstacle hampering large-scale production.[20] But despite the fact that many general plans modelled on examples implemented throughout the Soviet Union were drawn up in Tallinn, nobody had the money to realise them—the drawings were mainly intended to serve propaganda purposes. These general plans foresaw small central settlements, often designed for just one hundred families. They mostly used a scheme of zoning, designating an administrative centre, a production area, and a residential district consisting of single houses. The term "agro-town" was already being used here and there.[21] During the Stalin era the intention was to create these central settlements on empty land; in reality however they all started to develop around existing settlements.

THE KHRUSHCHEV ERA—COLLECTIVE FARMS GET GOING

From the mid-nineteen-fifties, many concessions were made to collective farms with the aim of encouraging agriculture. State prices for agricultural produce were increased, sales quotas to the state were reduced and wages were paid out in money. As the economy generally improved, the collective farms were able to buy more tractors and equipment. The many strange campaigns, such as the compulsory project to encourage the growing of maize implemented following Khrushchev's visit to America (although it was an unsuitable crop for the Estonian climate and could only be used for green fodder), did not cause any great economic damage. Slowly people learned to manage collective farms; barns and other collective farm buildings were built and new homes began to appear. The latter were mainly two-storey buildings with four small apartments.

THE BREZHNEV ERA—LARGE-SCALE PRODUCTION ON COLLECTIVE FARMS

Intensive large-scale production, which is characteristic of all modern economies,[22] began in the late nineteen-sixties. While the economy of the USSR generally stagnated in the nineteen-seventies, the collective farms based on collective ownership had more economic independence and Estonian kolkhozes were able to make the most of this. The Soviet production plans assigned the role of meat and dairy producer to the Estonian SSR. On the basis of the distribution programme in the USSR, most of these products were taken out of Estonia, mainly to the Leningrad region, which with its population of more than three million absorbed everything that arrived without the shelves in the shops even having a chance to fill. Even though the collective farms earned well from this exchange, the distribution programme was unable to supply the towns in Estonia adequately, so the selection of meat products was limited.[23] This extraction of agricultural produce from Estonia cannot strictly be called colonialism. In part, it was just an expansion of a more successful economic unit into a neighbouring market. Estonian collective farms were very interested in exceeding sales quotas because this was rewarded with the distribution of additional resources such as a larger allowance for buying machinery and equipment, fertilisers or building materials.

In the nineteen-seventies, the agricultural productivity in Estonia was twice that of the average in the USSR. By the early nineteen-seventies, the number of people involved in agriculture was just one-third of the number of people who had been working as farmers in 1939, although they were producing 1.5 times as much agricultural output.[24] Even so, rural areas were plagued by a shortage of good workers. During peak seasons, students and other urban citizens were sent to the countryside to help out and augment the rural workforce. This fact actually reveals the low levels both of productivity and of mechanisation, although by that time most pre-war productivity indicators had been exceeded anyway. For example, in 1971 one dairy cow in Estonia yielded 3,199 kilograms of milk per year,[25] compared to 2,950 kilograms in 1938.[26] By comparison in 1970, the average Soviet cow produced 2,110 kilograms, while the average Danish cow gave 3,950 kilograms of milk.[27] The further development of pre-war breeding programmes, extensive land improvements, the more widespread use of fertilisers, mechanisation, and more effective management were all factors that had helped to increase production levels.

Large farms accommodating over 1,000 cows were built in Estonia, with a blind belief in the efficiency of large-scale production. Huge pork farms were established near Viljandi and Pärnu, where 54,000 and 24,000 animals respectively were fattened each year.[28] Since development in rural areas occurred much more rapidly than in cities, it was not surprising that, by 1972, Estonian urban and rural wages were on a par,[29] and that by the beginning of the nineteen-eighties they were even clearly higher in the country.[30]

Urban Planning of Kolkhoz Central Settlements

After the shock of collectivisation in the Stalin era and during Khrushchev's thaw, the country started to get back on its feet, but by now the small kolkhozes that had been created and planned as ensembles in the nineteen-fifties had become unviable. The period from 1962 to 1967 saw the creation of long-term plans for all the regions (fifteen in all) of the Estonian SSR[31] (▶ 2), and in terms of the breadth and complexity of the task this was really a huge step forward in territorial planning. Besides architects, specialists in agronomy, energy, geography, land use, and economics were also working on the project. These long-term plans determined the location of residential areas, public institutions, industry and farming, transport, communication and electrical networks as well as civil engineering. The average size of collective farms was now set at 8,000 hectares, which meant that they were still forced to merge in order to form larger units, as in the nineteen-sixties the average size of kolkhozes or sovkhozes was only 3,300 hectares (▶ 3). Increasing their size was supposed to be economically more lucrative, and also made it easier to mechanise production processes and to use the workforce in the most effective way. Under the conditions of the planned economy the state investments were decided according to these long-term plans. Alongside these schemes, general plans were also developed for specific kolkhozes and sovkhozes, providing more details in addition to the general directions defined in the regional plans.

The regional plans selected 650 potential settlements out of more than 2,000 existing villages. Of these, 315 were planned to become central settlements for collective farms, accommodating approximately 800–1,200 people, and a further 335 villages were to be auxiliary settlements with about 300–600 inhabitants. The auxiliary settlements were usually existing villages that may have previously served as centres for older and smaller kolkhozes. Thus

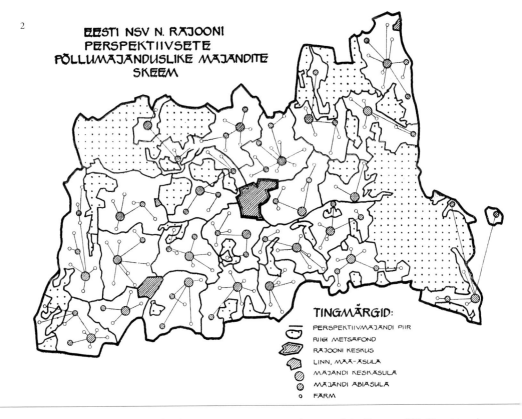

2

**EESTI NSV N. RAJOONI
PERSPEKTIIVSETE
PÕLLUMAJANDUSLIKE MAJANDITE
SKEEM**

TINGMÄRGID:

PERSPEKTIIVMAJANDI PIIR
RIIGI METSAFOND
RAJOONI KESKUS
LINN, MAA-ASULA
MAJANDI KESKASULA
MAJANDI ABIASULA
FARM

2   Long-term plan for agricultural enterprises in an unnamed region of the Estonian SSR. Disguising the Tartu region as region N reflects the Soviet mania for secrecy.

something had already been built there, but they had become auxiliary settlements following the amalgamation into larger collective farms.

The development of such a new network of settlements became a contentious issue, giving grounds for much discussion. It seems that the main concern was the "agro-town"—a settlement of 2,000–4,000 inhabitants, which was recommended by the Soviet Union, but feared by Estonians. Everyone taking part in the discussion seemed to be convinced that

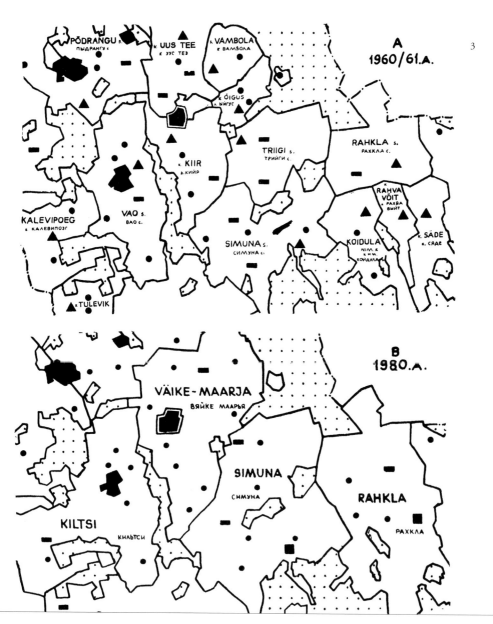

3 Part of a plan showing the borders and centres of agricultural enterprises. A: current situation, B: plan for the future. Squares and rectangles mark settlements, triangles mark current centres of collective farms, circles designate farms.

there was no way to achieve large-scale production without a more compact settlement system, but the problem arose from the question of the concentration of these settlements. Boris Mirov, the chief architect of the architectural office *Eesti Maaehitusprojekt* (Estonian Rural Construction Bureau), the main bureau for building design in the country, proclaimed that the benefits of the traditional diffuse settlement—for example, proximity to nature, a healthy lifestyle, quiet surroundings and the preservation of the natural face of our landscape—were self-evident, whereas the supporters of agro-towns needed to prove their point mathematically, based on calculations.[32]

Economic calculations for the future were very fashionable in the USSR in the nineteen-sixties, but they lost their importance in the next decade, since nothing ever really turned out as they had foreseen. Even though Mirov was responsible for the typical urban apartment buildings constructed on the basis of standard designs, and his work proved to be the greatest millstone for the nationalist discourse despising kolkhozes, at least he had the courage to stand up to the party programme and say that the city was not the ultimate ideal and that the country had advantages to offer that could not be found in the city. Paul Härmson—an architect with scholarly interests—did some calculations and proved that there was no point in dreaming of new agro-towns, since there was no money to build them.[33] Besides, all the construction projects that had just got under way in the country would have to be stopped at once as they were being carried out in small villages with no future. He was also worried that greater settlement concentration would increase transport costs—building and maintaining roads, buying and keeping cars and buses and also the time spent on travelling to and from work are all important and costly factors. Härmson warned that if the people living in the agro-town had to start using vehicles to get to their fields, number of cars would have to be increased tenfold—and the Soviet industrial structure would not be able to cope with this. There were also a number of other calculations that were troublesome—for example, "access to cultural services" could not be shown in terms of its monetary value.[34]

As urbanisation continued and the number of people involved in agriculture continued to fall, opinions also changed—in the nineteen-eighties, the general opinion was that by the beginning of the twenty-first century around 400–600 inhabitants would remain in the kolkhoz centres.[35] This shift in thinking was characteristic of the stagnation period when utopias were generally abandoned.

Building the Central Kolkhoz Settlements

From the nineteen-sixties, the Estonian landscape underwent dramatic changes. The use of tractors demanded bigger fields, so extensive land improvement was employed to make way for large stretches of field. As a result of the industrial approach to agriculture, farms in forested areas became desolate and overgrown; neglected farms were then turned into more fields. Villages earmarked as centres for the collective farms grew, whilst others dwindled as people continued to move away, some of them to the new centres. This became known as

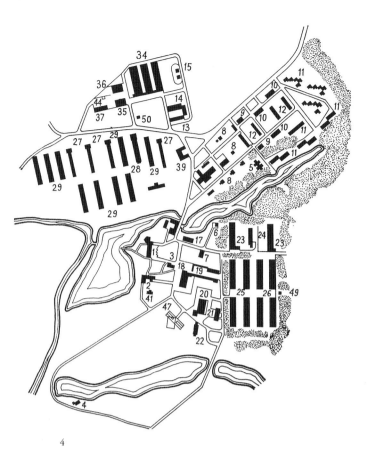

1: office;
2: canteen;
3: service centre;
4: Finnish sauna;
5: kindergarten-crèche;
6: sauna;
7–12: housing;
13: garages for private cars;
14: boiler house;
15, 39: pump houses;
17, 35–38: storage buildings;
18, 19: garages for agricultural machinery;
20–22: industrial buildings;
23–29, 34: chicken coops;
41: greenhouse;
44, 47, 49–50: technical structures.
The plan is based on a master plan by Valve Pormeister, which was significantly changed during its construction. In the plan, the shopping centre is unmarked and lies between positions 8 and 39. The settlement was developed using the former core of the village, the manor, as a basis; the well-known office building by Valve Pormeister replaced the wooden manor house. No. 17, etc., are former manor structures. No. 8 marks the nineteen-fifties single-family dwellings from the period before the apartment blocks were built. Instead of terraced houses in the NE corner (No. 11), a primary school / kindergarten was built in the late Soviet period. The development of Kurtna was influenced by its proximity to Kiisa, an old pre-war commuter garden suburb of Tallinn.

the borderland syndrome—characterised by a huge contrast between the developing centre and the remaining villages which were in a state of decline.[36] Another outcome of these developments was the partially-built settlements that were initially scheduled to become centres, but later downgraded to auxiliary settlement status at some point during the unification processes, meaning that all development was stopped there.

The dream of having completely new settlements built on completely new sites remained a dream; in reality collective farm centres developed along more pragmatic lines on the basis of existing villages and their existing infrastructure. During Stalin's rule, old parish centres with churches had been seen as ideologically unsuitable as collective farm centres, but during Khrushchev's time this was no longer considered important although, ironically, this was when the fight for atheism was gathering real momentum. Collective farm centres also made good use of the old manor houses that had been left empty after the land reform in 1920. Before the war some difficulty had been found in making full use of them—although

4   Master plan for the (Experimental Aviculture) Farm in the (central) settlement of Kurtna, Harju region.
5   Central settlement of Lungu Sovkhoz in the Rapla region in the nineteen-sixties. The axial placement of buildings around the central square betrays an underlying nineteen-fifties Stalinist master plan. On the left, a traditionalist late nineteen-thirties revival house with four apartments built in the late nineteen-fifties. The two-

schools, cultural centres, sanatoriums, leprosy clinics, and so on, could be easily housed in the main building, outbuildings such as stables and cattle-sheds stood empty, since small farmers had nothing to store there. But collective farms found them easy to put to use, although they already started to abandon them again in the nineteen-sixties. Nevertheless, the most common way for a collective farm centre to develop was by growing up around the old manor houses, and thanks to this the collective farm settlements did not contrast too starkly with the surrounding environment.

Central collective farm settlements such as this were not built overnight—it took more than thirty years to develop them.[37] The process lasted from the end of the nineteen-fifties to the beginning of the nineteen-nineties, when the kolkhozes and sovkhozes ultimately collapsed (▶ 4). The concentric development in these settlements can often still be seen, with older and smaller buildings at the centre and increasingly larger buildings towards the outer limits. This can best be seen in the case of residential buildings.[38] At the centre there are even traditionalist buildings from the nineteen-fifties, normally with two to four apartments and a gabled roof. These are usually followed by apartment houses built in the nineteen-sixties —two-storey buildings containing small apartments, built of silicate bricks and covered with a flat roof (▶ 5). Most often these were built for cattlemen close to the new cattle-sheds so, in those villages that had ceased to develop, they often stand as single buildings among the farmhouses—and as such they appear especially mournful, even symbolically reproachful of the kolkhoz system. In 1964, Mirov had already created standard designs for three-storey dwellings that also had a completely flat roof, and there was already some storage space available in the apartments. Three-storey pre-fabricated concrete buildings remained the most common type of residential building in the country towards the end of

5

storey houses represent early nineteen-sixties standard designs; the house on the left is built of large blocks and the two on the right of silica bricks. In the centre is a shop following a modernist standard design. The barn behind the shop seems to be a remnant from the time of the manor, as it is detached from the plan of the central settlement.

6

7

6   Hummuli, the central settlement of the former Hummuli sovkhoz in the Valga region. The former Neo-Gothic red brick manor house, used as a school, can be seen at the back; in the middle ground there are apartment blocks for the sovkhoz employees, in the foreground their garden plots. On the left the four-storey apartment building, partly disused, is from the standard series 1-317. The output of urban construction plants was occasionally used to construct such buildings in the country.

the Soviet era, though in time their modernist architecture became a little less harsh and more traditionalist, thanks to the influence of postmodernism. The level of pre-fabrication also increased, and the apartments became more comfortable. In the nineteen-seventies, pre-fabricated concrete buildings of up to five storeys also made occasional appearances— these were produced in the construction plants in Tallinn, Tartu, or Narva, and once they were installed in the village, there was no way of telling the difference between the village environment and dormitory suburbs (▶ 6). In contrast to the everyday urban quality of the apartment buildings, the groups of detached family dwellings were usually positioned in a beautiful location on the edge of the manor park or even outside the settlement on the banks of a river or lake, in order to emphasise their elite status. But despite the presence of the enormous residential buildings in the central kolkhoz settlements, most country people remained on their farms. The general pattern was that young people moved into the new settlements and older people stayed on the farm.

Was the Urban Lifestyle Able to Bring Happiness?

An apartment building in the kolkhoz offered a real contrast to life in a farmhouse. In a private farmhouse people had been used to living only with other members of their own family, whereas now there were always neighbours around and plenty of opportunities for

8

7   Central settlement of the "9 May" collective farm in Väätsa, Paide region. In the foreground there is a shop/canteen, completed in 1971; in the mid-ground an office/club completed in 1969 according to a Lithuanian standard design (1964); in the background, apartment blocks and, in between the fields, the pre-war farms and farm buildings of the collective farm can be seen.
8   The office building of the Kurtna Experimental Aviculture Farm in the Harju region, designed by the architect Valve Pormeister, 1965–66.

9

social intercourse—it was a little as though every day was a "church day." At the same time, television and radio became more accessible and little by little farms even became connected by phone lines—all this reduced the feeling of isolation that prevailed on secluded farms. Cars helped even more. In general, the Soviet Union became motorised very slowly, but thanks to the relative wealth of Estonian kolkhozes and sovkhozes, the number of cars per inhabitant was several times higher here than the average in the USSR.

It was believed that one of the main advantages of an urban development was the conveniences it offered. On traditional farms there were always animals around, but now their sheds were situated outside the settlement, which meant there was no cattle odour and it was much easier to keep the village clean. However, real comforts in the apartment buildings appeared very slowly. Since the first standard designs for apartment buildings had extremely small—*Existenzminimum*—apartments, the uninstalled bathroom was often used as a pantry. Taking into account their wooden stove, dry toilet, and the fact that sometimes water even had to be brought in from the well, it was only the architectural form that was modern. In the second half of the nineteen-sixties, a transition was made to the building of mostly three-storey buildings. This was due to the fact that there was now more money and the cost per square metre of constructing larger buildings had fallen;[39] thus sewerage systems could be built and older houses were also linked to the system. With the building of boiler houses, central heating was then installed.

Another advantage for living in such a settlement was the proximity of all the services (▶ 7). Inhabitants could reach their workplace on foot or an organized bus was available— this was much better than having to walk or go by horse drawn cart, bicycle or car all the way to the centre. Most of the people who moved into the central settlement were young.

9   Swimming pool and sauna, laundry, doctor's surgery and hairdresser's in Oisu, the central settlement of the collective farm "Estonia" in the Paide region (architect: Ain Õun, 1978–88). The economically successful "Estonia" kolkhoz was not concerned with architecture; if they used an architect at all, their buildings were mainly designed by lesser-known architects rather than large architectural firms. Today the building is partially unoccupied; only the doctor's surgery, pharmacy and beauty salon are in use.

They had some kind of special agricultural education and they mostly worked in the settlement, at the kolkhoz administration or at a workshop nearby. The most dominant building in the central settlement was the office-club symbolising the power of the collective[40] (▶ 8). The kolkhoz office was often combined with the club because the large hall used for general meetings by the kolkhoz could also be used by choirs and theatre groups for rehearsals at other times. At that time a lot of people still lived in the country with limited means of mobility, so the club also operated as a cinema; professional theatres from the cities also often came to the kolkhoz clubs to give performances. Schools and kindergartens were also close by. In addition, kolkhozes and sovkhozes built canteens where everybody could have lunch. And considering that in the Soviet Union shortages were the rule, it was strategically important to live close to a shop. The loss of the traditional farm sauna was compensated for by the provision of a local "public sauna," and since all the people going there knew each other anyway, it took on the function of a tavern on Saturday evenings. In the nineteen-seventies, kolkhozes and sovkhozes also started building sports grounds and swimming pools—once again to the benefit of the inhabitants of the settlement (▶ 9).

The people who lived in the flats also had their small garden plots outside the centre. On the one hand this was positive as it meant that they were not completely removed from

10

10   "Kullipesa" (Hawk's Nest) single-family dwelling, Põlva kolkhoz, 1972—a standard design from 1971 by the architect Tõnu Kull from the EKE Projekt office, which subsequently became popular throughout Estonia.

country living; but on the other hand, it seemed absurd to have to bring the greens for the soup from a considerable distance away. So some amenities were not so close to the central settlement (▶ 6).

Inhabitants of central settlements were also permitted to keep animals. Outside the settlement there was a separate village made up of small sheds and barns, like a small caricature of the larger central settlement. It seems comical that a person living in an apartment, who may for example have worked in the kolkhoz dairy farm, also had to keep their own cow, sheep, pig, rabbits, and chickens, but this was an opportunity to save on food rather than buying it from the shop. It also meant that they had a better food supply, as the shop counter was usually empty. For these country people, keeping animals was not considered tedious, it was a natural part of country life, something they had always done. What was considered tedious was the trip from the apartment to the animals; furthermore it was strange keeping animals so far from home where you could not see or hear them as you went about your everyday tasks as you would on a farm.

Even though the standard designs of kitchens gradually became bigger, they were still not suitable for the preparation of home-grown produce. The fact that animals were kept also indicates that the inhabitants of a central settlement had excess time and energy. The wide range of leisure activities possible in the city was simply not available. It is also thought that the confined conditions in the standard apartments forced people to seek activities outside the home.[41] The residents of the apartment blocks in central settlements can be viewed as the estate labourers of the Soviet period—people without roots who had the mentality of wage earners without a sense of ownership of the collective kolkhoz property—something that the people who had been forced to give their animals and equipment up to the kolkhozes when they were first established still had, at least to some extent.

However, it seems that during the nineteen-sixties the urban euphoria prescribed by the party programme passed, and the merits of country living were recognized once again. In other words, the urban concept metamorphosed into that of the garden city. In the early nineteen-sixties it was only possible to build apartment houses consisting of four to eight small flats, but as the economic situation improved more money became available for the construction of residential buildings. Terraced houses, though closer to the ground than apartment buildings, never became very popular, and in the mid-nineteen-sixties detached family houses began to be built once again. Standard designs were created in Tallinn, inspired by Scandinavian models, and in the nineteen-seventies and nineteen-eighties, kolkhozes used these to create new residential buildings adjacent to the core of the settlement (▶ 10). They were larger than flats, consisting of four to six rooms; in the back garden fresh vegetables could be grown for cooking and at the front, flowerbeds reminiscent of a suburban city lifestyle blossomed as symbols of affluence. These family houses were usually given to the technocratic elite of the kolkhoz—the success of the collective farm depended on their work, and they had to be rewarded with concessions and privileges. Family houses either belonged to the kolkhoz and the resident paid a nominal rent, as was usual for the apartment blocks, or a group of family houses were joined together to form a housing co-operative. Often, in the case of good workers, the membership fee was graciously waived by the kolkhoz. A private house was a powerful and important instrument for rewarding the best workers. If the happy goal of a symbiosis of urban and rural life was ever achieved, it was in these buildings. But since the average central settlement of a collective farm had about one hundred flats in apartment buildings and about ten to twenty new family houses, one can say that happiness was not really evenly distributed in Estonian kolkhozes.

Conclusion

In the nineteen-sixties and nineteen-seventies, the kolkhozes and sovkhozes were committed to the industrial large-scale production of agricultural produce, and settlements emerged where the rural way of life gave way to a semi-urban lifestyle. The communist ideology had always considered country life as backward and undeveloped, and in this regard it might have seemed that it would make people happy if the urban lifestyle was transferred to the country; however in Estonia the rural population responded with considerable distrust. In Estonia, farmers were regarded as wealthy and innovative members of society. Thanks to their working habits and the extremely favourable market situation, Estonian kolkhozes and sovkhozes quickly became relatively wealthy compared to their counterparts in the other states around the USSR. In addition, the central settlements of these collective farms were built up in a more integral way than elsewhere. The kolkhoz and sovkhoz centres combined elements of urban and rural life; the happiest people were the privileged few who belonged to the technocratic elite and could live in a private house. In this way, the noble image of happiness in the communist ideology took on a relatively petty-bourgeois form.

Endnotes

* This research has been carried out as a part of the Estonian Ministry of Education and Research Grant no. SF 0160047s09

1 Vera Nikolayevna Kalmykova, *Arkhitektura sovetskovo sela* [Architecture of the Soviet Village] (Moscow: Stroiizdat, 1975), 147–77.

2 For example "The History of Estonian Agriculture," published by the Estonian University of Life Sciences, deals thoroughly with the first period of Estonian independence in 1919–40 (150–215), but the section covering the Soviet period from 1940–91 is much more general (216–34); Rein Lillak, *Eesti põllumajanduse ajalugu* [History of Estonian Agriculture] (Tartu: Eesti Põllumajandusülikool, 2003).

3 Eesti Põllumajandus XX sajandil. II köide. Ülevaade põllumajanduse loost okupatsioonide ajal. Aastad 1940–1990. I osa. Inimene ja ühiskond [Estonian 20th Century Agriculture. Vol 2. Survey of the Story of Agriculture during the Occupations. 1940–1990. Part I. Man and Society] (Tallinn: Põllumajandusministeerium et al., 2007).

4 Lauri Vahtre, "Stagnatsioon ja venestuskampaania [Stagnation and the Campaign of Russification]," in *Eesti ajalugu* [History of Estonia] VI, ed. Sulev Vahtre (Tartu: Ilmamaa, 2005), 314–17.

5 Rein Lang, "Vanemate pattude lunastamine [Redemption of the Sins of Parents]," *Postimees*, August 28, 2006, http://www.postimees.ee/280806/esileht/arvamus/215128.php (accessed January 14, 2009); see also: Rein Raudvere, "Lagunev Eesti tuleb lammutada [Decaying Estonia must be demolished]," *Maaleht*, April 19, 2007, http://paber.maaleht.ee/?page=Uudised&grupp=artikkel&artikkel=8367 (accessed January 15, 2009).

6 Karl Marx and Friedrich Engels, "Manifest der Kommunistischen Partei," in *Deutsche Geschichtsphilosophie. Ausgewählte Texte von Lessing bis Jaspers*, ed. Kurt Rossmann (Munich: dtv, 1969), 281.

7 Friedrich Engels, "Korteriküsimusest [The Housing Question] (1872)," in Karl Marx and Friedrich Engels, *Valitud teosed kahes köites, 1 köide*. (Tallinn: Eesti Riiklik Kirjastus, 1957), 503.

8 Le Corbusier, *La ville radieuse*. (Paris: Vincent, Fréal & Co, ²1964 [1933]), 331.

9 Henri Lefebvre, "The right to the City," in *Architecture Culture 1943–1968. A Documentary Anthology*, ed. Joan Ockman with Edward Eigen (New York: Rizzoli, 2000 [1993]), 430.

10 *Nõukogude Liidu Kommunistliku Partei Programm* [The Programme of the Communist Party of the Soviet Union] (Tallinn: Eesti Riiklik Kirjastus, 1961), 78.

11 Ants Mellik, "Asustusvormi perspektiivse ümberkujundamise küsimusi Eesti NSV-s [The Issue of the Long-term Restructuring of the Form of Settlements in the Estonian SSR]," in *Linnaehituse küsimusi Eesti NSV-s. Artiklite kogumik* [The Issue of Urban Planning in the Estonian SSR] (Tallinn: Riiklik Ehituse ja Arhitektuuri Komitee, 1963), 17. He most probably adopted the utopian idea of the communist settlement from Russian authors. Compare: Alexei Gutnov et al., *The Ideal Communist City* (New York: G. Braziller, 1971).

12 David Crowley and Susan E. Reid, "Style and Socialism: Modernity and Material Culture in Post-War Eastern Europe," in *Style and Socialism: Modernity and Material Culture in Post-War Eastern Europe*,

ed. David Crowley and Susan E. Reid (Oxford: Berg, 2000), 5.

13 For an overview of similar processes in Russia see: Judith Pallot, "Living in the Soviet Countryside" in *Russian Housing in the Modern Age. Design and Social History*, ed. William C. Brumfield and Blair A. Ruble (Cambridge: Woodrow Wilson Center Press & Cambridge University Press, 1993), 211–31.

14 Concerning the genesis of the landscape see: Vello Lõugas, "Põllumajanduslike maastike ajaloost Eestis [The History of Agricultural Landscapes in Estonia]," in *Põllumajanduslik maastik Eestis* [Agricultural Landscape in Estonia] (Tallinn: Valgus, 1980), 50–84.

15 See lists of deportees: http://www.okupatsioon.ee/english/lists/index.html (accessed January 16, 2009).

16 Karl Siilivask, comp. by, *Eesti NSV ajalugu, II osa* [History of the Estonian SSR, part 2] (Tallinn: Valgus, 1980), 293.

17 Lillak, (see note 2), 223.

18 See also: Enno Tammer, comp. by, *Nõukogude aeg ja inimene* [Soviet Time and Man] (Tallinn: Tänapäev/Postimees, 2004), 31.

19 Liina Jänes, "The Stalinist Collective Farm Village. Attempts to Establish Town-type Settlements in the Estonian Landscape," in *Constructed Happiness. Domestic Environment in the Cold War Era*, ed. Mart Kalm and Ingrid Ruudi (Tallinn, 2005), 184–99.

20 Vsevolod Tihhomirov, "Kolhoosiasulate planeerimise aluseid Eesti NSV-s [Principles of Planning in Kolkhoz Settlements in the Estonian SSR]," in *Eesti NSV kolhoosiaslute planeerimisest ja ehitamisest* [On the Planning and Constructing of Kolkhoz Settlements in the Estonian SSR] (Tallinn: Eesti Riiklik Kirjastus, 1953), 5.

21 August Muuga, *Kolhoosiasulate planeerimine* [The Planning of Settlements for Kolkhozes] (Tallinn: Eesti Riiklik Kirjastus, 1950), 39.

22 Maths Isacson, "The Highly Industrialised Period in the Nordic and Baltic Countries." in *Yhdyskuntasuunnittelu. The Finnish Journal of Urban Studies* 41 (2003:3): 33.

23 See also: Tammer, (see note 18), 130–34, 236, 239–40.

24 Juhan Kahk and Karl Siilivask, *Eesti NSV ajalugu* [History of the Estonian SSR] (Tallinn: Perioodika, 1984), 136.

25 Edgar Tõnurist, "Sotsialistliku põllumajanduse arengust Nõukogude Eestis [On the Development of Socialist Agriculture in Soviet Estonia]," in *Sotsialistliku põllumajanduse areng Nõukogude Eestis* [The Development of Socialist Agriculture in Soviet Estonia], ed. Edgar Tõnurist, comp. by Väino Järv and Juhan Kahk (Tallinn: Valgus, 1976), 28.

26 Lillak, (see note 2), 171.

27 Romualdas J. Misiunas and Rein Taagepera, *Balti riigid: Sõlteaastad 1940–1990* (Tallinn: Koolibri, 1997), 217 [*The Baltic States: the years of dependence, 1940–1980*. Berkeley, Los Angeles: University of California Press, 1983].

28 Siilivask, (see note 16), 293.

29 Misiunas and Taagepera, (see note 27), 214.

30 Vahtre, (see note 4), 316.

31 Adolf Käsper, "Perspektiivplaneerimisest Eesti NSV-s [Long-term Planning in the Estonian SSR]," *Ehitus ja arhitektuur* [Construction and Architecture] (1967:4): 11–14.

32 Boris Mirov, "Maaehituse probleeme [Problems of Construction in the Countryside]," in *Eesti arhitektuur. Artiklite kogumik* [Estonian Architecture. Collection of Essays] (Tallinn: Valgus, 1969), 74.

33 Paul Härmson, "Perspektiivse asustusvormi kavandamisest Eesti NSV-s [Planning of Long-term Forms of Settlement in Estonian SSR]," *Sotsialistlik Põllumajandus* [Socialist Agriculture] 20 (1964): 916–19.

34 Endel Arman, "Kas üks või mitu kolhoosiasulat? [One or More Kolkhoz Settlements?]," *Sotsialistlik Põllumajandus* [Socialist Agriculture] 14, (1961): 654–57.

35 Leonid Volkov, *Eestimaa asustus* [Settlement in Estonia] (Tallinn: Eesti Raamat, 1980), 199.

36 Lillak, (see note 2), 226.

37 For the construction activities of kolkhozes see: Mart Kalm, "The Oasis of the Industrialised Countryside in Soviet Estonia," in *Industry and Modernism. Companies, Architecture, and Identity in the Nordic and Baltic Countries during the High-Industrial Period*, ed. A. Kervanto-Nevanlinna (Helsinki: Finnish Literature Society, 2007), 352–71.

38 See the typology of residential buildings: Mihkel Karu, "Kus pidi kolhoosnik elama? Kolhooside tüüpelamuehitus Eestis kuni 1980. aastateni [Where did a Member of a Kolkhoz Have to Live? Standardised Housing of Kolkhozes in Estonia until the Early nineteen-eighties] (Bakalaureusetöö [BA thesis], Tallinn Eesti Kunstiakadeemia, 2005). Manuscript in the EKA KTI (Estonian Academy of Arts, Institute of Art History).

39 Vello Viirmaa, "Mitmekorruseliste elamute püstitamisest maa-asulais [On Erecting Multi-storey Housing in the Countryside]," in *Maaehituse küsimusi Eesti NSV-s* [On Constructing in the Countryside] (Tallinn: Riiklik Ehituskomitee, 1964), 36–38.

40 Liina Jänes, "Kolhoosikeskus Eesti NSV-s: arhitektuurne resistance sovetiseerimisele [The office-club of the Kolkhoz in Estonian SSR: an Architectural Resistance to Sovietisation] (Bakalaureusetöö [BA thesis], Tallinn Eesti Kunstiakadeemia, 2000). Manuscript in the EKA KTI (Estonian Academy of Arts, Institute of Art History)."

41 Heiki Pärdi, "Eesti maa-arhitektuur XX sajandi pööristes [Estonian Country Architecture in the Turmoils of the 20th Century]," in *Eesti Põllumajandus XX sajandil. II köide. Ülevaade põllumajanduse loost okupatsioonide ajal. Aastad 1940–1990. I osa. Inimene ja ühiskond* [Estonian Agriculture in the 20th Century. Vol 2. A Survey of the Story of Agriculture during the Occupations. 1940–1990. Part I. Man and Society] (Tallinn: Põllumajandusministeerium et al., 2007), 273.

NEW HORIZONS

The Representation of Ideal Practices in a
Modern City:
Firminy-Vert 1959

Clarisse Lauras

"Utopia is Reality in the Making" (Edouard Herriot)

Urban planning poses a problem when a divergence arises between the envisaged city and the actual way inhabitants live and interact within an urban environment. How does the concept of a city look as far as the decision-makers, the city planners, or anyone who has an influence on the future of cities is concerned, and what impact do these representations have on the daily life of the people who actually live there? Firminy-Vert (Green Firminy) is a perfect case study for the discrepancies that can occur between the conception of a city and the practicalities of everyday life there. Since 1954, the small city of Firminy-Vert in the Ondaine valley (Département Loire) has been the subject of a master city planning project aimed at creating an entire neighbourhood whose residential and overall structure is planned on the basis of modern, hygienist philosophy. The instigator of the project and the driving force behind it was Eugène Claudius-Petit (responsible for the rebuilding efforts in France after the Second World War), who was elected mayor in 1953. He engaged several famous architects, including Le Corbusier, to work on the realisation of the project, which was to be carried out according to the principles of modernism in which he strongly believed. The neighbourhood he envisioned incorporated 1500 apartments, schools, a sports stadium, a cultural centre and a church.

However, initial investigations carried out by the new mayor and his team revealed that things were not as they should be in the area; the existing blue collar population was plagued with all kinds of problems, alcoholism being the worst of them. The first assertion was that the practices and daily habits of the inhabitants could be strongly influenced by the newly created environment that was to be built around them. The entire neighbourhood was designed according to this vision; the idea was that a building can have a positive influence on individuals and on the community as a whole. Urban morphology is seen as possessing the power to transform social morphology. Claudius-Petit also believed that these changes would provide his city with a strong sense of identity, give it a place within the national context, set an example.

However this little urban utopia, where the life of the community has been thought through from the cradle to the grave, would prove to be thoroughly out of touch with the expectations and lifestyle of its inhabitants. If we are interested in how a perfect modern city is likely to work, it is essential to begin by taking a close look at how people have been used to spending their lives up until now, in an environment where, traditionally, work and living have been closely intertwined. One of the challenges is also to envision the level of discrepancy or coherency likely to arise between the inhabitants' wishes and the new rules as defined by the decision-makers.

In acknowledgement of the challenges facing them, the city council—led by Claudius-Petit—published an illustrated booklet entitled *New Horizons*, which was given to all new inhabitants moving into the area. This booklet explained the benefits and special features of the new living space, the quality of the construction materials and the general rules to be observed in striving towards a "new way of living."[1] It bears witness to the decision-makers' firm belief in this experiment; they were quite convinced that the urban environment could improve the daily lives of its inhabitants. In the following, we will investigate the statements made in the booklet with the actual changes occurring in the neighbourhood. Here we will see a constant wavering between the ideal representation of the urban environment on paper and the reality of the daily life of its inhabitants, the inconsistencies between the planned and the real version of a city.

Urban Dystopia: Firminy after the Second World War

One cannot understand Firminy without investigating the background against which Claudius-Petit's visions and ambitions arose. For eighteen years, he was fully devoted to the creation of a completely new city; it was to be a renaissance, a utopia that would change the life of his contemporaries.

For a long time, little was known about this craftsman who became a member of the government under Charles de Gaulle. Claudius-Petit, a man of character, was a member of the French Resistance network during the war; in the ensuing years he became extremely active on the political arena, both at national and local levels. He greatly admired the work of Le Corbusier. For a long time, his life was described in a series of short sharp assertions, some of them wrong; in any case written accounts fail to capture various aspects of his character. *A Politician in the World of Architecture,* a biography[2] published by a Ph.D. student a few years ago, finally gave a chronological description of the active life of a single-minded man and underlined the importance of his special relationship with architecture and the work of architects. Firminy is the logical outcome of this liaison between two worlds.

Born in 1907 in Angers, from a modest background, Claudius-Petit lost his father when he was very young. He finished his primary education and sough texile in various workshops throughout the region   stables, jewellery studios, and finally fell in love with the world of wood and carpentry. Just like his older brother, he quit school to study drawing and sketching, map design, even oil painting. He attended evening classes in Angers, Paris, and Lyon and became acquainted with the work of the trade unions, taking a special interest in the ideas of Marc Sangnier. At the age of sixteen he became the union representative of his workshop; his dedication to the cause was evident in every new workplace he entered. A man of action, wishing to share his knowledge, he turned towards teaching at the Ampère high school in Lyon and discovers the neighbouring province, the Loire Département. Claudius-Petit became familiar with modern architecture in the early nineteen-thirties, devouring the works of Le Corbusier. Of this mentor and future friend he says: "…in his speaking and writings he really knows how to get people to abandon their cocoon of indifference."[3] In fact, this was one of the main goals Claudius-Petit set for himself.

At the outbreak of war Claudius-Petit, true to his own convictions, enrolled in the French Resistance movement in the Rhône and Loire regions. In 1943 he left for Algiers where he met a number of architects at the Unitec Congress in 1944. He was well-read, and had always been passionate about architecture and city planning. He felt a close affinity with the specialists who were gathering forces, ready to rebuild France after the war. He believed, however, that the task at hand demanded far more than a pure rebuilding effort; he wished to create a new vision in which the mistakes of the past were eliminated. Immediately after the war, he rejected the position of Veteran Minister, and subsequently agreed to become head of the Ministry of Rebuilding in 1948; a strategic decision, in keeping with his ambitions, ideas and knowledge. He held the position for five years, in spite of all the turbulences affecting the French government at the time. His administration consisted of architects, technicians, and city planners, all of whom are carefully chosen for their joint belief in his vision and his ideas.

Claudius-Petit juggled between local and national involvement. Although the constituency of Firminy had been consigned to him, he spent less and less time there; this sad industrial city with its joyless main street marked with the scars of the industrial revolution represented the opposite of all that he believed in. It was far removed from the brand new architecture of the United States district in Lyon, designed by Tony Garnier, or the skyscrapers in Villeurbanne by Maurice Leroux. As a teacher, he had urged his students to realise how "materialism, self-interest and money could destroy a wonderful landscape"[4] and often brought them to Firminy to prove his point. The landscape and the surrounding areas were indeed beautiful, but the small city with its 20,000 inhabitants bore all the signs of intense industrialisation (steel, coal) and labour. The main sources of employment were found within the heavy industries, and there was no form of planning—the mines and the river dictated where the houses were built.

In 1952, Claudius-Petit was invited to visit the city by a delegation of *appelous*,[5] some of whom he had met whilst working in the Resistance. Afterwards, he recounted how filthy everything was, with slums everywhere, and remarked that the houses have been built one after the other without any concessions to planning or overall coherence. He went out to meet the inhabitants, and for a long time afterwards he was haunted by the memory of children whose ears had been chewed by rats. This encounter between a government official and people from the poorest classes, of course, provoked typical questions from the inhabitants: "Mr. Minister, are you staying with us for good or are you abandoning us?" But Claudius-Petit was definitely there to stay. In 1952 and 1953 he dedicated himself to winning the local election, and succeeded against the communist party. As head of the city council, and subsequently the president of the public housing committee, he was in an excellent position to put some of his ideas into practice. Firminy provided the perfect experimental ground—the town was important enough to have interesting needs but small enough to allow him to keep a close eye on the way it developed.

Industrial Valley—for Claudius-Petit, as for most of his contemporaries, these words belonged to the elementary vocabulary of geography. Everything seemed grey, monotonous, irreversible, sad:

> The trees have been replaced by factory chimneys. The fires in the great furnaces never stop, the railways, contained by the hills, suddenly sprawl out towards the workshops, the deafening hammering of the steelworks, the strident alarm that goes off before the crowds of exhausted faces, men and women, fill the streets after a hard working day.[6]

Firminy, however was far from being an exception; in the early nineteen-fifties most of the surrounding cities were faced with the same issues and environmental problems. Until the nineteen-sixties, the neighbouring city of Saint-Etienne won all the awards for being the worst French city with over 100,000 inhabitants. Firminy was light-years away from even the basic requirements stipulated in a study published by the National Council for Social Studies in the United States in 1946. In order to retain the dignity of its inhabitants, urban housing should have fulfilled at least the following conditions:[7] running water, a toilet, a shower or a bath, central heating, direct sunlight, and a good airflow system, it should be close to schools, transport and playgrounds, and it should have at least one room per person living in the apartment. Firminy was a typical example of overpopulation coupled with poor living conditions.

The new mayor decided to have a survey completed to define the existing living conditions and the general state of available housing. The surveyors were instructed to identify the relevant facts required to analyse the level of poverty as a whole—they were to comment on the family's behaviour (social standards) and the state of their accommodation (hygiene).[8] In the case of hygiene, the researchers were to comment on negative aspects only (e.g., if not enough cutlery and crockery is available) and on the general state of the apartment; they were even requested to comment if a lack of taste is evident in the interior decorations and design. These studies revealed the extent of the work to be done and the close relationship between a disorderly and chaotic exterior and the poverty of the inhabitants. In 1965, Maryse Dufaux summarised her perceptions as follows:

> One cannot say that this city is a beautiful one, in fact we must confess that it is not beautiful in the least. Whilst driving the ten kilometres from Saint-Etienne I saw nothing but a coalmining environment, the road is lined with factory chimneys, the buildings seem to be coated in black. Firminy, appearing in the basin of the river Loire, is a dark city, which would have fitted every single description found in Emile Zola's book *Germinal*. Although we are in the south, the sun seems unable to brighten the stones of the sad houses, everything seems joyless. Only labour seems to have a role to play and we quickly forget how beautiful the surrounding countryside is.[9]

Copyright Mairie de Firminy

This was the face of Firminy, then: a dark city with low-rise buildings, overshadowed by the factories and the black chimneys. This is how it was presented in the introductory booklet *New Horizons* (▶ 1): a city in decline, a dying city, a miserable place; there is no one out on the streets, dying trees are scattered here and there, a succession of soulless houses. Even the church tower seems worn down by time, unable to stand up with pride.

Eugène Claudius-Petit described the housing from his own perspective, coloured by a general vision of industrial cities as well as his memory of his first visit to the city:

1   Leave Firminy-Noir for Firminy-Vert, extract from *Horizons nouveaux*, 1959.

Whole families are crammed into these two-storey houses which have been built up hastily on uneven ground using bad construction materials, very often without proper foundations, even without qualified construction workers. The design is always the same from one house to another—there are always two large rooms opening out onto the main street if they are on the ground floor, or reached by a stiff wooden staircase if they are upstairs, a coal heater close to the sink (if there is one) in the room which serves as kitchen and dining room. In the other room, the bedroom, there are several beds and one or two pieces of furniture. If the family is large, it is not unusual to have a bed in the kitchen. The facts are much more vivid and real than descriptions from the nineteenth century, yet people are living in such conditions in the first half of the twentieth century.[10]

In Firminy it was not the material damages of war that need to be repaired, but the wounds caused by a lack of urban planning and policies. Firminy had been sacrificed to industry, and industry had abused the city and the people who live there. "Industry conquers, devouring everything. … The industrial era … paid no heed to the needs of the living population." Claudius-Petit criticised the lack of coherent policies and the fact that nothing had been done for fifty years:

If industry does not adapt, it dies, it must continually reinvent itself to awaken new desires and attract new customers. When it comes to dealing with cities however, conservatism and stagnation prevail most of the time, no new taxes are introduced, the pavements are falling apart, the sewers are overflowing and the street lights go off one after another. No more taxes? There is no water in summer. No new taxes—young people leave the city, taking the workshops with them, the city falls into a slumber and prepares to die.[11]

In Firminy the schools and the hospital were out-of-date and overcrowded; there were insufficient supplies of clean drinking water most of the time:

The sewerage network is inadequate, water is collected by a dam built in 1897 and redistributed without being properly filtered and treated. The development of electricity and gas networks is not coordinated, electrical lines dangle haphazardly between one building and another. The few remaining street lamps do not even succeed in creating the illusion of a city. The city has grown, but its infrastructure is lagging behind.[12]

Eugène Claudius-Petit's opinion on the existing situation was uncompromising: "Wherever you looked, the lack of proper means and the urgency of the situation were apparent. Essential and basic tasks had not been done when they should have been and the extent of repair work required was daunting."[13] Even though these statements were made in the middle of a political campaign, the surveys and audits confirm the lack of investment and the need to take immediate action. In 1953, out of 7,653 apartments, around 5,000 of them (70 per cent) have a sink, 1,000 (13 per cent) an inside toilet and 500 (6.5 per cent) their own bathroom. The housing authority could not cope with the requests that flooded in; only thirty-two new apartments had been built after 1948. So the new mayor was faced with a clear, vast and urgent task. The challenge was huge, but he had the conviction and the means to achieve some of his goals.

Creating and Offering a New Living Environment: the Happy City

The immediate needs in the city were overwhelming and cried out for urgent solutions. Claudius-Petit, however, had no desire to rush headlong into the issues. His team was diverse and extremely competent; the architects and engineers had all worked with him previously at the Ministry and they were reunited with a common aim. The mayor was convinced that it was not enough to be content with rebuilding the defect housing areas, even though new norms would, of course, be introduced. Creativity was required. The demographic studies and surveys reinforced him in his ideas, forecasting that there would be 35,000 to 40,000 inhabitants by 1985. The team moved in, established itself in a sheltered spot in the south, sharpened its pencils and got down to work on producing designs for a vast project. 1000 apartments were to be built, followed by a unit of 314 apartments, all designed by Le Corbusier. It was necessary to think big, be daring, whilst keeping costs down to a minimum. It was after all a social housing project, dedicated to producing accommodation for low-income families and as such it was under the strict constraints of French regulations. The team envisaged a modern living environment set within green spaces. Fresh air, space, and sun were to play an important role, in order to provide the framework for a better life. In 1961, the project was awarded the Urban Planning Prize for outstanding achievements. Important for the essence of the district were the new shapes and colours—white and green as opposed to grey and black. A new face was to be found for the city, creating a new landscape, refocusing on the human being. From then on, "high apartment buildings" were to overlook the factory chimneys and the church. Even the cemetery itself, which would have been forgotten in most cities, was completely rebuilt and landscaped, in acknowledgement to the growth and needs of the future population. The mayor presented the plans and discussed the details with everyone, but the master plan was not negotiable. There was no room for participative democracy.

The building site became a popular destination for sightseers; everyone was surprised by the speed and efficiency of the new construction techniques. In order to create a sense of community and to ensure that the inhabitants and the entire community felt involved in the proceedings, the team created a welcoming handbook for the first people moving into this new district, to which they give the name Firminy-Vert. The team set to work.

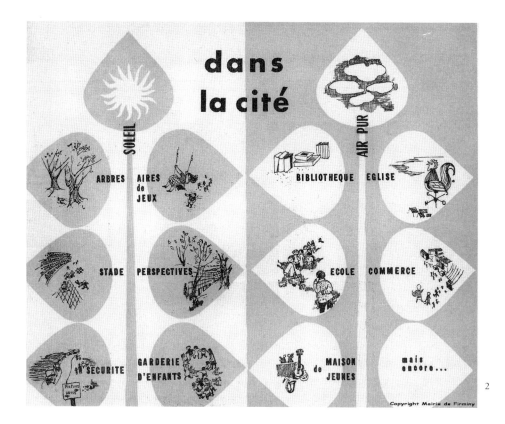

Nothing could be left to chance. The project was entirely innovative and the time had to be taken to explain it in a simple way. At a time when comics were becoming more and more popular, the team decided to use drawings and keep text to a minimum—after all, a brand new concept could not resort to traditional forms. Jean Claude Vertongen, a student at that time, was appointed with the task. He vividly recalled spending several weekends in Claudius-Petit's office in Firminy, poring over every sketch and drawing. He worked on a motif, Claudius Petit corrected it, producing a completely new version. The artist drew it again, simplified it still more. Jacques Bador wrote most of the text. The task of the authors was to explain a new way of life to the newcomers who came from a completely different environment.

To cut down on costs, the booklet dispensed with red and blue in favour of the colour green, which was omnipresent in the initial overall design. However in real life, when the first newcomers arrived, there was hardly a trace of green to be seen (▶ 1). The landscaping was far from finished, nothing had had a chance to grow, and people often complained about the mud and craters everywhere. "The inhabitants are walking on the moon! A right royal entry. Just what they should be doing in these times of space travel!"[14] The handbook

2   The checklist of a modern city, extract from *Horizons nouveaux*, 1959.

advised the inhabitants to forget about removal vans, all they needed to do was leave the anarchic and deadly city behind them and start a new life just a few metres away but not, the mayor insisted, in a new city. The city still exists, Firminy-Vert was simply a new district, a "happier" district, and the mayor asserted that the new inhabitants should be conscious of the fact. The booklet and poster portrayed an organic city, represented by a plant thriving in the clear air and sunshine (▶ 2). Everything was within close proximity, all that was required to produce a healthy mind within a healthy body: schools, libraries, playgrounds, churches, cultural centre, stadium. The last three of these projects were left in the hands of Le Corbusier. The traffic lanes were segregated, a common idea going back as far as the utopian ideals of the Renaissance. The booklet indeed took some of its inspiration from those maps from medieval or early modern times, where an idea, an ideal is represented rather than reality. At Firminy-Vert the "Cours des marronniers" (Horse Chestnut Walk), the main thoroughfare leading through the district like a backbone, is a pedestrian zone. The term "Cours" (Walk) signifies the importance of moving around on foot, which is designated as the main form of transport in the entire area.

Every single element of a happy city is here. Work, which shaped the entire identity of the previous city, was not even mentioned in the booklet. Sceptics who claimed that the whole construction was likely to collapse like a house of cards were given the answer "solidity." The seventeen-storey tower block was built high in order to take advantage of the green spaces surrounding it as much as possible. The trees, flowers and lawns, were not supplementary features, but an integral part of the overall architecture of the site. The white walls with glass and wooden panels were designed to "play with the colours of the sky."

But the ideal city we see in the photographs was soon to clash with the world of the inhabitants and their everyday practices and habits. The lawns and greenery were barely given the chance to grow before being trampled underfoot; the white façades were hung over with carpets and washing. The housewives received several warnings, they were asked not to beat their carpets over the heads of the passers-by, shown how to install a system for hanging up washing over the bathtub, but all to no avail; old habits die hard. After all it is healthier to hang out washing to dry in the fresh air and sunlight.

The designers made an attempt to adapt, for instance by creating circular rooms for the purpose of drying laundry. However, in a district where people hardly know each other, it was not as easy as it seems to leave clothes unattended; furthermore for some inhabitants the drying rooms were too far away from their apartments and the distance is a strong deterrent. The designers tried again, and came up with the idea of installing drying cabinets in the apartments. However, this plan also failed due to financial restraints. People continued to hang their washing out of the windows (▶ 4).

The mayor and the architect strictly refused any idea of giving up on the original plans and design. They told people to take a walk around the district, gain a new perspective, begin to see that the walls looked considerably better without washing hanging up in front of them.

Education was seen as the answer, the only way of changing the inhabitants' approach towards their own environment, both outside and inside the apartments.

Housing in the Happy City: Comfort and Organisation

The text and illustrations in the handbook described in detail how the new accommodation differed from the old (▶ 3). The purity and constancy of water supplies was guaranteed, thanks to a new water-cleansing station. There were elevators in the two highest buildings, which became a landmark for the city and a popular viewing point for visitors. The large bay windows allowed ample sunlight to enter the apartments, yet they were placed so that people did not look directly into one another's apartments, in order to ensure privacy. Direct sunlight, a source of harmony, well-being and health within the family—references to hygienist theories were never far away. Gas and electricity were supplied, and the materials used were all easy to care for. There was the comfort of central heating in a place where, as Claudius-Petit reminded everyone, only one building was equipped with central heating when he was elected. Central heating signalised the end of the pollution caused by coal heating. But in a city where the miners had ample supplies of a natural resource to provide them with warmth, urban central heating was not always seen in a positive light; one of the future tenants who had just bought a brand new coal heater wrote to the mayor to complain how expensive it would be for him to switch to central heating. The booklet reminded him of the purpose of all the new comforts—they were there so that all members of the family would lead a pleasant, relaxed, and cheerful life, both inside and outside of the home. Just as the neighbourhood outside was organised, the living space within was also required to follow certain rules. The booklet gave advice and examples of how the rooms should be furnished in each type of apartment. Vertongen remembers that it was seen as a key issue to find a way of making the designs easy to read by everyone, not only by specialists. Finally, it was decided that the plans would take the form of simple drawings from an aerial view, with a stylised depiction of the materials, accessories and people. People are omnipresent in the drawings, perhaps to underline the fact that the apartments, which were often accused of being mere architectural objects, were in fact functional and there to be used by people. The position of the windows is indicated by a wavy line, a curtain. The insert at the top left denotes how many children the couple has. The human being and the family are at the centre of this new habitat, which had been conceived with them in mind. The booklet gave them advice on how to place their furniture; if they had none, they were advised to take their time when choosing new furnishings. The old family furniture will find its place, but most of the drawings featured functional furniture of a far more modern design. In fact, some families refused to move into the apartments for fear that their furniture would not fit in there. The educational measures went so far as to construct a special model apartment, fully furnished, to help future tenants choose new furniture.

3

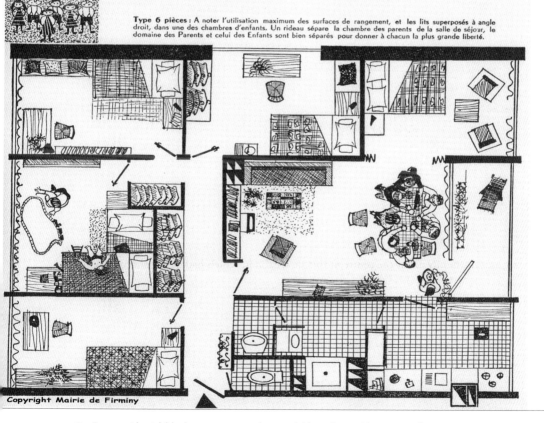

3   From residential block to apartment: the good life in Firminy-Vert, extract from *Horizons nouveaux*, 1959.

Postcards were printed, but the prime target of the advertising was not the real tenants. According to an employee of the public housing agency, the demand for the apartments was so high that most of the future tenants did not bother to visit the sample apartment; in fact most of them did not even know it existed. This apartment remained a model, once more, to be admired by visitors who could imagine, as they wished, that all the apartments in Firminy-Vert were furnished and decorated like this one. However, at the time the local *appelou* furniture salesman Martinez had more success with the sale of such items as dining-room furniture in the style of the "Spanish Golden Age" (▶ 5) or copies of wall tapestries; sometimes there was fabric draped from the ceiling. It was very different from what the designers had envisaged, but the new tenants were beginning to establish themselves. People were encouraged to create some of the fittings themselves in order to develop their creativity; there were descriptions of how to make a lamp out of a glass bottle. However, they were not to play around with the wall paintings, and they certainly had to stay well away from the electrical fittings! The booklet also provided explanations on the use of sanitary equipment (a novelty for a lot of the newcomers) and the common rooms.

From Utopian Designs to the Ideal Community

Being a local government officer is a serious job with a lot of responsibilities. We do not make decisions for ourselves, but for the entire population. We are not working towards minor goals—our aim is to provide a meaningful life for our fellow citizens. We are trying, on a small scale, to achieve what we would like to achieve for France as a whole. Our limited financial means do not hold us back in any way—audacity brings far richer rewards than false modesty.[15]

Providing a meaningful life to a whole population is one of the best ways of describing Claudius-Petit's vision of the happy city. His dream was to give life a meaning, without labour and toil being the sole function of the city and its inhabitants; a dream that lives on to the present day. Inhabitants were encouraged to invite one another to each other's homes, to get to know one another and play an active part in community life. The booklet was mainly targeted at women and children. A community laundry room was described as the ultimate forum for forging friendships, and Claudius-Petit did not hesitate to use a reference to the "boudoir." The women are shown knitting, talking or reading as they wait for their washing. The drawings in the booklet show children playing in a playground—the team responsible even went on study trips to Switzerland, the most advanced country for the design of open spaces at that time. The girls play with dolls, the boys with trains and miniature cars (▶ 3). The playground was seen as a unique opportunity for children to use their fantasy and create imaginary worlds, in keeping with the psychological trend of the time which emphasised the importance of the childhood years. An abundance of nurseries and primary schools

Copyright Mairie de Firminy

Collection Privée G. Roux

4

4   Drying laundry: ideal practice and real practice, extract from *Horizons nouveaux*, 1959, and photograph from the private collection of Georges Roux.

The show-flat

Collection Privée G. Roux

Son style vous a plu
son prix vous étonne
sa qualité vous enchantera

C'EST VRAIMENT LE STYLE A LA PORTÉE DE TOUS

Salle à Manger en Chêne massif
et bois de placage traité ébénisterie.
Décor bronze vieilli comprenant :
- 1 buffet 221 x 150 x 50,
- 1 table 146 x 94 - 2 allonges à
  l'italienne,
- 1 argentier 125 x 135 x 45 assorti,
- 6 chaises chêne massif garnies
  plastique rouge.

les 9 Pièces

3280 Fr

SALLE A MANGER HAUTE ÉPOQUE ESPAGNOLE
c'est une sélection

MARTINEZ

FIRMINY   SAINT-ÉTIENNE   LE PUY
85, Rue Jean-Jaurès   31, 34, 36 Rue   39, Boulevard Saint-Louis
57, Boulevard de Fayol   du 11 Novembre   46, Boulevard Saint-Louis

Copyright Mairie de Firminy

5

5   Conflict of practices: model apartment, ideally furnished in keeping with the concept of the architects, and a picture of the furniture that fires the imagination of the inhabitants. Undated postcard, probably post 1960, and advertisement in the local Firminy newspaper, 1962.

quickly appeared, within easy reach of the apartment blocks. Firminy was slowly becoming a symbol of urban renewal. Photographs show trees in full blossom and laughing children. After all, this architecture was built for the future, for the children; they were the ones who would implement the changes necessary to ensure its continuing success.

There was much more on the agenda here than accommodation and city improvements; what was envisaged was the complete transformation of society. Sandpits and swings for the children, washing machines and kitchen devices for the women, pipe, newspaper, peace and quiet for the men, and culture for everyone. The type and size of the apartments were mixed to ensure that various age groups, income brackets, and types of family were brought into contact with one another. Just as the apartments were perfectly organised with everything in its rightful place, each inhabitant was carefully placed and integrated within an environment where mutual respect was the rule and healthy leisure activities could be enjoyed by all.

> Social care and equipment will never be cost efficient in the usual sense of the word. We should consider them from a wider perspective, for a city or the country as a whole. In the end, sending a child to a cultural centre will cost twenty times less than dealing with a delinquent child.[16]

The beginnings of collective dwelling proved difficult for the newcomers, who were un-used to living at such close quarters. The housing office received complaints, even petitions protesting about the noise level. The agency reminded people that we will always have neighbours to contend with, even though most of us dream of having our own home and garden.[17] The change was a radical one; people had to get used to living in concrete blocks with flat roofs, quite different from their stone houses with pitched roofs. Years later, some of the garages next to the blocks would even be given traditional tiled roofs. Former inhab-itants remembered being annoyed by the noise coming from the children playing outside, or an argumentative elderly couple constantly shouting at each other on the stairs. The mixing of ethnic communities also presented some challenges; there is a general fear of the unknown, of unfamiliar customs. As the war in Algeria began, people told stories of sheep being slaughtered in the bathrooms.

The booklet failed to forecast such problems. The last sentence was hopeful: "And now in-vite your friends!" (▶ 6) The neighbours discovered in the first pages of the booklet became firm friends; in just a few pages the booklet had created a community. The mayor would promote this idea in his political campaign in 1965: "Every piece of equipment will take its place, making its contribution to the shape and character of the city, to its beauty. The inhabitants will be proud to belong to a community such as this."[18]

The family was at the heart of the project and the booklet emphasised that children should be made aware of the beauty of the well-managed architecture and city planning around them. According to Claudius-Petit, education was the cornerstone and the starting point of everything; he believed that people, especially children, have to be introduced to new things in order to awaken their receptiveness and interest in the arts. The design and decoration of the schools, entrusted to well-known artists, were essential as far as this is concerned. Claudius-Petit had always fought hard against the dangers of alcoholism (one of his most famous sayings was "Frenchmen drink away half of their homes") and aimed to create an alcohol-free city—quite a challenge in a working-class area with a traditionally high number of bars. The only vice to be seen in the booklet was the use of tobacco, which in the nineteen-sixties was not even considered to be a public hazard.

New Horizons also drew up a checklist of the things required to build a successful city, a magic recipe that is universally applicable. The mayor, however, understood that the meaningful life the new city was capable of creating was not always the life people were willing to live, and in the run-up to the municipal elections he explained:

> Can a mayor still do anything to change the life of his fellow citizens? … Yes, if he has a long-term goal and is not afraid of being misunderstood. The common good is not always recognised by the population at the right time, but in the end it will prevail. There is a fatal gap between the decisions of a local government, based on sociological studies, and the population's immediate needs.[19]

Science was up against the individual's resistance to change. Claudius-Petit believed that education would finally close the gap.

When a delegation of tenants protested against the high rents, the political opponents from the communist party did not hesitate to take advantage of the situation, stating their version of municipal politics in their local bulletin:

> Our mayor demonstrates once more his disdain for a working population, not catering for its real needs, boasting about his architectural achievements. We are the ones living in the apartments, we are the ones who have to spend most of our lives in Firminy-Vert, we are not as ecstatic as our mayor, we can see that we do not live in a perfect world and we are not afraid to say so.[20]

The community described in the booklet is a friendly, family-oriented one, yet somehow it seemed a little disconnected from real life. During the first years, the designers regarded the project as an experiment. Although they did see some of the "malfunctions of the system," this was always from an external, almost scientific perspective. The community they showed in the booklet consisted of children discovering life and nature, men at work, women who, thanks to modern machines, had more time to spend on cultural pursuits and helping with their children's education.

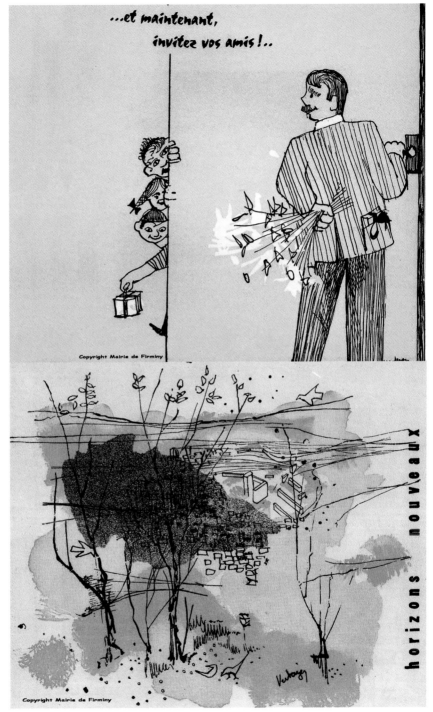

6

6   A community of inhabitants on their way to new horizons. Extract from *Horizons nouveaux*, 1959.

Strangely enough, teenagers did not feature anywhere in this idyllic picture. Is it because of the nature of the drawings, which did not allow for such distinctions to be made, or were they left out on purpose? Although psychology was beginning to turn its attention towards them, teenagers still hovered between the two different worlds of adulthood and childhood; this was particularly obvious in an industrial environment such as Firminy where the majority of them had already started working.

Alfred Sauvy's[21] ideas penetrated the entire concept of the city: young people represent a chance, an opportunity to be taken hold of. Firminy-Vert focused on youth, while the elderly did not even feature in the booklet anymore. Young couples with children were seen as the future of the city, they were the ones who would contribute to its rebirth. However, this overall scheme came to a sudden end at the outset of the economic crisis. Many of Firminy's factories closed down, with a dramatic effect on the entire region. *La montée des jeunes* (The Rise of the Young) by Alfred Sauvy quickly became *Le péril jeune* (The Peril of the Young) by Cédric Klapisch.[22] In 1959, when the booklet was first published, the anxiety caused by the new wave of trouble-makers amongst the young had reached its peak. An article entitled "From school uniform to black jackets" appeared in *Opinions*, one of the local newspapers of which Claudius Petit was the political director, promoting the idea of a huge public effort to help the nation's youngsters: "We need to understand and remember that the city of Paris employs 1200 street cleaners to maintain and keep its streets clean, how many youth clubs are available for the city's youngsters to guide them onto the right path and keep the gutters clean?"[23] The cleansing of the cities, the cleansing of society: the parallels between the vocabulary chosen, the methods used, are striking.

The idealised image of society shown in this booklet, the high hopes placed in this new habitat and its perfect tenants, mirror an entire era and some of its utopian visions—those of the decision-makers being sometimes at odds with those of the inhabitants—and the ideals of the real urban planning therapy that the urban planners wished to put into practice.[24]

> Urban planning is a powerful means of encouraging human and cultural development. It allows the city to develop in a harmonious way. It establishes public order as far as construction, utilities, traffic regulations are concerned. … It is also a source of well-being; it restores the framework required for a healthy living environment. It is the task of our team to make Firminy-Vert a better, happier, more human city.[25]

New horizons are indeed created, and new horizons are given back in return. Some of the goals are partly achieved, based on surveys and studies; however the better society, the ideal community shown in the booklet, is to remain but a dream.

Endnotes

1   Speech made by Eugène Claudius-Petit at the inauguration of the Marseille housing association, 14 October 1952, quoted in: Jean Jenger, *Le Corbusier, l'architecture pour émouvoir* (Paris: Gallimard, 2002), 144–45.

2   Benoît Pouvreau, *Un politique en architecture. Eugène Claudius-Petit (1907–1989)* (Paris: Le Moniteur, Architextes, 2004).

3   Eugène Claudius-Petit, "Le Corbusier que j'ai connu" in *Église Saint-Pierre de Firminy-Vert—Ensemble reprenons le chantier*, (Paris: Association Le Corbusier, 1995), 20.

4   Interview given by Eugène Claudius-Petit in *Positions* 102 (1965:1).

5   The inhabitants of Firminy are known as *appelous*.

6   Typescript by Eugène Claudius-Petit on the industrial city, undated, probably between 1960 and 1967. Archives Nationales de France, 538_AP_82.

7   Jean Cellier, "Le logement à Saint-Etienne," (Doctoral law thesis, Grenoble, 1949), 126.

8   Survey on defective housing, note made by a researcher undated, probably after 1955. Archives Municipales de Firminy, D 16_1 [3 D_1].

9   Maryse Dufaux, "Firminy," *Femmes d'aujourd'hui*, September 16, 1965.

10 Text by Eugène Claudius-Petit, typescript for a book project about Firminy, undated, probably between 1960 and 1967. Archives Nationales de France, 538_AP_82.

11 Text by Eugène Claudius-Petit, typescript on the industrial city, undated, probably between 1960 and 1967. Archives Nationales de France, 538_AP_82.

12 Text by Eugène Claudius-Petit, typescript for a book project about Firminy, undated, probably between 1960 and 1967. Archives Nationales de France, 538_AP_82.

13 Eugène Claudius-Petit in *Urbanisme. Revue française* 104 (1968): 7.

14 Letter by Marcel Roux to Eugène Claudius-Petit, 9 May 1961. Archives Nationales de France, 538_AP_91.

15 Speech made by Eugène Claudius-Petit on the occasion of his re-election as mayor. Archives Municipales de Firminy, registre des délibérations municipales, séance du 29 mars 1959.

16 Eugène Claudius-Petit, "Construire est un acte redoutable," *Opinions... contre toute contrainte, surtout celle de l'esprit*, April 18, 1960.

17 Institut National d'Etudes Démographiques, *Désirs des Français en matière d'habitation urbaine. Une enquête par sondage* (Paris: Presses Universitaires de France. Travaux et Documents. Cahier no. 3, 1947).

18 Eugène Claudius-Petit, "Habiter—Circuler—Travailler—Se cultiver. Administrer une ville au XXème siècle c'est répondre aux besoins des habitants en créant les conditions d'une vie meilleure," *Opinions... contre toute contrainte, surtout celle de l'esprit*, March 10, 1965.

19 Claudius-Petit, (see note 18).

20 *Le drapeau rouge*, section edited by the communist cell of Firminy-Vert, undated, probably late 1960 or early 1961. Archives Nationales de France, 627_AP_67.

21 In particular see : Alfred Sauvy, *La montée des jeunes* (Paris: Calmann-Lévy, 1959). This work is dedicated to "the young people who will save France."

22 Cédric Klapisch, *Le péril jeune*, 1994.

23 "Des blousses grises... aux blousons noirs," *Opinions... contre toute contrainte, surtout celle de l'esprit*, September 12, 1959. The author concludes his article as follows : "En 1933, un homme a su canaliser le besoin de violence des jeunes. Il a trouvé des milliers de petits cerveaux capables d'absorber vite une morale élémentaire. ... Cela s'appelait les jeunesses hitlériennes."

24 Louis Cornille, "Thérapeutique urbanistes pour les petites villes," (PhD diss., Institut d'Urbanisme de Paris, 1945).

25 Claudius-Petit, (see note 18).

"ON HOLIDAY 365 DAYS A YEAR" ON THE OUTSKIRTS OF ROME

Urban Form, Lifestyles, and
the Pursuit of Happiness
in the Suburb of Casalpalocco,
ca. 1955–1980

Bruno Bonomo

In a volume dedicated to the relationship between urban planning and the pursuit of happiness, it seems appropriate to deal with an experience that most people in our time would presumably consider the happiest ever possible: being on holiday 365 days a year. What is rather surprising about this quite exceptional experience is that it was intended to take place in an urban environment which, in contrast, sounds pretty ordinary—that is, on the outskirts of Rome. More specifically, its setting was supposed to be a place called Casalpalocco:[1] a vast middle-class suburb with around 15,000 inhabitants, located approximately ten kilometres to the south-west of the Italian capital.

This essay first focuses on the planning and promotion of Casalpalocco, examining in particular the ideas and values—including that of happiness—with which living in this suburb was associated, and the distinctive lifestyle that was proposed to its prospective inhabitants. The first section provides an introductory overview on Casalpalocco. The second deals with the suburb's plan and the general aims its promoters intended to give it, while the third looks at the promotional campaigns for Casalpalocco's dwellings. The fourth section links Casalpalocco's features to the evolving values and aspirations of the Roman middle classes at a time of great change, both in the economy and in the social and cultural spheres. Shifting to a different perspective, the fifth section discusses the dwellers' appropriation of this (sub)urban space and some key aspects of living in Casalpalocco. Finally, the penultimate section analyses a number of critical representations of Casalpalocco and the lifestyle it embodied, whilst the last one provides some concluding remarks on the main issues raised in the essay.

Casalpalocco: an Overview

Casalpalocco was developed between the mid-nineteen-fifties and the mid-nineteen-seventies by the Società Generale Immobiliare (SGI), one of the leading Italian real estate and building companies of the time, and the most prominent among those operating in Rome.[2] The SGI had acquired the large rural estate of Palocco in 1936, and in the early 1950s it started some preliminary reclamation work on the area, with the intention of building "a model district" to be presented on the occasion of the 1960 Olympic Games, which were to be held in the Italian capital.[3] However, mainly due to the considerable delay in reaching an administrative agreement (*convenzione*) with the municipality, the development required much longer than expected, and the new suburb could not be completed until approximately twenty years later.

Once completed, however, this low-density suburban settlement—with its wide parkways, ample green space and thousands of single- and multi-family houses (▶ 1)—showed quite different features from most contemporary Roman middle-class districts. 'Ordinary' districts, in fact, lay within the city, typically consisted of multi-storey blocks of flats, often built rather close to one another, and tended to suffer from problems such as lack of green space and high traffic congestion.

In order to gain an idea of the problems affecting such districts, one can look at the one that virtually epitomised the Roman bourgeoisie: Parioli. The development of this district had begun in the first decades of the twentieth century and was completed in the period following the Second World War in a series of individual building initiatives lacking appropriate coordination and control. The buildings that had been constructed before the war were surrounded, and in some cases substituted, by a mass of functionalist blocks of flats. This led to the progressive densification of the area, which in the end reached a point of saturation. Thus, in the early nineteen-sixties the planning historian Italo Insolera could write that while up to 1950 Parioli had "undoubtedly provided a fairly comfortable environment, with many gardens, high-class dwellings, villas and tranquil streets," subsequently "speculative building completely massacred it: the usual wave of blocks of flats submerged everything like magma, transforming beautiful panoramas into 'the opposite façade'. … In the extremely narrow streets there is no place left to park, not only for the [large] 'Americans' that abound in the district, but even the [small Fiat] '600s' and the 'Vespas.'"[4]

Casalpalocco's plan, on the other hand, was inspired by some American suburban estates (in all probability including the first Levittown, located on Long Island) that had been observed by two SGI executives during a trip to the US in the post-war period.[5] It is widely known, in fact, that suburbanisation was a distinguishing feature of urban development patterns in Anglo-Saxon countries in the twentieth century, especially in England and the US. Here,

1   An aerial view of the northern area of Casalpalocco, ca. 1972.

cities expanded in quite an irregular and amorphous manner, sprawling into the surrounding countryside and sometimes encircling non-urbanised areas, while in continental Europe they tended to grow around their cores in a more compact way.[6]

Location and layout, however, were not Casalpalocco's only distinctive features. Additionally, this was the first time in Rome, and presumably in the whole of Italy, that a private company had planned and built an entire suburb of such a considerable size, and administrative procedures similar to those adopted for Casalpalocco were subsequently introduced in both local and national planning legislation.[7] Thus, to quote Stephen Ward, this should be seen as one of those cases when—instead of urban planning being organised by the state, as is the norm—"profit-seeking developers were the implementing agents of planning innovations."[8]

The Plan: "An Alternative to Traditional Urban Ways of Life"

Casalpalocco was planned by the SGI's planning office in collaboration with some of the major Italian architects of the post-war period: Adalberto Libera, Ugo Luccichenti, Mario Paniconi, Giulio Pediconi and Giuseppe Vaccaro. The basic structure of the plan was rather simple, consisting of a network of main roads giving access to the various

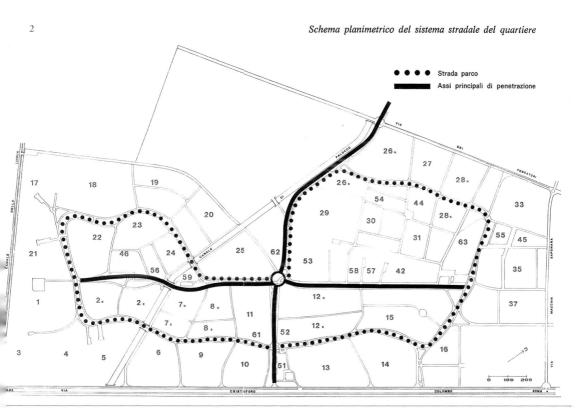

2   *Schema planimetrico del sistema stradale del quartiere*

● ● ● ●   Strada parco
▬▬▬   Assi principali di penetrazione

2   The main road network and the isole.

subdivisions of which the suburb was composed. Casalpalocco was connected to other areas (Rome towards the northeast and the Tyrrhenian coast towards the southwest) by two tangential roads running north and south of it: respectively via dei Pescatori and via Cristoforo Colombo. These tangential roads were connected by a transverse road (via di Casalpalocco), at the ends of which the main accesses to the suburb were located. In addition, the main road network included a road set at right angles to via di Casalpalocco and a long curved parkway (▶ 2).

The subdivisions, which were called *isole* (islands) and marked by numbers, consisted of both residences and public or private facilities. These facilities—which included, for instance, the schools (*isole* 54, 55, and 63), the shopping centres (*isole* 45, 46, 51, and 53), the church (*isola* 58), the residents' club (*isola* 61) and the sporting centre (*isola* 62)—were located along the main roads. As for the residences, the building types adopted were single- and especially multi-family houses, usually two storeys high (▶ 3); in addition, a small number of blocks of flats with particular characteristics were built in the final phase of the development. Almost every dwelling had its private garden, and many also gave access to shared areas and amenities, such as children's playgrounds, tennis courts, and swimming pools.

3

3   Single- and multi-family houses, isola 7.

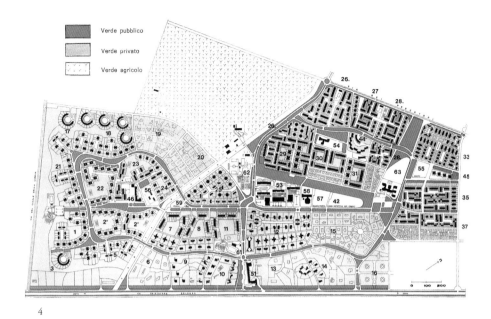

Verde pubblico

Verde privato

Verde agricolo

4

Great importance was placed upon the quality of public spaces. The road system was carefully planned to allow a smooth circulation of traffic and avoid any problems of congestion. The open-air pedestrian areas of the shopping malls were designed to play an important role in social relationships. For instance, according to the SGI's annual promotional magazine, the main mall, called Le Terrazze, was to be "rather than [just] a shopping mall … a 'centre of life and a meeting place', a centre that, together with the adjacent church, will form the physical heart of the community."[9] Finally, the plan included approximately twenty-seven hectares of public green space, mostly located along the suburb's main roads, where the residents could go for walks, do sport or simply have a rest.

In fact, one of Casalpalocco's distinguishing features was intended to be the abundance of green space, both public and private (▶ 4). According to an informative volume edited by the SGI, green space was to represent "the development's connecting fabric and contribute in a decisive way to favour the new way of life to be offered to the inhabitants."[10] With regard to this, it is important to stress that Casalpalocco's overall aim was "to offer an alternative to traditional urban ways of life, maintaining their substantial advantages (consisting of an environment with facilities provided) and at the same time avoiding their numerous disadvantages (bad traffic congestion, separation from nature, lack of opportunities to relax, etc.)."[11]

If considered in a wider historical perspective, this statement is hardly surprising. Since they first developed in nineteenth-century England, suburbs had attracted the middle

4   Casalpalocco's green spaces (public areas are shown in dark green, private areas in light green).

una casa nel verde per una vacanza di 365 giorni all'anno

5

classes looking for alternatives to living in the urban cores, which were increasingly per-ceived as squalid places due to the concentration of industrial premises—which were often very noisy and caused relevant problems in terms of air and water pollution—and run-down residential areas occupied by the lower working classes and the poor (the so-called 'slums').[12] Analogously, some of the main forces that encouraged the process of subur-banisation in the twentieth century were dissatisfaction with the living conditions in the urban cores, the aspiration to dwell in larger and more comfortable homes, possibly with a garden, the desire to benefit from airy environments and the attraction of a life somehow closer to nature.[13]

On a general level, it is almost needless to say that urban planning is a response to the problems of existing urban environments (thus, according to Peter Hall, twentieth-century town planning on the whole "essentially represents a reaction to the evils of the nineteenth-century city").[14] From this point of view, what is of particular interest in relation to this essay is that Casalpalocco was not only planned but also promoted precisely in opposition to some of the major problems of Rome's 'ordinary' urban districts, such as air pollution, noise, high building density and lack of green space.

5 "A home in a green environment for being on holiday 365 days a year", promotional booklet 1967.

The Promotional Campaign: "On Holiday 365 Days a Year"

Casalpalocco's dwellings were advertised like no other Roman residential building initiative of the time. While most builders and developers stopped at describing their residential units on sale in basic black-and-white advertisements published in the local press, the SGI's pervasive promotional campaigns featured sophisticated ads with photographs and illustrations, both black-and-white and colour, as well as stylish and colourful brochures.[15] These promotional materials strongly associated living in the suburb with ideas such as modernity, freedom, youth, leisure, healthiness, and serenity, promising a better quality of life and ultimately happiness to prospective buyers.

For instance, in a promotional brochure from the mid-nineteen-sixties, Casalpalocco was presented as "the most modern residential district,"[16] and in a later one it was stressed that the suburb had been "conceived in a new way that meets the requirements of today's life."[17] Another brochure, entitled *A new way of living for the youth of yesterday, today and tomorrow*, assured that in Casalpalocco one would find "a home in a green environment for being on holiday 365 days a year" (▶ 5). It was argued that "in Casalpalocco life is better" by virtue of the weather, which was milder than in Rome, the proximity to the sea and the Castelfusano pine wood, the purity of the air, which was oxygenated by the surrounding green space, the absence of urban noise, and the availability of a range of leisure facilities including a large swimming pool with solarium, a residents' club, and numerous tennis courts.[18]

According to an advertisement published in the press, unlike urban districts, in Casalpalocco one would find "no concrete beehives, no noise: only a lot of green space, … plenty of serenity and a new way of conceiving the home."[19] In addition, another ad promised not only "a new home, different from the usual city flat, a garden of your own, part of the huge garden represented by Casal Palocco, sporting facilities and shopping malls," but also "plenty of fresh air and a sense of freedom never experienced before."[20] The theme of freedom was a crucial one in the marketing of Casalpalocco. One advertisement, for instance, guaranteed that "a home in Casalpalocco equals living in freedom"[21] (▶ 6). Furthermore, one of the above-mentioned promotional brochures emphasised that "many things that are lacking in large urban agglomerations are, in contrast, available in Casalpalocco," including "an almost forgotten sense of freedom that expresses itself in a casual style of clothing, easier and more spontaneous social relationships, and in the joy of living in a place so different from others."[22] These are very significant issues, and I will come back to them later in this essay.

On the other hand, it is important to highlight that, in order to enjoy this freedom, one basic condition had to be met: that is, the possession of a car. In fact—rather paradoxically for a district that in one ad was presented as "300 hectares of clean air,"[23] but consistently with its location and layout (and in particular with the lack of rail connections and the shortage of public transportation to and from Rome)—Casalpalocco was closely associated with that veritable epitome of post-war modernisation, the private car. For instance, in an advertisement published in 1969, the image of a child in a toy car being refilled with a petrol

una casa a Casalpalocco e' vivere in liberta'

CASALPALOCCO
sulla via C. Colombo a 10 minuti dall'E.U.R.

è alla portata di tutti:
appartamenti
con giardino
a partire da L. 11 milioni

SOCIETA' GENERALE IMMOBILIARE
Piazzale dell'Agricoltura, 24
Roma - E.U.R. ● tel. 5904

l'Ufficio Vendite (tel. 60.90.787) è aperto tutti i giorni tranne il martedì

6 "A home in Casalpalocco means living in freedom", 1969.

casalpalocco: un pieno d'aria pura

..ed anche un pieno di serenita', di spensieratezza, di gioia di viv
à Casalpalocco, nel quartiere piu' giovane di Roma, c'e' la casa
ivete desiderato da sempre.

e nel nuovo
centro residenziale
"gli ULIVI"
sconto di UN MILIONE
per appartamento
fino al 30 Giugno 1969

CASALPALOCCO
sulla via C. Colombo a 10 minuti dall'E.U.R.

è alla portata di tutti:
appartamenti con giardino
a partire da L. 11 milioni

**SOCIETA' GENERALE
IMMOBILIARE** Piazzale dell'Agricoltura 24
Roma - E.U.R. • tel 5904

I Ufficio Vendite • tel 60.90.787 • è aperto anche nei giorn

7   "Casalpalocco: refuelling with pure air", 1969.

un' Aria di vacanza
un Ambiente giovane e sereno
un Ampio giardino
un' Abitazione con l'A maiuscola

Stiamo parlando di Casalpalocco - l'argomento del giorno - ed in particolare dei nuovi villini dell'Isola XXV. Tre o quattro camere da letto al piano superiore, tripli servizi, salone e sala da pranzo, sala hobby, garage per due macchine, solarium, giardino privato e, in più, l'atmosfera inimitabile di un centro immerso nel verde a due passi dall'E.U.R. e dal mare. Inoltre, favorevolissime condizioni di pagamento. Se non avete mai pensato seriamente ad una vera casa, fatelo adesso: vi renderete conto di aver fatto

un Acquisto felice

CASALPALOCCO
Isola XXV

sulla via C. Colombo a 10 minuti dall'E.U.R.
Ufficio Vendite tel. 60.90.787

SOCIETA'
GENERALE
IMMOBILIARE
Roma - E.U.R.
Piazzale dell'Agricoltura, 24
tel. 5904

8 "Holiday air; a young and serene environment; a large garden; a Home with a capital H; a happy purchase", 1969.

pump was accompanied, with presumably involuntary irony, by the slogan: "Casalpalocco: refuelling with pure air"[24] (▶ 7). In another ad, everyone buying a dwelling was offered "a temporary discount to allow for the purchase of a car."[25]

Finally, in illustrating the features of the dwellings in one of Casalpalocco's isole (three or four bedrooms, living room and dining room, three bathrooms, hobby room, garage for two cars, and private garden), features that made each of them "a Home with a capital H," another advertisement promised prospective buyers "holiday air," "a young and serene environment" and ultimately "a happy purchase"[26] (▶ 8). Similarly, an ad published in one of the first issues of the suburb's local magazine underlined that in Casalpalocco, thanks to the abundance of green lawns and trees that offered plenty of opportunities to play, "there are only happy children."[27]

Thus, in the SGI's promotional materials, the idea of happiness was explicitly associated with living in Casalpalocco. This connection is hardly surprising for such an American-style suburb, bearing in mind the fact that the American Declaration of Independence included the pursuit of happiness among the unalienable rights of citizens.[28] However, in terms of this essay it is important to stress the spatial dimension of this happiness and its new and unprecedented character. In fact, what would allow the suburb's future inhabitants to live a happy life was precisely the setting and layout of Casalpalocco, a residential environment that was depicted as being radically different from the urban districts of Rome and, above all, free from their severe shortcomings and problems. In such an innovative environment, as I shall argue in the following section, the Palocchini were supposed to experience an entirely new way of life.

A New Lifestyle for the Middle Classes of the 'Italian Miracle'

It should be apparent from the above that Casalpalocco's promotional campaigns—with their frequent use of images of children, their emphasis on the theme of youth and their stark anti-urban stances- –were targeted at young (or youthful, to be more precise) middle-class families who were dissatisfied with the living standards and costs of the urban districts and their blocks of flats. More specifically, the SGI intended to especially attract people who worked in areas with a high concentration of tertiary workplaces situated relatively close, or at least well connected by road, to Casalpalocco. These included EUR, a modern office and business district developed in the post-war period, and the new intercontinental airport of Fiumicino, opened in 1960.[29] Data from the early nineteen-seventies, when the development of Casalpalocco was almost completed, shows that its social composition basically reflected these objectives. In fact, 91 per cent of the inhabitants came from other districts of Rome; as for their professional profile, 62 per cent of the breadwinners were executives and clerks (with pilots and other airline employees alone accounting for 14 per cent), 11 per cent were professionals, 9 per cent traders and 5 per cent industrialists and managers.[30]

One of the most important points emerging from this essay is that Casalpalocco's planning and promotion were aimed at matching—and at the same time influencing—the values and aspirations of these youthful and dynamic sections of the Roman middle classes. In this regard it must be taken into account that in the post-war period, especially from the late nineteen-fifties onwards, Italy was undergoing considerable change both in its economy and in the social and cultural spheres. After the hard years of the *ricostruzione* (reconstruction), the country lived through a period of extraordinary economic growth that is usually referred to as 'the boom,' 'the economic miracle' or 'the Italian miracle' (1958–63).[31] A brief slowdown followed in the mid-nineteen-sixties (the so-called *congiuntura*), but then the economy continued to grow until the 1973 oil crisis, which marked, in Italy as in the rest of the western world, the end of 'the golden age' and the beginning of 'the crisis decades.'[32] When the crisis broke out, Italy had evolved from a relatively poor and largely agricultural country, as it still was some twenty years earlier, to one of the most advanced industrial economies of the world.[33] Along the way, it experienced a massive increase in per capita income, substantial social mobility and a significant expansion of the urban middle classes due to general economic progress and the huge internal migration flows from rural areas and small towns to medium and large cities. A substantial shift in consumption patterns also took place, with the middle classes playing the leading role. A rapid growth in per capita private consumption (which doubled between 1956 and 1970) was accompanied, in percentage terms, by a reduction in expenditure for basic needs (especially food) and a parallel increase in outlay for durable goods (above all cars, furnishings, and household appliances), leisure, beauty and body care, and services.[34]

Even more importantly, while up to the nineteen-fifties Italy was governed by a set of values centred on the predominance of saving, a consumer culture subsequently imposed itself, with the view of consumption as a primary means of self-fulfilment and an essential form of social integration. This cultural shift, as various scholars have noted, was largely influenced by the model of the 'American way of life.'[35] At the same time, especially from the mid-nineteen-sixties onwards, other cultural transformations led to a veritable revolution in manners and lifestyles, involving aspects such as gender roles, sexual behaviour, and the relationships between different generations and social groups. With regard to this last aspect, traditional hierarchies and forms of deference weakened considerably, while more informal attitudes in social relationships started to prevail.[36] In addition, in this period young people and youth culture had an unprecedented influence on the rest of society: in Arthur Marwick's words, "such was the prestige of youth and the appeal of the youthful lifestyle that it became possible to be 'youthful' at much more advanced ages than would ever have been thought proper previously."[37]

In the context of these momentous transformations that were re-shaping Italian society, the promise made by the SGI to the prospective buyers of Casalpalocco's dwellings was not just a home, however different from the 'ordinary' city flat, but also a new and distinctive lifestyle. A lifestyle that had as its main hallmarks high levels of comfort both within and outside the home (with particular attention to the opportunities of outdoor life and the overall quality of the residential environment), an emphasis on leisure and relaxation, private motorisation, youthful attitudes and rather informal social relationships. By virtue of these elements, which were integrated in a suburban environment that was quite novel for the Italian capital, Casalpalocco came to embody an 'American' model of modernity that matched the aspirations of many youthful and dynamic members of the increasingly affluent Roman middle classes.

Living in Casalpalocco: the Dwellers' Appropriation of (Sub)Urban Space

The articles and letters published in the local monthly magazine *La Gazzetta di Casal Palocco*, the first issue of which came out in November 1968, are an excellent indication of why people decided to move to Casalpalocco and what life was like in this suburban residential environment. Between November 1969 and February 1970, for instance, a report entitled "What do you think about Casal Palocco?" was published, in which more than thirty residents were asked about their reasons for moving to the suburb and their present feelings about living there.[38]

With regard to the former point, the vast majority of the answers focused on the opportunities for outdoor life, the possibility of raising children in a healthy, green and airy environment that would allow them to grow up in freedom, and the perspective of relaxing in a tranquil and serene place. Many residents explicitly pointed out contrasts between the opportunities offered by Casalpalocco and the problems of life in the urban core, which they saw as spoiled by traffic congestion, air pollution, noise, and stress. Some also mentioned the desire not to live in a block of flats but in a house with a private garden and, in some cases, with shared areas and amenities. High school student Lucia Zei, for example, said that she and her parents had been "charmed by the idea of not having a lift and of having our own entrance gate," while the jeweller Marcello Cecchini expressed his desire to escape from "the massive cages of airbricks, where from inside you can count each step taken by the lady living upstairs, and from outside the fume from the exhausts of buses and motorcycles come in, along with shouts, the noise of trams, bad smells and so on."[39]

Similar reasons for moving to Casalpalocco emerged both from interviews with well-known residents appearing in other issues of the magazine and from the letters sent to its editor by 'ordinary' readers, who expressed their opinions on the most diverse matters. Actor Nando Gazzolo, father of three, explained that he had chosen Casalpalocco because "the city … is an insurmountable restriction on children's freedom. … They need a free and unrestricted environment, where they can lead a life out in the open air, as is their right." His colleague Umberto d'Orsi summarised his choice by saying that he had opted for Casalpalocco "because here I can sleep in peace." Analogously, engineer Anna Maria De Rossi wrote that she had bought a house in the suburb "with the sole aim of having a tranquil, relaxing and serene place to come back to in the evening after a working day," while Claudio Scalone emphasised that he had left Rome "in order to escape the city's noise and chaos, and try to find a green oasis where nature could freely show its marvels."[40]

A house with a garden, a residential environment different from the urban core, plenty of green space, tranquillity and relaxation, and a focus on children's needs and 'freedom': in these residents' statements on the reasons why they chose Casalpalocco, it is not surprising that we find many of the themes on which the SGI's contemporary advertising campaigns were centred. On the other hand, particular attention should also be paid to what residents said about living in Casalpalocco and how they felt about their new residential environment. Here it is noteworthy that the majority of those who were interviewed for the above-mentioned report expressed their basic satisfaction with Casalpalocco. For instance, Alitalia pilot Giovanni Cattaruzza, one of the 'pioneers' of the suburb, who had been living there since 1960, declared: "I can certainly say that my family and I are pleased to live here, and my expectations have been fulfilled." Final-year university student Mario Gianandrea, aged twenty-two, stated: "I like living here very much: if I moved back to the city, I would feel like a fish out of water." It was not just the absence of urban noise, the abundance of green space, the purity of the air, the opportunities for children to play outdoors and for adults to relax, and the availability of leisure facilities such as swimming pools and tennis courts that were appreciated by residents. Lawyer Domenico Pugliatti, in fact, said that one of the reasons why he was satisfied with Casalpalocco was that "human relationships are on a level of simplicity that frees us from the burden of the formalities of the city and helps us to become more genuine again."[41] This point is a particularly important one and should be analysed in more detail.

As shown in one of the previous sections, the SGI's promotional materials stated that "easier and more spontaneous social relationships," "a casual style of clothing" and the related "sense of freedom" were important elements of the new lifestyle that residents would experience in Casalpalocco.[42] Various articles published in *La Gazzetta* seem to confirm this point, providing evidence of the Palocchini's youthful attitudes and rather informal social relationships. For instance, in the first issue, the informal and youthful behaviour of Casalpalocco's residents was called into contrast with that of the inner-city dwellers: "In Prati wives do not go shopping by bike, in via del Tritone you do not see distinguished gentlemen digging the earth, in Trastevere children do not caper on the lawns. In Casal Palocco such things happen every day, people are used to them, and many could not do without."[43] Informality and youthful attitudes were also apparent in the modes of self-presentation, as shown by an article published three years later that argued: "In conformist Italy, Casal Palocco is an island apart, where everybody feels young. Ladies of all ages wear miniskirts, enjoying the beneficial sun, or go shopping with curlers hidden under a headscarf, the American way, and ride their bicycles, … while men show enviable tans under their grey hair."[44] Analogously, in one of the oral history interviews that I have conducted for this research, Fabrizio Schneider, one of Casalpalocco's first inhabitants and for a long time the editor of *La Gazzetta*, explained:

> At the beginning there almost was a uniform: the tracksuit. Everybody went around wearing a tracksuit, that is, a pair of trousers and a sweatshirt. Nobody—the tie doesn't exist anymore. If you go around looking for somebody wearing a tie, you would find just one or two people: because nobody wears a tie anymore. You go out dressed in the same way as you would at home. … This was the thing that was most appreciated: "Finally we don't need to change; we go out in the clothes we wear at home: after all, they are people we know and we don't have to observe any kind of formality.[45]

Thus, Casalpalocco appeared to be quite an informal residential environment in comparison with the 'ordinary' middle-class areas where more traditional etiquette and forms of behaviour tended to persist. An important element that favoured the development of informal social relationships among the residents was the presence of various residential complexes with shared areas and amenities, such as gardens, children's playgrounds, swimming pools and tennis courts. As a matter of fact, from the late nineteen-fifties onwards, such complexes started to proliferate in middle-class areas all around Rome. As a result, while up to the early post-war period private swimming pools and tennis courts were still an exclusive privilege of the well-to-do who lived in the most luxurious villas, they subsequently lost their exclusive nature and became important middle-class status symbols. This represented a clear instance of the process of 'democratisation of comfort' that was linked to the above-mentioned profound transformations in the economy and in the social and cultural spheres that Italy was experiencing from the years of the 'economic miracle' onwards. In addition, the proliferation of such residential complexes implied a substantial redefinition of the relationship between private and public space. In fact, their shared areas and amenities offered the inhabitants the opportunity of spending their leisure time 'at home', albeit outside their own domestic walls, thus constituting a sort of intermediate sphere (one could call it 'semi-private') that modified the sharp separation between domestic life and the outside world that was a key trait of the traditional middle-class lifestyle.

The influence of these shared areas and amenities on the residents' patterns of sociality is clearly revealed both in articles published in *La Gazzetta* and in my oral history interviews. In November 1974, for instance, the magazine reported that an internal tennis championship was being organised on the shared tennis court of isola 22, "with the aim of making this sporting event an opportunity to meet and get to know each other, in order to render the relationships among the residents as friendly and informal as possible."[46] Four years later, a brief account of a summer party amongst the residents in the shared garden of isola 2 was published, highlighting how "this pleasant occasion … allowed new friendships to be made or neighbourly relationships to be strengthened."[47] As for my oral history interviews, Rita

Chiodoni gave the following description of the informal social life she experienced in isola 33 in the nineteen-seventies:

> I used to go out wearing, I will not say [just] my swimsuit, but a loose-fitting blouse, sometimes with a bath towel over my shoulder, to go to the swimming pool. … Then we used to get together. Because after the swimming pool, I do not know, perhaps a game of ping-pong … or a tennis match was organised. And that was a meeting place: because in these residential complexes next to the swimming pools there are … clubs. … There was a club with sofas where you could sit—you went to the club … and had a chat with your friends, you spent your time there. So you were always socialising. … Adults, perhaps—my father and the others—organised games of poker. Mothers talked about cooking or other things: "So let's have dinner at so-and-so's"; but in the American way, that is, everybody brought some food along. This was also a different way of life. … Let's take an example: when my mother went to my aunt's—perhaps just because it was my aunt—she used to say: "I will bring something [to eat]." But otherwise you just went to somebody's house, maybe you could bring some dessert, but you didn't bring pans of food, because it could be offensive; one could think: "Why are you coming here with a pan of pasta! Do you think I don't have enough money to prepare pasta?" Here in Casalpalocco, it was different: it became normal to go round to so-and-so's and bring a dish with you, somebody else came with something else, so that families met up together. … It was a continual socialising with everybody. Parents were also always with friends, with other people. It was rare to have no guests at home.[48]

It is significant that Rita Chiodoni points out that dinners in Casalpalocco were organised "the American way," just as women used to dress casually to go shopping according to the article in *La Gazzetta* quoted above. In fact, as mentioned in the previous sections, in the Roman context Casalpalocco stood out as a residential environment with a marked American character. As well as its suburban location and layout, the types of housing built and the residents' informal behaviour and social relationships, some particular places also gave Casalpalocco a further touch of the American feeling—for instance, the shopping malls or the drive-in cinema (something quite unusual in Italy) situated adjacent to the suburb.[49] With regard to this, the architect and Professor of Architecture Pippo Ciorra, who spent his youth in Casalpalocco, emphasised that because of these and other elements—including a white Mustang roadster that the mother of one of his friends used to drive around the suburb—Casalpalocco seemed "a bit like *American Graffiti* taken to extremes."[50]

This being said, let us go back to Rita Chiodoni, who had moved to Casalpalocco in 1963 at the age of ten. In her interview, she emphasised the intense sense of freedom she enjoyed there as a child and then a teenager: the opportunity of spending a lot of time outdoors, playing in the shared garden, riding her bike around the suburb, going out wearing a T-shirt, shorts and flip-flops, meeting her friends at the bar or in the hobby rooms that most houses had in their basement, and so on. All of this, she argued, "gives you more freedom, it makes you grow in a different way; … if I compare my years between ten and eighteen here in Casalpalocco with [those of the people living in] Rome, there was a gulf, a total gulf." Later in the interview, she added:

> You were always in contact with people, you were not isolated. This is something that does not happen in Rome. I mean, in Rome you go out: but you go out with a friend of yours, you go to the city centre, you go somewhere. You don't have all these people who—this involvement. For instance, you open your garden gate, you are watering the plants, you see somebody and you ask them: "Ah, what are you doing, are you watering the lawn? Why don't you come to my place for a coffee?;" so you stopped watering the plants and went to the neighbour's, you chatted, had coffee and spent some time there, then maybe you had dinner together. That is to say, it was as if you were on holiday: a holiday all year round.[51]

Significantly, life in Casalpalocco was likened to being on holiday by other interviewees as well, who also highlighted the particular sense of freedom they enjoyed there. For instance, when asked about his first impressions of the suburb, where he moved to with his wife and his daughter in 1969, building surveyor Franco Proietti replied:

> My first impressions were that when [I was not at work and] I could spend time here, I felt I was on holiday. … Because you could go for a walk outside without the stink of cars, you went to the sports club and played tennis. In Rome it was difficult to do such things, unless you belonged to some private sports club. Here, by contrast, this seemed a [natural] thing to do, something you could just do because you belonged to this district. So it was a different way of life, so to speak. When my parents, who lived in Prenestino, came to see me, they felt like they were on holiday, too. And indeed, coming from the periphery of Rome, a place like this was another kind of life: entirely different.[52]

And photographer Claudio Santoni, whose father opened the first newspaper kiosk in Casalpalocco after being the director of the drive-in cinema, recounted:

> Before coming here I lived in a flat [in Ostia, a suburb of Rome]: a beautiful large flat, 4–5 rooms, on the fourth floor, with a view of the sea. Only you had problems with the people living downstairs, problems with the people upstairs, you had condominium meetings, and other annoying things. Here, in contrast, if I want to go out walking or

make a noise, I can do it: it doesn't annoy anybody. I don't do it, because I'm not the type, however— … Nobody gets up my nose. I don't have any problems. Whereas in a block of flats you can't, absolutely. Furthermore, until recently I had three dogs and a cat—can you imagine them in a block of flats? It would have been impossible. Here you can, you can do as you like—there's nothing to prevent you. In my garden, I can keep all the animals I want. … Then, the idea of cycling around, peacefully, without anybody attacking you or robbing you—here you could do it in peace. Everywhere, every shopping centre is easy to get to on foot. You don't have to drive, you can simply walk. You are free. This is the point—you are free. Then you could do any sport you wanted, from tennis to swimming: [in the sporting clubs] there were swimming pools, tennis courts, everything. In addition, [many] isole had their own swimming pools, tennis courts, and so on. … So you lived in the greatest freedom, doing whatever you wanted. You worked until Friday, then the idea of coming back here—it was a different atmosphere. And then, Saturday and Sunday, did you ever see anybody dressed in formal clothes? People wore tracksuits, shorts, out on their bicycles, on the way to the swimming pool—the tennis courts were always full. It was a way of life: a holiday, it was a holiday.[53]

It is apparent that these residents' accounts of their life in Casalpalocco basically reflect the slogans of the SGI's promotional campaigns: "a new way of living," "on holiday 365 days a year," "living in freedom," etc. Nevertheless, it would be simplistic to assume that living in Casalpalocco was a bed of roses. Going back to the above-mentioned report "What do you think about Casal Palocco?," for instance, it must be stressed that the three interviewees quoted earlier in this section (Cattaruzza, Gianandrea, and Pugliatti), although expressing their satisfaction with Casalpalocco, also referred to some problems that affected the suburb: the lack of schools and cultural activities and the inadequacy of public transport. In addition, the housewife Lia Mele highlighted that she and her husband had been more satisfied five years earlier, when "there was still total peace and tranquillity," while at present "it is only peaceful inside our residential complex." Finally, set designer Maurizio Monacelli said that he and his wife were disappointed because a shared area of their residential complex close to their house "has been transformed into a football pitch. When the kids are not playing football, they play hide-and-seek, and often adults take part in their games making just as much noise. In the afternoons it is bedlam: it is impossible to sleep."[54]
These remarks are significant. As witnessed by numerous articles published in the magazine, schools and public transport remained problematic issues also in the following years. Given the high concentration of young families with children, the few schools that had been built in the suburb soon became overcrowded, and students had to be divided into split shifts.[55]
As for public transport, the bus service linking Casalpalocco with the urban core of Rome and the neighbouring settlements of Acilia and Ostia was largely insufficient, reinforcing

the residents' dependency on their private cars.[56] Even more importantly, in terms of this essay, the progressive completion of the various isole and the consequent demographic growth of Casalpalocco (which had around 4,000 inhabitants in 1968, 10,000 in 1971 and 15,000 in 1974) were accompanied by an intensification of the conflicts linked with the dwellers' appropriation of the (sub)urban space.

Some of these conflicts concerned the use of motor vehicles. The articles and letters published in *La Gazzetta* show that many residents complained about the excessive speed of cars and motorcycles, which increased the risk of road accidents. Others protested about the widespread practice of improperly parking the cars on the lawns or along the streets instead of putting them in the garages or in the appropriate car parks, claiming that this ruined the green spaces and caused difficulties in driving and manoeuvring, especially in the narrowest streets[57]. In addition, motor vehicles were blamed for being noisy, above all the roaring mopeds and scooters with altered engines, which in a resident's letter of complaint were polemically referred to as "eardrum-busters."[58] It is noteworthy that an article dedicated to the annoying noise produced by such mopeds and scooters argued that, following the numerous readers' complaints, it was necessary to denounce "this bad habit of some individuals who believe, wrongly, that they can behave in absolute freedom, riding roughshod over any rules of civilised life, rules that are crucial for those who chose Casalpalocco as a place of tranquil residence."[59] These words hint at a key point, which I will come back to later in this section.

Before that, however, it is important to stress that motor vehicles were not the only cause for concern. In fact, the residents' coveted tranquillity and relaxation were menaced by other agents as well, for instance dogs and the young. As regards the former, by virtue of the abundance of green space, Casalpalocco was an excellent environment for dogs, and a lot of residents indeed had one or more. On the other hand, many protested that dogs barked too loudly or that they were allowed to roam freely around the district without a muzzle, frightening or even biting the passers-by. In May 1975, for instance, an article whose subheading read "Casalpalocco is a dogs' paradise: even too much so, somebody says" informed that "dogs go around our district's roads and lawns, uncontrolled, as undisturbed masters," with the consequence that "at least one person a day … is bitten by a dog: it happens to children who are playing on the road …, to messengers who deliver the mail, to night watchmen placing control tickets on the gates, and to ladies out shopping."[60]

As for the young, a distinction between children and teenagers must be made. The rowdy behaviour of some of the latter was criticised in several articles published in *La Gazzetta*. Apart from riding noisy mopeds and scooters, not only on the roads but also on the lawns and on cycle lanes, teenagers were blamed for acts of hooliganism, vandalism, or juvenile delinquency. In the spring of 1972, for instance, various episodes that had recently occurred in the suburb were reported, including children being chased away from the parish football field where they were playing by teenagers who insulted and beat the adults who had intervened in favour of the children; a child being hit on the head during a party in the garden of a house by a stone thrown from outside; wallets being stolen from the swimming pool's changing rooms; the church's stained-glass windows being broken by stones and airgun pellets; and "youngsters 'from a good family'" being caught stealing in a house.[61]

On the other hand, complaints about boisterous children, similar to that made by Maurizio Monacelli described above, abounded in the magazine, as in the case of an article that described the problematic situation of isola 35. Due to the noisy games and bicycle races organised by the children, a resident protested that "in the afternoon, whether one wants to rest or has to work, one is driven crazy: how is it possible with such a din?" As a result, he claimed: "here one does not live better—I would show the people from the SGI—one simply cannot live anymore!" Then, he explained that parents had been repeatedly asked to intervene, but refused to do so. Finally, the author of the article commented that the arguments some of these parents put forward—"But we came here [to Casalpalocco] precisely in order to let our kids run free in the open air"—was inappropriate, since children could run and shout as much as they wanted, but "not in the streets, under the residents' windows: there are open green spaces available to everybody, why not use them?"[62]

The crucial point is that in all these cases a conflict on the issue of freedom was at play. On the one hand, there was an idea of freedom as the liberty to exploit all the possibilities offered by Casalpalocco in order to do whatever one wanted, regardless of the potentially negative consequences for other people, including driving fast, parking in areas where it was not allowed, riding roaring motorcycles on green spaces or cycle lanes, letting dogs loose around the suburb without control, or allowing children to play outside loudly at any hour. On the other hand, there was a vision that placed emphasis on freedom understood as the liberation from the evils of urban life, the opportunity of benefiting from a carefully planned and well-kept residential environment, and the possibility of relaxing in peace: all things that required a shared respect for the basic rules of communal life. In other words, in the appropriation of the (sub)urban space by Casalpalocco's residents, a quite individualistic idea of freedom met and clashed with one that, in contrast, was more focused on collective well-being. Going back to the article about noisy mopeds and scooters quoted above, it was precisely the clash between behaving "in absolute freedom" and observing the "rules of civilised life."

Furthermore, these conflicts in the appropriation of the (sub)urban space were tightly linked to another important process: the (re-)emergence, in a residential environment that had been depicted as being radically different from the city core, of some typically urban phenomena. Such were, for instance, the problems linked to road traffic and to the presence and behaviour of neighbours described above. In addition, the impact of a distinctive urban phenomenon of the nineteen-seventies has to be taken into account, that is, the diffuse violence between members of opposing political groups, which—alongside the clashes between militants and the police, and the terrorist activities of underground organisations—marked Italian history between the late nineteen-sixties and the early nineteen-eighties.[63]

Albeit not on a large scale and fortunately without any loss of human life, Casalpalocco was affected by the violent confrontation between left-wing and right-wing groups as were many other areas of major Italian cities. For instance, on the eve of the important referendum on divorce that was held in May 1974, motorised gangs formed by "some dozens of young people (and some adults as well), all belonging to the extreme wings of the opposite political sides" chased each other armed with sticks: "One could breathe hatred, one could breathe violence, one could breathe the desire to come to blows," *La Gazzetta* commented, until "the carabinieri's powerful intervention … managed to avoid the worst."[64] Four and a half years later, the magazine reported that on a Saturday night approximately forty right-wing youths assaulted a group of left-wingers, some of whom required medical treatment for the bruises and wounds they suffered; afterwards "the air remained full of tension" and the following morning further clashes occurred. The editor of the magazine claimed that the contingent of *carabinieri* in Casalpalocco should be increased, since it was utterly clear that the suburb was not "an oasis detached from the situation of the rest of Italy" and, therefore, it had to be "defended from violence as any other district."[65] Finally, between the end of April and the beginning of May 1979, two cars belonging to a young man and a member of Parliament elected for the Communist Party were set on fire, and a bomb exploded in isola 20 in front of the house of a right-wing sympathiser, destroying two gates, breaking all the window panes in the vicinity and seriously damaging two cars parked in the street.[66]

It is apparent that all of this contradicted the image of Casalpalocco as a tranquil and relaxing residential environment, living in which—as stated by a SGI's advertisement—"means forgetting the inconveniences and problems of city life."[67] As a matter of fact, the possibility that Casalpalocco might begin to suffer from the same defects as the urban core was deeply feared by its inhabitants. As early as 1970, the member of Parliament Ruggero Villa, interviewed with other residents for a report on the problems of Casalpalocco, argued that "we must at all costs avoid that, in the suburb, the same evils are reproduced which caused the majority of the residents to flee from the city. So we must declare war on overcrowding …, chaotic traffic and noise."[68] The building of new isole and the consequent densification of the suburb (which Villa termed "overcrowding") were also perceived as dangerous by another resident, Oscar Guarnieri, who observed three and a half years later that Casalpalocco had become "the same as any other district of Rome, albeit fairly green, with the additional inconvenience of being far away from the city centre and ill-served by public transport." "There will be less and less green space—Guarnieri went on—since it has to make room for the houses. … As for tranquillity: well, better not to mention it."[69] Finally, in 1979 an article dedicated to the state of the suburb's green spaces denounced that "Casalpalocco, the satellite of a chaotic city, has assumed its few good qualities and its numerous defects," including a sheer disregard for the green spaces, where domestic rubbish and old pieces of furniture were thrown away and cars parked.[70]

Thus, both on the pages of the local magazine and in some oral history interviews with 'pioneers' of Casalpalocco, it is not surprising to find a sense of nostalgia for its early years, which tend to be idealised as a 'golden age' in contrast to the suburb's subsequent decline. As far as *La Gazzetta* is concerned, this attitude is already apparent in a letter sent in by a reader in July 1970, which argued that, although the number of dwellings and inhabitants was increasing alongside the level of comfort, the peace, green spaces, and the residents' civility were diminishing.[71] Two and a half years later, commercial executive Ettore Carletti concisely answered the question "What more would you want from Casalpalocco?," wistfully recalling "the tranquillity of not so long ago, when Casalpalocco was 'an oasis of peace and safety.'"[72] In March 1977, finally, on the occasion of its hundredth issue, the magazine collected the memories of a number of residents who had been living in Casalpalocco for a long time. On the whole, the tone of the accounts was rather nostalgic; Sergio Perissi, who had moved to the suburb thirteen years earlier, stated:

> I remember a different climate: bucolic and unaffected. Palocco was inhabited by people who came from the city with a certain way of life in mind, a different form of education for the young, perhaps based on the model of the village, where everybody knows each other and everyone is friends. It was a way of escaping from the isolation of the city. We had in mind a more proactive, communitarian, Christianly understood social life. All of this actually developed, but lasted only until five or six years ago: then it all came to an end. The settlement has expanded; the type of inhabitants has changed, maybe many came here thinking of it as a posh district, bringing with them complexes and frustrations accumulated in the city. Their impact with Palocco has caused a division between old and new [residents], and the former have ended up retreating into their shells. Not finding that climate any more, some also went away. I miss, as many others do, those times that now seem so far away, when we believed that this could be a model district, not only for its green spaces and tranquillity, but also in terms of human relationships.[73]

Though in a different sense, the idea of the transformation and decline of Casalpalocco being linked with a contrast between 'old' and 'new' residents—in other words, between those who moved to the suburb before the late nineteen-sixties, when it still was a relatively small settlement, and those who moved there later and contributed to its growth to the current size—also emerged in the oral history interview with Claudio Santoni. He linked this aspect with the different housing types constructed in the early years of the suburb, when the SGI built villas and large houses in order to set its social tone, and in the subsequent period, when smaller dwellings were also built:

[Initially] there were actors, directors, scriptwriters, embassy staff: there were only such people. There was a good standard of people. It was an extremely tranquil place. You went out without locking the door, and nothing happened. Just imagine, there was a single policeman, called Antonio, who rode his motorbike around the suburb; when somebody lost their keys, he arrived [and said, giving the keys back]: 'Claudio, you lost your keys.' Whilst today: are you crazy? It is absurd to imagine anything like that. … There were no robberies, there was nothing, nothing at all. It was a really tranquil life. … And there were only villas. … Then, little by little, it started to turn into isole with … mini flats, not villas anymore: super-mini-houses … with gardens the size of this table. … And then it filled up with people—it was within everybody's reach. … All kinds of people came here, including people rather—let's say that it would have been better if they had not come. Several times people were arrested who were hiding here: swindlers, and so on. … Almost anybody could come here, so to say. So that elite thing that there had been before was lost. And now it is an ordinary district: just with a lot of green space, because otherwise … I mean, a property here costs the same as in Rome: no more, no less.[74]

On a general level, nostalgia is a natural and common feature of people's memories of the past.[75] In the Roman context, however, Santoni's account sounds particularly interesting in that it represents an inverted version of recurring memory narratives according to which a significant improvement in living conditions and in the quality of the residential environment was accompanied by a deterioration in social life. This is, for instance, a key theme in the memories of the numerous former shanty town dwellers who moved to social housing estates between the nineteen-fifties and the nineteen-seventies. When asked about their feelings regarding their transfer from hovels to flats, many of them typically expressed regret for the loss of the everyday solidarity and the old-style communitarian life of the shanty town, where everybody knew everyone and one could 'leave the door unlocked' without anybody stealing anything from the dwellings.[76] In Santoni's account, in contrast, it is a deterioration of the quality of the dwellings and the social composition of the residents that causes the end of the 'golden age' and a decline in the conditions of life for Casalpalocco's inhabitants: an original bourgeois inversion, one could say, of a typical lower-class memory narrative.

"Why Did You Move Here?" Critical Representations of Casalpalocco

In the previous section, we saw that on various occasions the residents of Casalpalocco pointed towards neighbours' or other people's forms of behaviour that, in their opinion, negatively affected the quality of life in the suburb. In addition, a further element must be taken into account. Everybody who is familiar with the wide and long-standing debates on suburbanisation in the Anglo-Saxon countries—from Lewis Mumford and Jane Jacobs in the early nineteen-sixties to the New Urbanism planning movement and the Urban Task Force, chaired by the architect Richard Rogers, in more recent times—knows that a large amount of criticism has been directed towards this pattern of urban development and towards the alleged defects of suburban life.[77] Similarly, a number of drastically critical representations of Casalpalocco per se—rather than just condemnations of specific aspects causing a deterioration in the conditions of life for the residents—were given by both internal and external observers.

As far as the former are concerned, severe criticism of Casalpalocco was expressed by a very limited number of residents on the pages of *La Gazzetta*. In the context of the above-mentioned report "What do you think of Casal Palocco?," for instance, the university student and theatre director Stefano Mastini said that he had a negative opinion of the suburb because of its being "a sort of island, far from the rest of the world," characterised by "an affected way of life and of thinking, too distant from the living reality of our society." He argued that the diffuse apathy and the "human … and intellectual poverty" of Casalpalocco stemmed from the fact that this residential environment was made so as to attract "uniquely those people with a certain way of thinking and of living, who are used to comforts and also privileges, people who belong to a minority and not to the majority." Finally, when asked about his proposals for improving life in Casalpalocco, Mastini concluded that he had only an individual solution: "I will move back to Rome as soon as possible."[78] Some years later, similar comments were made in a letter sent to the magazine by another resident, Francesco Capriglione, who polemically defined Casalpalocco as "a dormitory for alienated bourgeois," where there was "no risk of seeing and feeling the actual problems of the people, or of having unwanted encounters with poverty, the exploited and the oppressed."[79]

These remarks, albeit few and isolated, are noteworthy in that they questioned precisely the element that, according to its promoters, should have represented Casalpalocco's strong point: its separation from the urban realm and its related problems. In fact, what Mastini and Capriglione ultimately criticised was the distance, not only geographical but above all social, that separated those living in a middle-class suburban residential environment such as Casalpalocco from the issues of contemporary society, in particular the problems of the underprivileged. This was an aspect that, in a period of widespread engagement in politics and in social struggles such as the nineteen-seventies, appeared intolerable to them. Interestingly, such radical views of Casalpalocco's defects are in some measure echoed in Pippo Ciorra's narrative about his youth in the suburb. Ciorra recounts that he was a member of a local group of young activists with a fundamentally anarchic line, whose main aim was to "react to this condition of small suburban paradise" and "mess up" the area through acts of "micro vandalism" such as sticking posters on the walls or going into the sporting club at night and throwing all the chairs into the swimming pool.[80]

If Ciorra and his friends were rebelling against Casalpalocco's tidiness, tranquillity and 'middle-classness,' these were precisely the elements that made a negative impression on an external observer such as the writer Lidia Ravera when she first visited the suburb in the mid-nineteen-seventies. In a narrative report written in 2002, Ravera recounts that she moved from Milan to Rome as a twenty-year-old radical activist in 1975. After staying at a friend's place in the city centre for a while, she went to Casalpalocco, where another friend's parents had offered to rent her an attic room in their house. Ravera recalls that Casalpalocco struck her because everything was new, there were plenty of trees and chirping birds, and a salty breeze blew from the nearby sea, giving her the impression that Rome was "one thousand miles away." The attic room she saw was in a detached house "all made of glass and bricks, with three bathrooms, three bedrooms and a living room with polished parquet," which reminded her of her parents' flat in a residential area of Turin. Feeling it was like home, she desired "more than anything else in the world to escape and go back to the dust and traffic, on the ancient ground, strewn with condoms and bottle shards." Only more than twenty years later—having learned to enjoy the silence and love the grass, the trees and the breeze coming from the sea more than noise, concrete and the polluted air of the city—did she start to appreciate "this Roman Beverly Hills."[81]

Finally, a well-known critical representation of Casalpalocco 'from the outside' was given by Nanni Moretti, one of the major living Italian directors, in his film *Caro Diario* (1993). In the first of the three episodes that make up this film, Moretti rides his Vespa around Rome, going through several districts. When he reaches Casalpalocco, he comments: "Passing near these houses I sense a smell of tracksuits worn instead of clothes, a smell of videotapes, dogs on guard in the garden and ready-made pizzas in cardboard boxes." Then, he stops a local resident who is parking his car near his home with a couple of videotapes in his hands, and polemically asks him why he had decided to move to Casalpalocco some thirty years before, when Rome "was a wonderful city". In this scene, Moretti portrays Casalpalocco as an extremely tranquil, informal, even slightly impersonal and artificial residential environment, reflecting—in Vittorio Vidotto's words—"a more deep-rooted aversion to Casalpalocco's residential affected respectability."[82] This is in all probability true, but on the other hand, it seems to me that Moretti is looking at Casalpalocco from a rather traditional bourgeois viewpoint, thus failing to acknowledge the strength of the aspirations and values that—as shown in this essay—drove thousands of Roman families to leave the city and move to this suburb.

Conclusions

This essay has argued that, in the context of post-war Rome, Casalpalocco was a quite atypical middle-class residential environment that had been planned as an alternative to the urban core and its perceived problems. The SGI's pervasive promotional campaigns not only emphasised Casalpalocco's difference from the 'ordinary' urban districts, but also promised its prospective inhabitants a new lifestyle based on high levels of comfort, a focus on leisure and outdoor life, youthful attitudes and informality in social relationships. Relaxation, healthiness, and freedom were other cornerstones of a way of living that was explicitly associated with happiness. By virtue of these elements, at a time of intense economic growth and great changes in the social and cultural spheres such as the nineteen-sixties and early nineteen-seventies, Casalpalocco came to embody an 'American' model of modernity in keeping with the aspirations and values of many youthful and dynamic members of the Roman middle classes.

Shifting to a different perspective and discussing what it was like to live in this suburb, it became evident that some of the elements emphasised in the SGI's promotional materials actually corresponded with real features of life in Casalpalocco and that the residents fundamentally enjoyed the opportunities offered by this particular residential environment. On the other hand, in the course of time a series of conflicts arose among the dwellers as far as the appropriation of this (sub)urban space was concerned, especially in relation to the use of shared areas and public spaces. Underlying these conflicts, it has been stressed, were two different concepts of freedom, one starkly individualistic and the other more focused on collective well-being. Furthermore, some typically urban problems (re-)emerged, causing residents to feel increasingly dissatisfied with the living conditions in the suburb and to develop a sense of nostalgia for its early years, which tended to be idealised as a 'golden age.'

In relation to this, it must be taken into account that, between the nineteen-sixties and the present day, Casalpalocco—originally an isolated settlement between the urban core of Rome and the Tyrrhenian coast—has been engulfed in the massive expansion of the city towards the southwest. Nonetheless, even once absorbed into the sprawling metropolis, Casalpalocco has maintained its specificity in comparison to the unplanned and haphazard development of many surrounding suburbs, such as Infernetto, Axa, and Canale della Lingua. Interestingly, these differences have been underlined by Casalpalocco's residents on various occasions, both on the pages of *La Gazzetta* and in the oral history interviews I conducted for this research project. For instance, an article dedicated to the suburb argued that Casalpalocco "has to be considered a model, especially in comparison with the neighbouring settlements of S. Giorgio, Infernetto and Dragona."[83] In addition, the architect and Professor of Architecture Pippo Ciorra highlighted that Casalpalocco was developed on the basis of "a beautiful plan" and features "nice houses," while "at Axa they bastardised; they started to build taller and lower-quality buildings: it was a real debasement."[84]

To conclude with a remark on the issue of happiness: in 1969 Loya Chattergjie, the 16-year-old daughter of a FAO (Food and Agricultural Organisation of the United Nations) official, said in an interview published in *La Gazzetta* that she and her family had been living in Casalpalocco for two years and were "happy to be here."[85] In this case, Casalpalocco's promise of happiness was evidently kept. Thereafter, by contrast, no similar assertions by other residents appeared on the pages of the local magazine, and on the basis of what has been said in this essay it is not difficult to understand why. As we have seen, the reality of living in Casalpalocco proved to be more complex and problematic than the joyful and alluring image of the suburb given by the SGI's advertisements. If the latter cheerfully promised a happy life to the prospective purchasers of the dwellings, one can consider their subsequent experiences in the suburb to be a confirmation of the Italian saying: "*la felicità non è di questo mondo*" ("happiness is not of this world").

Endnotes

1   "Casalpalocco" is habitually spelled both as a single word (as in this essay) and as two words: "Casal Palocco." In addition, the abbreviated form "Palocco" is sometimes used as well. As for the local residents, they are usually called "Palocchini."

2   For a profile of the SGI and an analysis of its building initiatives in post-war Rome, see: Bruno Bonomo, "Grande impresa e sviluppo urbano: l'attività della Società generale immobiliare a Roma nel secondo dopoguerra," *Storia urbana* 112 (2006): 167–95.

3   Archivio Centrale dello Stato (ACS), Società Generale Immobiliare Sogene (SGIS), Verbali delle Assemblee generali degli azionisti, b. 3, reg. 10, April 15, 1957, 92–93. This and all the following quotations from Italian sources have been translated into English by the author.

4   Italo Insolera, *Roma moderna. Un secolo di storia urbanistica 1870–1970* (Turin: Einaudi, 1993 [1962]), 191.

5   ACS, SGIS, Emilio Pifferi, *Note per una analisi della SGI*, memoirs (1995), 39–41.

6   Mark Clapson, *Suburban Century. Social Change and Urban Growth in England and the United States* (Oxford, New York: Berg, 2003), 13–14. For a recent account of research on suburbanisation and an interesting discussion on consolidated and new approaches to this field of study, see: Ruth McManus and Philip J. Ethington, "Suburbs in transition: new approaches to suburban history," *Urban History* 34 (2007:2): 317–37.

7   Piero Ostilio Rossi, *Roma. Guida all'architettura moderna, 1909–2000* (Rome, Bari: Laterza, 2000), 222.

8   Stephen V. Ward, *Planning the Twentieth-Century City. The Advanced Capitalist World* (Chichester: John Wiley & Sons, 2002), 4.

9   Realizzazioni e studi nel settore edilizio, 1971, 16.

10 Casalpalocco Società Generale Immobiliare, special issue of the *Quaderni della Società Generale Immobiliare*, 1973, 4.

11 *Casalpalocco Società Generale Immobiliare*, (see note 10), 11.

12 Harold J. Dyos and David A. Reeder, "Slums and Suburbs," in *The Victorian City. Images and Realities Vol. 1*, ed. Harold J. Dyos and Michael Wolff (London: Routledge & Kegan Paul, 1973), 359–86. For a more recent account of these issues, see: Richard Rodger, "Slums and Suburbs: The Persistence of Residential Apartheid," in *The English Urban Landscape*, ed. Philip Waller (Oxford: Oxford University Press, 2000), 233–68, 236–44.

13 Clapson, (see note 6), 51–78.

14 Peter Hall, *Cities of Tomorrow. An Intellectual History of Urban Planning and Design in the Twentieth Century* (Oxford: Blackwell, 2002 [1988]), 7.

15 In more general terms, the post-war period was one of great evolution in advertising techniques and language. On Italy, see: Adam Arvidsson, *Marketing Modernity: Italian advertising from Fascism to post Modernity* (London: Routledge, 2003), 67 ff.; Daniele Pittèri, *La pubblicità in Italia. Dal dopoguerra a oggi* (Rome, Bari: Laterza, 2006 [2002]).

16 *Casalpalocco*, promotional brochure (ca. 1965). This brochure was kindly given to me by Franco Proietti, one of the residents of Casalpalocco I interviewed for my research. I thank him for this.

17 ACS, SGIS, Ufficio pubblicità, b. 3, f. Roma dépliants, *Le si legge in faccia la gioia di vivere a Casalpalocco*, promotional brochure (July 1969). The classification of these documents, which are temporarily held in the depository of via del Serafico, is provisional.

18 ACS, SGIS, Ufficio pubblicità, b. 3, *Un nuovo modo di abitare per i giovani di ieri, di oggi, di domani*, promotional brochure (September 1967).

19 *Il Messaggero*, April 4, 1970, 9.

20 *Il Messaggero*, January 11, 1970, 13.

21 ACS, SGIS, Ufficio pubblicità, b. 1, f. Raccolta pubblicità 1969 quotidiani e periodici, *Una casa a Casalpalocco è vivere in libertà*.

22 ACS, SGIS, Ufficio pubblicità, b. 3, (see note 17).

23 *Il Messaggero*, October 3, 1970, 17.

24 ACS, SGIS, Ufficio pubblicità, b. 1, f. Raccolta pubblicità 1969 quotidiani e periodici, *Casalpalocco: un pieno d'aria pura*. On the role of the private car in the Italian post-war modernisation, see: Federico Paolini, *Un paese a quattro ruote. Automobili e società in Italia* (Venice: Marsilio, 2005).

25 *Il Messaggero*, January 3, 1969, 14.

26 ACS, SGIS, Ufficio pubblicità, b. 1, f. Raccolta pubblicità 1969 quotidiani e periodici, *Un'Aria di vacanza …*

27 *La Gazzetta di Casal Palocco*, December 1968, 15.

28 "We hold these Truths to be self-evident, that all Men are created equal, that they are endowed, by their Creator, with certain unalienable Rights, that among these are Life, Liberty, and the Pursuit of Happiness." The Declaration of Independence, which was approved by the Second Continental Congress on 4 July 1776, is reproduced on the Library of Congress web site, http://www.loc.gov/rr/program/bib/ourdocs/DeclarInd.html (accessed January 19, 2009).

29 Casalpalocco Società Generale Immobiliare, (see note 10), 13.

30 Pensioners and housewives accounted for eight per cent; people doing "other activities" for five per cent—Casalpalocco Società Generale Immobiliare (see note 10), 24–26.

31 Guido Crainz, *Storia del miracolo italiano. Culture, identità, trasformazioni fra anni cinquanta e sessanta* (Rome: Donzelli, 1996); Antonio Cardini, ed., *Il miracolo economico italiano (1958–1963)* (Bologna: Il Mulino, 2006).

32 Eric J. Hobsbawm, *Age of Extremes: the Short Twentieth Century, 1914–1991* (London: Michael Joseph, 1994).

33 Paul Ginsborg, *A History of Contemporary Italy: Society and Politics, 1943–1988* (London: Penguin, 1990), 212.

34 Emanuela Scarpellini, *L'Italia dei consumi: dalla Belle Époque al nuovo millennio* (Rome, Bari: Laterza, 2008), 129 ff.

35 On the 'conquest' of Italy (and Europe as a whole) by the American way of life and consumer culture, see: Victoria de Grazia, *Irresistible Empire. America's Advance through 20th-Century Europe* (Cambridge/Mass., London: Belknap, 2005). With regard to the domestic sphere, see: Paolo Scrivano, "Signs of Americanization in Italian Domestic Life: Italy's Postwar Conversion to Consumerism," *Journal of Contemporary History* 40 (2005:2): 317–40.

36 Vittorio Vidotto, *Italiani/e. Dal miracolo economico a oggi* (Rome, Bari: Laterza, 2005), 81–82.

37 Arthur Marwick, *The Sixties. Cultural Revolution in Britain, France, Italy and the United States, c.1958–c.1974* (Oxford: Oxford University Press, 1998), 17.

38 The report was published in four parts: November 1969, 1–5; December 1969, 10–12; January 1970, 3–5; and February 1970, 3–4.

39 "Che ne pensate di Casal Palocco?," *La Gazzetta di Casal Palocco*, November 1969, 3; January 1970, 4.

40 "Incontro con Nando Gazzolo. Sherlock Holmes a Casal Palocco," *La Gazzetta di Casal Palocco*, December 1968, 1–2; "Vuole fare il cattivo ma è un quiet-man," *La Gazzetta di Casal Palocco*, February 1969, 3–4; "A colloquio coi lettori," La Gazzetta di Casal Palocco, October 1969,

17; "A colloquio coi lettori," *La Gazzetta di Casal Palocco,* January 1970, 18.

41 "Che ne pensate di Casal Palocco?," *La Gazzetta di Casal Palocco,* November 1969, 2, 4; December 1969, 11.

42 ACS, SGIS, Ufficio pubblicità, b. 3, (see note 17).

43 "Noi e gli altri in un ambiente così," *La Gazzetta di Casal Palocco,* November 1968, 1–3, 1; Prati and Trastevere are two districts of Rome and via del Tritone is a well-known street in the city centre.

44 "I prezzi salati del 'vivere meglio,'" *La Gazzetta di Casal Palocco,* July 1971, 8.

45 Interview with Fabrizio Schneider (retired journalist, born in 1921), March 21, 2008. Audio files of all the interviews that have been conducted for this research are held and can be accessed at the Archivio Franco Coggiola of the Circolo Gianni Bosio, Rome.

46 "Una buona idea per sentirsi più vicini," *La Gazzetta di Casal Palocco,* November 1974, 24.

47 "Si sono divertiti anche i rimasti: braciolata notturna," *La Gazzetta di Casal Palocco,* September 1978, 8.

48 Interview with Rita Chiodoni (advertising agent and painter, born in 1953), March 15, 2008.

49 According to Claudio Santoni, son of the director of the drive-in cinema, this was the only such facility in the entire country (Interview with Claudio Santoni, photographer, born in 1943, May 10, 2008).

50 Interview with Giuseppe Ciorra, known as Pippo (architect and Professor of Architecture, born in 1955), June 11, 2008.

51 Interview with Rita Chiodoni (advertising agent and painter, born in 1953), March 15, 2008.

52 Interview with Franco Proietti (retired building surveyor, born in 1937), April 14, 2008; Prenestino is a district of Rome.

53 Interview with Claudio Santoni (photographer, born in 1943), May 10, 2008.

54 "Che ne pensate di Casal Palocco?," *La Gazzetta di Casal Palocco,* November, 1969, 1–5; December, 1969, 10–12.

55 See, for instance, "Per le scuole elementari e medie incombe la minaccia dei tripli turni," *La Gazzetta di Casal Palocco,* June 1972, 7; "Nulla di fatto per le nuove scuole: è in corso una vibrata azione comune," *La Gazzetta di Casal Palocco,* June 1974, 6.

56 "Le carenze dei trasporti pubblici a Casalpalocco," *La Gazzetta di Casal Palocco,* February 1974, 17; "Palocco chiede un servizio di trasporti più civile," *La Gazzetta di Casal Palocco,* January 1978, 7.

57 See, for instance: "E gli altri si arrangino…," *La Gazzetta di Casal Palocco,* February 1972, 17; "Chiedo, prego, supplico: moderate la velocità," *La Gazzetta di Casal Palocco,* December 1973, 26; "Una questione di spazio?," *La Gazzetta di Casal Palocco,* November 1976, 7; "Come la velocità ha ucciso in via Prassilla," *La Gazzetta di Casal Palocco,* September 1979, 5.

58 "I soliti rompitori. Ennesima protesta contro i selvaggi in moto," *La Gazzetta di Casal Palocco,* October 1975, 29.

59 "Gli assordatori motorizzati sono soprattutto dei maleducati," *La Gazzetta di Casal Palocco,* June 1970, 3.

60 "Attenzione, c'è la legge," *La Gazzetta di Casal Palocco,* May 1975, 19.

61 "Atti di teppismo, prepotenze, gravi provocazioni: fatti di cronaca che denunciano il decadimento della vita di quartiere," *La Gazzetta di Casal Palocco,* April–May 1972, 10.

62 "Il diritto alla quiete e l'art. 659 del codice penale," *La Gazzetta di Casal Palocco,* February 1972, 7; Another article denounced a similar situation in isole 27 and 28, where "youngsters from six to twenty … behave in an uncivilised way," with the result that "more than one family starts to seriously think of leaving Casalpalocco and going to live among more polite people (granted that such people exist):" "Situazione insostenibile nell'isola 27–28," *La Gazzetta di Casal Palocco,* October 1973, 10.

63 For a synthetic work on the various forms of political violence in Italy from the late nineteen-sixties to the nineteen-eighties, see: Donatella Della Porta, *Social Movements, Political Violence, and the State: A Comparative Analysis of Italy and Germany* (Cambridge: Cambridge

University Press, 2006 [1995]). For an account of the major events that took place in Rome, see Vittorio Vidotto, *Roma contemporanea* (Rome, Bari: Laterza, 2006 [2001]), 325–34.

64 "Due episodi della campagna sul referendum," *La Gazzetta di Casal Palocco*, May 1974, 7.

65 "Week-end di violenza alle Terrazze," *La Gazzetta di Casal Palocco*, November 1978, 13.

66 "Pericolosa serie di atti di violenza," *La Gazzetta di Casal Palocco*, May 1979, 13.

67 *La Gazzetta di Casal Palocco*, October 1969, 19.

68 "I problemi di Palocco e i necessari interventi del Comune," *La Gazzetta di Casal Palocco*, May 1970, 3–4.

69 "Che tipo di quartiere stiamo preparando ai nostri figli," *La Gazzetta di Casal Palocco*, January 1974, 5.

70 "Se … se il verde è nostro, conserviamolo. Ne abbiamo 125 mq. a persona," *La Gazzetta di Casal Palocco*, March 1979, 3.

71 "Quando c'era Romolo," *La Gazzetta di Casal Palocco*, July 1970, 8.

72 "Cosa vorreste in più da Casalpalocco?," *La Gazzetta di Casal Palocco*, December 1972, 6–8, 7.

73 "Amarcord Palocco. Alcuni 'vecchi' palocchini ci hanno detto:," *La Gazzetta di Casal Palocco*, May 1977, 3, 13, here 3.

74 Interview with Claudio Santoni (photographer, born in 1943), May 10, 2008.

75 Raphael Samuel, *Theatres of Memory, Past and Present in Contemporary Culture, vol. 1* (London: Verso, 1994). Christopher Shaw and Malcolm Chase, eds., *The Imagined Past: History and Nostalgia* (Manchester: Manchester University Press, 1989). For a recent discussion of these issues in the context of another major Italian city, see: John Foot, "Micro-history of a house: memory and place in a Milanese neighbourhood, 1890–2000," *Urban History* 34 (2007:3): 431–52, 449–50.

76 See, for instance, Bruno Bonomo, "Dalla borgata di Prato Rotondo al quartiere Magliana. Storia di una comunità di immigrati nella Roma del secondo dopoguerra," *Giornale di storia contemporanea* (2003:1): 77–99; Franco Ferrarotti, con la collaborazione di Paola O. Bertelli, Marina D'Amato, Maria Immacolata Macioti, Maria Michetti, Laura Tini, *Vite di periferia* (Milan: Mondadori, 1981); Maria Immacolata Macioti, *La disgregazione di una comunità urbana. Il caso di Valle Aurelia a Roma* (Rome: Siares, 1988); Ulrike Viccaro, *Storia di Borgata Gordiani. Dal fascismo agli anni del 'boom'* (Milan: Franco Angeli, 2007).

77 The works I am referring to are Lewis Mumford, *The City in History. Its Origins, its Transformations, and its Prospects* (London: Secker & Warburg, 1961); Jane Jacobs, *The Death and Life of Great American Cities* (New York: Random, 1961); Andres Duany, Elizabeth Plater-Zyberck, Jeff Speck, *Suburban Nation. The Rise of Sprawl and the Decline of the American Dream* (New York: North Point Press, 2000); *Towards an Urban Renaissance. Final Report of the Urban Task Force chaired by Lord Rogers of Riverside* (London: Urban Task Force, 1999).

78 "Che ne pensate di Casal Palocco?," *La Gazzetta di Casal Palocco*, January 1970, 5.

79 "A colloquio coi lettori," *La Gazzetta di Casal Palocco*, February 1973, 19.

80 Interview with Giuseppe Ciorra, known as Pippo (architect and Professor of Architecture, born in 1955), June 11, 2008.

81 Lidia Ravera, "Casalpalocco," in *La città fuori le mura. Roma come non l'avete mai vista,* ed. Giuseppe Cerasa (Rome: Gruppo editoriale L'Espresso, 2005), 69–71.

82 Vidotto, (see note 63), 377.

83 "Casalpalocco è un quartiere riuscito?," *La Gazzetta di Casal Palocco*, November 1974, 13.

84 Interview with Giuseppe Ciorra, (see note 80).

85 "Sulla famiglia Chattergjie ci sarebbe da scrivere un libro," *La Gazzetta di Casal Palocco*, July 1969, 15–16.

A PARADISE BEHIND GATES AND WALLS

Gated Communities
in Eastern Europe
and the Promise
of Happiness

Jacek Gądecki,
Christian Smigiel

As the previous articles in this volume have shown, the promise of happiness in relation to urban planning is not an especially new concept. Throughout the last centuries, almost all innovative concepts and visions of urban planning and urban development have implied the idea of a better future and the promise of an improvement in the quality of urban life. In this regard, gated communities do not differ from their predecessors.[1] Furthermore, gated communities are not a particularly new idea in urban planning. Based on the reshaping of urban planning concepts from the beginning of the twentieth century, they promise a mixture of rural convenience and lively urbanity. The concept of gated housing is also no new phenomenon. In fact, one can find examples of gated and guarded housing throughout urban history since Roman times. Or, as the American regional planners Edward J. Blakely and Mary Gail Snyder put it: "Gated and walled cities are as old as city-building itself."[2] As a matter of fact, the novelty of gated communities is characterised by a network of dynamic parameters rather than by a single outstanding one. Certainly a major factor is that they reflect a concept of housing that goes far beyond the actual apartment or house in itself. Gated communities are promoted and presented as a post-modern lifestyle package. This kind of labelling and advertisement brings us to another level of analysis focussing on the actors, their strategic alignments and the rhetoric and imagery they use. In fact, the recent spread of this type of development is closely connected with a shift in urban governance reflecting a new relationship between public and private actors. The weakness of public institutions on the one hand and the strength of private developers on the other have had a severe impact on the proliferation of the housing product known as the 'gated community.'

This essay will focus on the presentation of gated housing estates in Central and Eastern Europe:[3] the rhetoric and images used by the sellers of these developments, their methods of argumentation and the ideas to which they appeal. The metaphor 'paradise' seems to be useful in describing the assumptions made concerning this type of planned community. Judging by their descriptions, gated housing estates are detached from the ordinary world and bathed in greenery; they offer a safe and harmonious way of life in the constantly changing and chaotic city. The essay uses the methods of critical discourse and media analysis, applied to a study of the housing environment. To a certain degree, this kind of approach allows the spheres of culture and economics to be investigated; discourse analysis within the context of urban research is used to highlight non-economical, cultural, or even non-rational aspects.[4]

The Emergence of a New Kind of Housing and Lifestyle

For European cities, gated housing estates represent rather a new trend in housing. Especially in Central and Eastern Europe, where this idea was little known before 1989, there has been a massive increase in privately governed residential spaces in recent years, and these are beginning to noticeably shape and alter the cityscape with their walls, gates, and barriers. But

1

gated communities are not only a new model of housing; they also imply a broader idea that can be labelled a spatial product or the expression of a new Zeitgeist.

If we examine the offers made by the developers, it quickly becomes evident that gated communities are above all being marketed as a form of lifestyle (▶ 1). Robert Freestone defines housing estates of this type as a form of development organised as a comprehensive and detailed product.[5] In the developers' advertisements (as well as in individual offers), gated housing estates are described as enclosed and monitored, but also as beautiful, neat, and clean places. They possess a private and exclusive character, offering security and harmony and a sense of escape from the overcrowded metropolis. Two examples from Poland and Bulgaria serve to illustrate that the sale offers refer to something more than a flat:

> The area covered with the project is over 70,000 square metres. Small but spacious streets, safe playgrounds, a courtyard, a tennis court, but most importantly the ample green vegetation will allow inhabitants to spend their free time here in a most agreeable way. We also did our best to make the dwellers feel safe in their development. Fenced area, a monitoring system as well as guards will prevent any disturbance of peace and quiet.[6]

> The Residential Park Sofia offers convenient homes in harmony with nature and the highest standard of living. Abundant green areas and parks, bicycle paths and pedes-

1   Brochure presenting a gated housing estate in Sofia.

trian zones contribute to the pleasant environment of the project. High-quality materials, excellent execution and professional property management make the project a unique living environment, ensuring the highest level of security and quality of life for the entire family.[7]

Advertisements like this one raise a number of questions for urban researchers: who has access to these gated communities and what are the factors regulating access? Why have gated communities become so popular in such a short time and what do they offer? Does the housing estate set itself apart from neighbouring spaces and the entire city, and in what way? What types of discourse influence these processes? These questions are particularly important if we wish to gain an understanding of the transformations taking place in the public sphere and a conception of what post-modern social space is about; they are directly associated with issues of power and privilege as well as with negotiations relating to urban space and divisions between the public versus the private spheres.

This leads us on to consider recent dynamics and transformations in metropolitan areas that would not have been possible without the participation of domestic and international property developers.[8] If we observe the real estate market since the beginning of the nineteen-nineties, it is noticeable that, in line with the rise in the share of developers in the market, the number of gated housing estates is also increasing. In 2006, 30 per cent of the newly-built housing market in Poland was already in the hands of companies, mainly in major cities. These companies are becoming important new players on the market, most often controlling the entire investment process, from the design of the real estate to the sale. In contrast to communal housing or individual housing construction, the new market players offer a much more complex product that goes beyond the mere concept of housing; a special lifestyle is also suggested to potential inhabitants. The developers apply strategies that appeal to fundamental needs. The most important features are security and nature, which are highlighted in order to "produce" a new kind of place evoking a vision of "paradise." This is presented as a synthesis of two worlds: the best of urbanity combined with the advantages of the countryside, resulting in a blend of safety, peace and health that proclaims urban happiness. This can be described as an "opposition of mythical nostalgias."[9] These oppositions seem to be amalgamated in the harmonious whole, guaranteeing a new life in a new world. The attempt to connect the two elements seems unlikely to succeed, although undoubtedly it is a worthwhile pursuit as far as investment is concerned, just as the Walt Disney Corporation invested in the creation of a perfect Celebrity Town (▶ 2, 3).

As Safe as Paradise—or the Game of the Fear of Crime

Crime prevention and the changeability of crime cannot be understood without considering changes in social and cultural sensitivity. Looking at various fields of society, we can even speak of a new "culture of fear." As the criminologist David Garland pointed out,

2

3

2 Traffic sign indicating a gated community in Sofia.
3 Faked landscape or paradise? Inside an American-style gated community in the suburbs of Sofia.

crime has gained a new dimension: that of fear. Whilst at one time it had more of a local and situational character, afflicting specific individuals or neighbourhoods, fear suddenly grew to become one of one of the most important social problems, not to say the trademark of an entire contemporary culture.[10] There are diverse causes for the current popularity of fear and security in media and politics as well as in urban planning. Nevertheless, the upswing has rather an elementary, ideological core that can be explored by looking at the very base of fear and security. First of all, both are socially produced values created by the distinction between norm and deviance.[11] Furthermore, security is something that is of essential benefit for every human being: nobody explicitly supports crime or danger. Therefore, security and crime prevention are important ideals for everyone, possessing universal importance. On the other hand, this makes them delicate values, which can be readily referred to by many actors for different purposes. For example, the fear of crime can be reinforced by public discourse on the subject of crime (i.e., crime talk), subsequently becoming part of a 'game with the fear of crime.' Against this backdrop we interpret the proliferation of gated com-

4

4   Security measures at a gated housing estate in Sofia. Nobody really knows what the gates, walls and cameras are actually supposed to protect the inhabitants against.

munities as a securitisation of housing. And indeed, fear and security materialise clearly in the form of the gated community, in which characteristic elements of the "culture of fear" are inscribed (▶ 4).

The need to provide security has not always been a big issue in Central and Eastern European societies. But nowadays the fear of crime is regarded as completely natural and rational, even though findings show that Bulgarians or Poles actually feel rather secure in their places of residence. Consequently, gated communities are becoming popular and even an accepted aspect of public discourse. In this regard the fear of crime, manifest amongst representatives of the richer strata, has caused security to emerge as an important component of marketing strategies. An entire branch of industry has developed, providing security services to private persons and communities on a level that state institutions are not able to provide. A striking example of this is the fact that there are 25,000 bodyguards at work in Warsaw. This is two and half times more than the number of policemen in the city.[12] They guard not only offices and shops, but also housing estates. Similar figures and trends are found in Sofia, where almost every apartment has a sticker at the entrance saying that it is regularly controlled by a security company.[13]

The above-mentioned aspects nevertheless indicate a new dimension in the marketing strategies of developers. A significant example of the close connection between the privatisation of security and the increased popularity of gated communities was the Open Conference on "Life Safety" organised in Wrocław in 2005 by one of the developers of gated communities. The conference was used to promote the new housing estate Archipelago of Green, which, according to the organisers, was Wrocław's first housing estate to be built in co-operation with a security agency. The programme of the conference stated explicitly that "the privatisation of security services" was the best solution for crime reduction at both local and national levels. This model of security, well-known from shopping malls, was successfully transferred to housing estates in only a couple of years. The motif of safety is subject to distinct privatisation: notions of security and fear constitute the basic, though not the only, advertising lever. Even the contents of brief newspaper articles bring over the message clearly:

> Investors take care to use the slogan 'guarded housing estate' in the offers they make. …
> It is a good sales trick. People are attracted by the notion of protection it infers—said
> Beata Święch, the Assistant Chairman of the Isan Invest SA Company.[14]

Real estate developers were one of the first to notice that a cultural change had taken place, using safety as a leitmotif in their marketing strategies. The concept of safety control gained primary significance, alongside the status and the "beauty" of buildings. The concept of safety became so important that advertisements and articles began to define housing estates not as fenced off or guarded, but as "safe housing estates":

The location induced us to design this safe housing estate. … There will be only two entries and one driveway here. … There are entry-phones by every gate. Moreover, cameras can be installed in the garage and the images from these places can be observed on several TV channels.[15]

Having summarised the fashion of security services and the societal output these infer, it is interesting to take a short look at the residents' perception of security. We have already mentioned the results of various studies showing that the majority of Bulgarians and Poles do not feel particularly insecure in their apartments and cities. And, indeed, a comparison of crime reports and statistics clearly shows that Sofia, Warsaw, or other Central and East European cities are no different from Amsterdam, Brussels, or Berlin in terms of crime levels.[16] When asked about safety in the city, respondents from Sofia stated that it was not actual physical danger that caused them to favour gated housing estates. Rather, a kind of desire for control seems to be the main motif inciting people to move into gated communities, a wish to escape from the uncontrolled (chaotic) post-socialist urban daily routine.[17] Furthermore, it can be concluded that the quest for privacy and social distinction seems to outplay the issue of security in Central and Eastern European cities.[18]

The Heavenly Landscape

The case of gated housing estates is not only challenging in terms of accessibility or inaccessibility. What seems to be a key element in understanding the phenomenon of such estates is, above all, the category of the landscape. Landscaping is more than a form of designing surroundings or of arranging space and places: it is a way of arranging and projecting social and cultural values. In critical geography, a landscape is not only a morphological entity (relating to its form), but also a representative of social and cultural meanings involving social relations. To use Henri Lefebvre's terminology, it is both a means and a result of production and reproduction processes.[19] Under the conditions of a consumer society, which inextricably links identity with possession, affiliation and access to a particular landscape constitutes one of the most serious indicators of identity, especially with regards to social class. Furthermore, landscape is a special set of goods. It is assigned to concrete spaces, it is geographically ordered and remains in place unlike other goods which circulate more freely.[20] One of the inhabitants of a gated community frankly confessed:

So I decided independently and spontaneously … a panoramic view was definitely crucial … The panorama accounts for more or less 50 per cent of the value of this apartment.[21]

If we analyse information delivered by developers in all kinds of promotional materials, press releases and interviews, it is immediately evident that the evocations of landscape are of considerable significance. The market-driven characteristics presented to potential buyers reveal that paradoxes and contradictions are consciously used and integrated in marketing strategies. Gated communities attempt to combine nature and culture: the gated housing estate offers untouched nature and at the same time provides fully subordinated, developed space:[22]

> Orchid Hills is a residential project that offers a modern solution, a living environment combining comfort with functionality. The gated character of the compound, the terrace-levelled park and the exquisite view of the Vitosha mountain give the residents the feeling of security, comfort and a high standard of living. [Orchid Hills] allows its inhabitants to live close to nature, yet still provides the comfort and ease of city life.[23]
>
> Marina Mokotów is situated in the centre of Warsaw, although over the half of its area is a landscaped parkland of sheltered nooks and small charming lakes.[24]

The importance of nature is especially obvious in the descriptions of gated housing estates provided not by the developers themselves, but by groups of designers or architects anxious to stress the advantages of new investment sites as far as the surroundings and their natural beauty are concerned, rather than concentrating on elements such as fences or gates. This change is clearly visible over a period of time: initially great emphasis was placed on their closed-in character, whereas subsequently developers changed the type of argumentation and focused more on their aesthetic and natural advantages. A conversation with the designer of the Eko Park housing estate in Cracow is an interesting example of this kind of rhetoric based on the discourse of nature:

> Until now it was enough to plant grass on the roof in order to talk about the ecological character of the construction … In our understanding, thinking about ecology means limiting the amount of pollutants which are being more and more frequently used during the technological processes involved in the production of construction materials. This does not stop us from designing and providing the best quality of flats; at the same time we make sure that all garages are built underground in order to keep motorised traffic separate from pedestrian walkways and to provide more green spaces. Of course, the housing estate will be enclosed and appropriately guarded.[25]

On the one side, the designer expresses a vision of the housing estate based on principles of sustainable development, combining high quality with a concern for the ecological dimension of the construction process and the safeguarding of nature. On the other side, at the end of his statement the designer states that the housing estate will "of course" be fenced in. This statement reflects the belief that a sustainable development and a harmonious relationship with the environment do not in any way exclude the putting up of fences and the creation of social inequality.

The landscape as an icon is, last but not least, a form of ideology: not only an appearance of space, but also a way of looking at and composing the world. In the case of gated communities, the landscape simultaneously works as an exclusion and as an inclusion factor, since it is appropriated and controlled by one group, and made unavailable to others. In this way the landscape at stake becomes a spatial manifestation of social relations—an ideology condensed to such a level that it manifests itself in a specific physical form. Constructing the landscape refers almost exclusively to the area occupied by the housing estate, rarely going beyond the actual and symbolic border of the wall or the fence, which separates the investment from the rest of the city. In determining idiosyncrasies of physical space, both access to and usage of "the world of nature" plays a significant role. Access to nature is firmly controlled by the fence, and the so-called "natural environment" is always professionally improved and maintained by gardeners. Just as in the early conceptions of environmentalists, the space of refuge becomes a kind of sanctuary offering "contemplation." It is often shaped in a way which utilises the 'natural firewall' (walls of green, artificial lakes, etc.). This romantic evocation of early environmentalists, adapted by the designers of gated communities, gives rise to many fundamental questions concerning public goods and social justice, such as the right of access to shrinking natural resources and different forms of landscape.[26] These questions do not only concern the access to newly-created green spaces, but (above all) the use of already existing public spheres for newly-built private investments. Gated communities tend to 'play the nature card' in an aggressive way by using public resources (e.g., urban parks). A journalist reports:

> A cosy housing estate at the Szczęśliwicki Park … named Lake Green owes its name to a small pond located on an adjacent plot which inhabitants can see from behind the fence. Szczęśliwice is a large construction site—the noise of machines and the roar of lorries are disrupting the pastoral life of its inhabitants.[27]

This leads us to another characteristic of the heavenly landscape promised by gated communities: the notion of history. In order to fully satisfy the high expectations of potential inhabitants, developers are beginning to take the history of the territory into consideration.[28] History is becoming the next element in the package; it is produced or reproduced for the purposes of making business transactions. Cultural and historical references allow a sense of belonging to arise. Developers use images embedded in the historical or master narrative of a city in order to underline the exclusiveness and prestige of their gated communities. A striking example of this is the fact that 90 per cent of the gated housing estates in Sofia are situated in the traditionally wealthy neighbourhoods that formerly housed the king's family and the socialist nomenclature. Furthermore, developers try to convince potential buyers that particular places, even if they are brand-new on the geographical and social map, are already steeped in "history":

> The name is intended to give the residence [Residence under the Eagle—the authors] importance and splendour. It refers to the monument crowned with the Polish Eagle

5   Advertisement of a gated housing estate in Sofia, promising a green, well-ordered and clean neighbourhood—an ideal place for families with children.

dating back to the Duchy of Warsaw, which stood in this place in the nineteenth century. For years it fell into disrepair; now it has been restored and placed on a new base in front of the main door of the residence.[29]

It is almost impossible to localise the founding myth, but certainly there are numerous strategies of shaping or redefining the identity of a place that are used to fulfil the promise of happiness to buyers, providing them with a sense of belonging. The suggestive power of the place not only consists of restricting availability, but also of expressing or constructing a sense of collective memory. To a large extent, a romanticised approach is employed here; great emphasis is placed on the past of the area, such in the case of Marina Mokotów which is presented as a "new town on Old Mokotów." These gated housing estates limit the access to a space by means of visible physical barriers and at the same time they create or process the history of this specific confined space. Developers use romantic names, mostly associated with nature and historical events: green hills, wild streams. In more advanced scripts, stories of other city sites are created or referred to:

> The new housing estate makes reference to many traditions. On the one hand we pay tribute to Ebenezer Howard and his garden city. Here we have an exceptional example of the realisation of this dream in the district of Giszowiec in Katowice. On the other hand we refer to exclusive residential developments from the inter-war period. (Designer T. Konior)[30]

This quotation reveals another feature of gated communities. It is quite evident that developers use and combine different styles of architecture and urban planning in order to attract as many potential buyers as possible. The majority of gated communities are designed according to an eclectic concept combining the idea of the garden city with the concept of standardised suburban detached or semi-detached housing. Additionally, developers employ specific features that relate to the local context, for example specific roof constructions. All in all, these architectural concepts are directed at promoting a particular sense of wellbeing and a feeling of security.

An important aspect of the whole package is the "myth of community" that somehow all gated communities are associated with. But in contrast to their North American or Latin American counterparts, Central and Eastern European gated community developers do not accentuate the meaning of a community with strong social relations between its members. Instead of promoting the idea of a homogenous community, developers focus on terms such as cosiness and neighbourly relations. In some way these strategies can be interpreted as being an adaptation to Eastern European circumstances, where the majority of potential buyers are not searching for a community, but rather for social distinction, privacy and the provision of services.

I don't have anything in common with my neighbours. You have to know that it is really difficult for us 'ordinary older Bulgarians' to feel comfortable here, because we are so different from all these young and rich people. We were raised differently with different values. This creates huge social differences in terms of attitudes towards life. … So we have moved here because of the landscape, fresh air and peace.[31]

The "beauty" of gated housing estates is one of the most important components distinguishing them from the chaotic post-socialist urban surroundings (▶ 5). Analysing the space of metropolitan areas in Eastern Europe, the luxurious and prestigious character of gated communities is mainly due to the provision of "exclusive" access to an aesthetically composed space. It is worthwhile taking note of the background against which gated developments are emerging. The current fragmentation of post-socialist cities is being intensified still further by chaotic and uncontrolled building developments, a lack of spatial regulations and gaps in the infrastructure. This stems from a loss of general public order, resulting in the financial incapacity and weakness of public institutions. Therefore, the gated communities are arising as a reaction to the poor quality of housing in Eastern European cities, where the randomness of architectural solutions has become the rule. In this context, the title of a conference which took place in May 2006 seems remarkable: "Warsaw—the Capital of the Third World." The provocative images presented during the event showed gated housing estates, chaotic development, a stark contrast between poverty and wealth. It is worthwhile regarding gated communities not only as one of the causes of such a city image, but also as an effect of spatial disorder. Within the context of ubiquitous chaos, the orderly and planned nature of the enclosed territory often becomes valuable in itself.

Such spectacular construction sites as Marina Mokotów or Residential Park Sofia, both officially known as "the city within the city," demonstrate a harmoniously constructed urban landscape which plays an important role in providing a sense of security for contemporary urban dwellers. Local examples of master-planned communities that have been realised are generally rather modest. However, within the context of the surrounding architectonic and urban chaos of post-socialist cities, they certainly deserve the description of "master-planned."

The presence of developers and planned investments on the Polish and Bulgarian markets is relatively new. After a period of initial distrust, an increasing number of buyers are deciding to place their trust in developers and purchase a flat or a house in a gated housing estate. Thus within a relatively short period of time (between the early nineteen-nineties and now) cities have adapted, more or less consciously, to a course of urban planning which has been functioning in the USA for several decades. The detailed planning of gated housing estates enables the estate's whole territory to be kept under control. Estates which are criticised as "islands of luxury" or "marble cages" by the press indeed constitute modern and aesthetic points on the map of the post-socialist cities. The spatial reality of many Central and Eastern European cities is quite accurately described by Rowland Atkinson and John Flintlock's concept of "time-space trajectories of segregation," in which segregation refers not only to gated housing estates, but a general "splintering urbanism" with its territories, corridors and objectives.[32]

The feeling of aesthetic cohesion serves to sanction and rationalise the practice of spatial and social segregation which, otherwise, could be the subject of much criticism. As mentioned above, security must be understood in a much broader sense than merely in the category of fear: security here is provided in a wider ontological sense. The aesthetic landscape, then, could be perceived as a way of implementing private politics of control, independent from local or national "zero tolerance" programmes, although they are based on the same assumptions. In this perspective, it is most useful to describe the reality of gated housing estates in terms of the theme park metaphor.[33] Gated housing estates, especially those of a higher standard, create a distinctive atmosphere by using unusual architectural solutions and high-quality materials. When one first enters a fenced and guarded building complex, one experiences a mixture of emotions, including uncertainty and excitement. Thus the analogies to a hotel lobby, used by many of the visitors and journalists to describe their emotions on first entering a gated community, are understandable. Gated housing estates create an "affective ambience," characteristic of a space of consumption.[34] Aesthetics play the key role here. In the chaos of the city, "islands of luxury" are becoming heterotopias and "forming another space, another real space, as perfect, meticulous and well arranged as ours is disordered,"[35] much like the case of the former Jesuit colonies described by Michel Foucault.

The Trouble with Happiness

The rhetoric of prestige and exclusivity is used by developers almost as often as the rhetoric of beauty and nature. Admittedly, not all newly-built gated housing estates have an elitist character; the standardisation of these developments in Central and Eastern Europe has at the same time led to a diversification of gated housing products. Nowadays they vary in size and concept, and some of them are aimed at fulfilling the needs of humbler middle-class strata, with a limited amount of floor space and rooms. Still the language of prestige and exclusiveness remains:

> Welcome to the new residential project 'sofia sky' … [Your] home in Bulgaria—a unique blend of Austrian quality and Bulgarian nature. In the district of Simeonovo on the slopes of the Vitosha Mountain, an international lifestyle is being offered in this matchless location.[36]

> The Deep Blue housing estate will be guarded and monitored (the monthly cost of this service is sixty złoty per flat). Investors are pleased to announce the construction of the recreational centre with a swimming pool, fitness club, golf course, tennis courts and

horse riding club. This will be carried out within two years. The kindergarten will also soon be open.[37]

The enclosed area, the system of monitoring and guards will not get in the way of the peace and the modern technology ... will provide the joy and satisfaction of being on holiday all year round.[38]

A house is presented here not only as a place to live, but also as a kind of feeling of "being on holiday." The comfort is derived from a set of activities that are included in the price of the flat. Gated housing estates—in Eastern Europe as elsewhere—provide leisure activities such as fitness rooms, tennis courts, swimming pools (for adults), beautiful playgrounds (for children), and man-made lakes (▶ 6).

This vision of happiness as described in the advertisements for gated communities often clashes with "reality." Real life does not appear to be as simple and peaceful as it is made

6   Inside a gated community in Santiago de Chile—the beauty of the landscape with a swimming pool.

out to be. To demonstrate some problems arising from this vision of paradise and happiness, it is worth taking a look at an example from popular culture. Because of the rising popularity of gated communities in Poland, Polish National TV, Channel 2 introduced a new TV show called The Bullionaires (Bulionerzy) in 2004. This TV show followed the changes in the lifestyle of the Nowik family, who moved from a pre-fabricated large scale housing estate to a gated community after winning a lottery organised by an instant bullion producer. The producer's short description of the show plot explains (that):

> Everything changes when they take part in a bullion cubes contest and win a luxury furnished apartment in an exclusive tower block in the centre of Warsaw, with the rent paid for an entire lifetime. All their dreams have come true. However, it soon turns out that living amongst the elite isn't at all simple.[39]

Differences between the "ordinary family" and the "elite" soon become clearly visible in the new environment. Moving to a new place of residence is tantamount to a change in the family's entire lifestyle—the protagonists develop new customs, change their mode of speaking, and go on a diet. The humour of this TV show relies on the relations between the "ordinary family" and the "elite," whose representatives are the members of a "new middle class": television producers and a journalist, a businesswoman, public relations agency owners, and a gay couple. The problem with happiness as revealed by the TV show seems to be crucial for understanding the expectations and reality of life in gated communities.

From the inhabitants' perspective, the image of gated communities and home owner associations does not so much correspond with North American examples, as presented by Evan McKenzie,[40] as with the reality of the American Wild West. Moreover, the metaphor of the "Wild West" arose completely independently in several interviews. Inhabitants used terms such as "ranchers" or "sheriff" to illustrate the behaviour of inhabitants and their way of managing the associations:

> There is [in our Board—the authors] a chairman who, at some point, felt he was a sheriff; the guy started bothering everybody … He became the boss of the Board and then suddenly started to behave like a sheriff. After that he resigned voluntarily, but even then he thought he was the sheriff here. He would sit at the porter's lodge all the time, giving instructions to the doorkeepers, telling them what to do. A new chairman was appointed, but even now he is still interfering. We tried to elect a new management board, but no one was interested.[41]

Conflict seems to be a major part of life in an "idyllic" gated community. It takes on diverse forms, involving both relations with the next-door neighbours and relations with people from "behind the fence." The framework of conflicts includes a considerable number of potential actors. Even when we look at the inhabitants only, it is possible to pinpoint a few characteristics of the conflicts. First of all, the relationships between owners as opposed to tenants of the flats in a gated housing estate are potential sources of conflict. Owners are strongly "ascribed to their role": because they actually own the place, they are more prone to conform to the rules of the associations; they are also more demanding, expressing their expectations to other inhabitants, to the estate's administration or to security officers. Their expectations grow in proportion to the amount of funds they have invested in the apartment. Furthermore, this leads to a juridification of relations between neighbours, arising from a strong sense of ownership.[42] Tenants display a much freer attitude to settling and cohabiting in the gated housing estate: they are more often the organisers of social gatherings and they are less willing to conform to regulations. This applies particularly to students and foreigners. The breaking of principles is often encountered with harsh reactions, such as for example the chairman of one of the gated housing estates in Warsaw imposing limits on the number of access cards given out:

> It turns out that we live in a penal camp, everyone is being punished because of those who rent flats out to students, who aren't registered as inhabitants—Mr Piotr is anxious—can the co-operative restrict access to my own flat?[43]

The second source of conflict is based on the relationship between childless inhabitants and families with children. The housing offers a guarantee of security and "peace," but the notion of "peace" strongly depends on the family situation of inhabitants. Families with children are looking for a suitable place to bring up their offspring: in most cases the gated housing estate offers them at least a small playground, greenery and a sense of security. However childless inhabitants, mainly the retired, are seeking peace in terms of silence and comfort. The diversity of lifestyles and the organisation of the settlement, as an effect of the second demographic transition, combined with the vague offers made by developers with the aim of satisfying the needs of all potential categories of purchasers, create another area of conflicts:

> The playground was built here, next to the porter's lodge in the corner. If the mother allows her child to go outside, it may go to the pond where she can't see it … That's why the mothers asked for a small sandpit to be put right next to the house, but an elderly gentleman [at the Board meeting—the authors] gets up and says that he has looked into the project and he chose to live in a part of the building where there wouldn't be any bloody kids.[44]

A further source of trouble and conflicts is a lack of communication between property management and residents. In spite of being advertised as luxury housing products, several gated communities have several shortcomings that can be traced back to a lack of housing quality and to a misunderstanding of the rules, regulations and covenants.

> In the beginning … we did not make clear contracts with the residents concerning the management. We were probably not ready for such things. That was in 2001. In 2002 they got the keys to their apartments. We didn't make contracts explicitly stating that the management of the complex had to be paid for. … Later on we tried to introduce this, but of course residents asked us "why are you asking us to pay if the others don't have to pay?" And so from 2001 until the beginning of 2007 we were maintaining the gardens for free. But this year we said either you pay 300 euros per year per apartment—which is not that high an amount—or we stop maintaining. So they had to decide.[45]

> When we decided to move here the developers told us that this would be a small gated housing complex with three or four apartment houses. But the developers kept changing their plans all the time. Instead of three or four apartment blocks, this area already has nineteen now … So we have been living on a never-ending construction site for the last four years.[46]

Another area of conflict, which is different to the situation on open housing estates as far as solving neighbourhood quarrels is concerned, arises from the continual presence of intermediaries. Internal conflicts in gated housing estates are mainly solved with the help of the security officers. One could gain the impression that the purpose of employing a security company is not so much to protect the inhabitants against danger from the outside world, but rather to supervise predictable internal affairs and regulate intra-community behaviour.

Conclusion

Gated housing estates as a product can be regarded as a sociocultural phenomenon that goes hand in hand with discontinuities in postmodern urban life. In the case of Central and Eastern Europe, gated housing estates are closely connected with societal uncertainty, the commoditisation of housing and a general privatisation of urban space. As described above, developers are using these discontinuities, along with a broad repertoire of cultural references, to promote their products. Furthermore, the gated housing estate can be seen as a milieu which plays a significant and specific role in redefining the social structure of a whole region. Gated housing estates are a modernised milieu, "perhaps even more effective in creating differences between social classes"[47] than other outward displays of income or education. That is why it is worth analysing this particular urban and architectonic form on a local, regional and global level, particularly in Central and Eastern Europe.

Endnotes

1 For the sake of readability we will use both the emblematic term 'gated community' (which has become an umbrella term or even a trademark in urban studies when talking about security-oriented, privately governed urban neighbourhoods) and 'gated housing estates' (which is less euphemistic and probably more appropriate for Central and Eastern Europe) interchangeably. Renaud Le Goix and Chris J. Webster, "Gated Communities," *Geography Compass* 3 (2008:2): 1189–1214.

2 Edward J. Blakely and Mary Gail Snyder, *Fortress America. Gated Communities in the United States* (Washington/D.C.: Brookings Institution Press, 1997), 3.

3 This article is based on field studies conducted by the authors in Bulgaria and Poland. Although there are differences between gated housing in Bulgaria and Poland, the similarities clearly prevail. Differences occur mainly in the public perception of gated housing estates (in terms of the range of public discussions); the marketing strategies and promising of happiness are almost identical (as they are in many other Central and Eastern European cities). Therefore, this essay focuses on the similarities between gated housing estates.

4 Sharon Zukin, *Landscapes of Power. From Detroit to Disney World* (Berkeley, Los Angeles, Oxford: University of California Press, 1991); Edward Soja, Thirdspace: Journeys to Los Angeles and Other Real-And-Imagined Places (Oxford: Blackwell, 1996).

5 Robert Freestone, Announcement of the forum "City Living: Creating Sydney's Sustainable Communities," http://www.unsw.edu.au/news/pad/articles/2003/oct/Master_planned_communities.html (accessed March 14, 2009).

6 http://www.osiedlebaltyk.com (accessed March 17, 2009).

7 http://residentialpark-sofia.com/en (accessed April 7, 2009).

8 In Bulgaria and Poland the proliferation of gated housing estates since the end of the nineteen-nineties is closely connected with the market-entry of international real estate developers, the establishment of local real estate companies and the consolidation of local housing markets.

9 Wojciech Burszta, "Miasto i wieś—opozycja mitycznych nostalgii [The Town and the Village—the Opposition of Mythical Nostalgias]," in *Pisanie miasta—czytanie miasta,* ed. Anna Zeidler-Janiszewska (Poznań: Humaniora, 1997), 95–107.

10 David Garland, *The Culture of Control. Crime and Social Order in Contemporary Society* (Oxford, New York: Oxford University Press, 2001), 11.

11 Bernd Belina, "Die kontrollierte Stadt" (Public Lecture held at the Jahrestagung Deutsche Akademie für Landeskunde, "Die kontrollierte Stadt," Friedrich-Alexander Universität Erlangen-Nürnberg, November 1, 2008).

12 According to data provided by the "Solidarność" trade union, there were 250,000 security officers employed in Poland in 2007, 25,000 of whom were working in Warsaw, see: http://www.10zl.org (accessed March 14, 2009).

13 Christian Smigiel, "Sozialräumlicher Wandel in Stadtregionen des östlichen Europa. Eine Bestandsaufnahme des Aufkommens einer neuen Wohnform: Geschlossene und bewachte Wohnkomplexe in der bulgarischen Hauptstadt Sofia," in *Modernisierung in Ost- und Ostmitteleuropa? Dynamiken innerstaatlichen und internationalen Wandels,* ed. Forschungsstelle Osteuropa Bremen, 2008, 83–86.

14 Małgorzata Zubik, "Strzeżonego Pan Bóg strzeże. Jak chroni się nowe osiedla? [Better safe than sorry. How are the new housing estates guarded?], Gazeta Wyborcza (Gazeta Stołeczna), May 19, 1999.

15 Jacek Kulesza, "Wśród zieleni. Co to będzie? [Amongst Greenery. What is going to be here?]," Gazeta Wyborcza (Gazeta Wrocław), October 20, 1999.

16 Cynthia Tavares and Geoffrey Thomas, "Statistik kurz gefasst. Bevölkerung und soziale Beziehungen. Kriminalität und Strafverfolgung," in Eurostat, 2008, 3–7.

17 Leibniz Institute for Regional Geography, *Gated and Guarded Housing in Eastern Europe, Forum Ifl 11,* ed. Christian Smigiel, 2009.

18 In this respect and in the motives of their residents, gated housing estates in Central and Eastern European seem to differ from the ones in Latin America and the USA. As several studies have emphasised, fear and the risks of urban life play a much more crucial role for residents in Latin America and the USA moving to closed neighbourhoods. Setha Low, "The edge and the center: gated communities and the discourse of urban fear," *American Anthropologist* 103 (2001:1): 45–58. Setha Low, *Behind the gates: life, security, and the pursuit of happiness in fortress America* (New York: Routledge, 2003). Teresa Caldeira, *City of walls: crime, segregation, and citizenship in São Paulo* (Berkeley/Ca: University of California Press, 2000).

19 Christian Schmid, *Stadt, Raum und Gesellschaft: Henri Lefebvre und die*

Theorie der Produktion des Raumes (Stuttgart: Steiner, 2005).

20 David Harvey, *The Limits to Capital* (Chicago: University of Chicago Press, 1982), 233.

21 Author's interview with a resident of a gated housing estate in Toruń, Poland.

22 Other paradoxes such as "uniqueness vs. standardisation" or "community vs. individual" can also be found. Concerning the paradox "uniqueness vs. standardisation" it can be said that although they are sold as unique neighbourhoods, gated communities are based on a concept of standardisation, see: Jacek Gądecki, "New social milieus—gated communities in the Polish urban landscape," in *Gated and Guarded Housing in Eastern Europe, Forum Ifl 11,* ed. Christian Smigiel, 2009. Therefore one can find dozens of similar gated housing estates all across Eastern Europe. The paradox "community vs. individualism" relates to the concept of a homogeneous community or neighbourhood that the developers are trying to sell. On the other hand, the same developers underline the individuality of each accommodation unit, designed to meet the requirements of each individual resident.

23 http://www.orchidhills-sofia.com (accessed April 8, 2009).

24 http://www.marinamokotow.com.pl (accessed March 21, 2009).

25 Adam Zyzman, "Nawiązać dialog z otoczeniem. Rozmowa z architektem Markiem Dunikowskim, współautorem projektu osiedla mieszkaniowego Eko Park [Establishing a Dialogue with the Surroundings. An interview with Marek Dunikowski, the architect and co-author of the Eko Park Housing Estate project.]," Gazeta Wyborcza (Gazeta Kraków), May 21, 2004.

26 Klaus Eder, "The Institutionalisation of Environmentalism: Ecological Discourse and the Second Transformation of the Public Sphere," in *Risk, Environment and Modernity. Towards a New Ecology,* ed. Scott Lash, Bronisław Szerszyński and Brian Wynne (London: Sage Publications, 1996), 203–223.

27 Malwina Buszko and Dariusz Bartoszewicz. "'Wyspy luksusu.' [The Islands of Luxury.]," Gazeta Wyborcza (Gazeta Stołeczna), July 1, 1998.

28 History has certainly become an important tool for promoting all kinds of housing or commercial products. Nevertheless, it seems that gated communities are even more strongly associated with the past by means of an eclectic idealisation of urban history.

29 Malwina Buszko and Dariusz Bartoszewicz, (see note 27).

30 Author's interviews with the designer T. Konior.

31 Author's interview with a resident of a gated and guarded housing estate in Sofia.

32 Rowland Atkinson and John Flint, "The Fortress UK? Gated Communities: the Spatial Revolt of the Elites and Time Space Trajectories of Segregation," in ESRC Center for Neighbourhood Research, CNR, Paper 17, 2004.

33 Michel Sorkin, *Variations on the Theme Park. The New American City and the End of Public Space* (New York: Hill and Wang, 1992).

34 Michel Maffesoli, *The Time of the Tribes: The Decline of Individuality in Mass Society* (London: Sage, 1996).

35 Michel Foucault, "Of Other Spaces: Utopias and Heterotopias," in *Rethinking Architecture: A Reader in Cultural Theory,* ed. Neil Leach (London, New York: Routledge, 1997), 350–355, here 356.

36 http://www.sofia-sky.com/v3/ (accessed April 9, 2009).

37 Information leaflet advertising a gated housing estate in Toruń (MT 2002).

38 http://www.osiedlebaltyk.com (accessed March 21, 2009).

39 http://www.filmweb.pl (accessed March 18, 2009).

40 Evan McKenzie, *Privatopia: Homeowner Associations and the Rise of Residential Private Government* (New Haven: Yale University Press, 1994).

41 Author's interview with a resident of a gated and guarded housing estate in Toruń, Poland.

42 Magdalena Mostowska, "Provision of private services and enforcing neighbours' behaviour in one of Warsaw's gated neighbourhoods," in *Gated and Guarded Housing in Eastern Europe, Forum Ifl 11,* ed. Christian Smigiel, 2009.

43 Jerzy S. Majewski and Tomasz Urzykowski. "'Kto im otworzy drzwi?' [Who is going to open the Doors to them?]," Gazeta Wyborcza (Gazeta Stołeczna), December 23, 2006.

44 Author's interview with a resident of a gated housing estate in Toruń.

45 Author's interview with the developer of MC—a gated housing estate in Sofia.

46 Author's interview with a resident of MC—a gated housing estate in Sofia.

47 Peter Alheit, "On a contradictory way to the 'learning society'. A critical approach," *Studies in the Education of Adults* 31 (1999): 66–81.

LIST OF AUTHORS

Arnold Bartetzky Dr. phil., studied History of Art, German Philology, and Philosophy in Freiburg i. Br., Tübingen, and Cracow. Researcher at the Centre for the History and Culture of East Central Europe (Geisteswissenschaftliches Zentrum Geschichte und Kultur Ostmitteleuropas) in Leipzig since 1995. Teaching experience at the Universities of Leipzig and Jena. Currently involved in a research project on "Imaginations of Urbanity in the 20th Century." Numerous publications on various aspects of architecture and urban planning from the Renaissance to the present day.

Marc Schalenberg Dr. phil., studied History, Art History, and Philosophy in Bonn, Oxford, Paris, and Berlin. *Wissenschaftlicher Assistent* at the History Departments of Humboldt University Berlin and the University of Zurich from 1999 to 2008. Research Fellow at Helsinki Collegium for Advanced Studies from 2008 to 2010. Co-editor of *Selling Berlin. Imagebildung und Stadtmarketing von der preußischen Residenz bis zur Bundeshauptstadt* (2008); various other publications in the field of modern European urban history. Currently preparing a comparative study on "urban icons" in German capital cities between 1648 and 1848.

Mohsen Aboutorabi PhD, Professor of Architecture and Director of Research Studies, Birmingham City University. Director of the architecture, landscape, and urban design practice 'urban synthesis' in Birmingham, with current projects in China, Iran, Finland, and the UK. Extensive teaching, research, and working experience in architecture, city planning and urban design. Involvement in city planning projects in Nigeria's new capital and townships in South Africa. Various publications on architecture and urban design with a focus on Islamic architecture, affordable housing, urbanisation processes, and rural housing in developing countries

Sándor Békési Dr. phil., studied History, Geography, and History & Philosophy of Science at Vienna University, scholar of the postgraduate programme "Culture and Environment" at the Institute for Interdisciplinary Research and Education (IFF) in Vienna from 1996 to 1998. Research Fellow at the International Research Center for Cultural Studies (IFK) in Vienna in 2005. Curator at the Wien Museum, Department of City Development and Topography, since 2004. Various publications on urban, environmental and transport history.

Mascha Bisping M.A., studied History of Art and German Philology in Marburg/Lahn. Scholar of the postgraduate programme "Klassizismus und Romantik" at Giessen from 1999 to 2002, Assistant in the History of Urban Design at the Swiss Federal Institute of Technology (ETH) in Zurich from 2003 to 2008. Currently completing a doctoral thesis on the city of Krefeld and the changes from the idea of the city as a work of art to the practice of urban planning as a process in the early nineteenth century. Various publications on the history of architecture and urban design (eighteenth and nineteenth centuries).

Bruno Bonomo PhD, studied *Lettere*, Modern History, and Urban History at Rome La Sapienza, Viterbo, and Leicester. Currently a research fellow at the University of Siena and adjunct professor of Modern History and History of Journalism at the universities of Tuscia-Viterbo and Rome La Sapienza. Various publications in the fields of urban history and oral history, including the volumes *Il quartiere delle Valli. Costruire Roma nel secondo dopoguerra* (2007) and *Città di parole. Storia orale da una periferia romana* (2006, co-authored with Alessandro Portelli, Alice Sotgia and Ulrike Viccaro).

Marina Dmitrieva Dr. phil., studied History of Art and History at the Lomonossov-University of Moscow. Lecturer at the Institute of Theatre in Moscow from 1982 to 1988 and at the Universities of Freiburg i. Br., Basel, Hamburg, and Bremen from 1991 to 1996. Researcher at the Institute of Art History of the Academy of Sciences in Moscow from 1988 to 1991 and researcher at the Centre for the History and Culture of East Central Europe (GWZO) at the University of Leipzig since 1996. Numerous publications on urban visual culture in Central and Eastern Europe, classical avant-garde and Renaissance art and architecture in Central Europe.

Jacek Friedrich PhD, studied History of Art in Cracow. Since 1990 lecturer at the Department of Art History, University of Gdansk. Numerous publications on twentieth century architecture and architectural culture, including the forthcoming book *Neue Stadt in altem Gewand. Der Wiederaufbau von Danzig 1945-1960* (2009). Currently working on a book about visual culture and ideologies in Danzig/Gdansk in the nineteenth and twentieth centuries.

Jacek Gądecki PhD in Sociology, associated with the Institute of Sociology in Toruń, currently working as a researcher and lecturer at the AGH University of Science and Technology in Cracow. Research interests: the anthropology of architecture (architecture and identity), the anthropology and sociology of the city (the public sphere, cultural economy), and architecture in general. Research scholarships at the Bauhaus Foundation (Dessau) and the City University in New York (subject: gated communities in the USA and Poland).

Mart Kalm PhD, Professor of History of Architecture, Dean of the Faculty of Art and Culture, Estonian Academy of Arts, Tallinn. Publications include: *Arhitekt Alar Kotli. Monograafia* (1994), *Functionalism in Estonia. A Guidebook* (1998), *Eesti 20 sajandi arhitektuur. Estonian 20th Century Architecture* (2001), *Toompea castle* (with Rein Zobel and Juhan Maiste, 2008). Currently participating in the research project "Visualising the Nation. Institutional Critique of 20th Century Art and Architecture in Estonia."

Christa Kamleithner Dipl.-Ing., Mag. phil., studied Architecture and Philosophy in Vienna. Research associate at the Technical University Graz from 2004 to 2005. Since 2006 research associate and lecturer at the University of the Arts in Berlin, teaching cultural sciences in the architectural course. Assistant lecturer at the Center for Metropolitan Studies at the Technical University in Berlin since 2007. Currently working on a doctoral thesis on the beginnings of modern urban planning in the nineteenth century, in connection with the evolvement of liberal forms of government. Various publications on urban development and the aesthetics of architecture.

Ana Kladnik PhD candidate at the University of Ljubljana, title of dissertation: *The Representation of Town Planning between "Future Euphoria" and "Utopia's Loss": The Formation of the "Socialist Town" in Yugoslavia and Czechoslovakia, 1945-1965;* since 2007 member of a research group within the project "Socialist Dictatorship as a World of Meaning. Representations of Social Order and Transformation of Authority in East Central Europe after 1945," run by the Institute of Contemporary History, Prague, and the Centre for Contemporary History, Potsdam.

Clarisse Lauras PhD student at the University of Lyon II, currently working on the thesis: *Living in a modern district in a medium-sized city: Firminy-Vert*, supervised by Jean-Luc Pinol. Research interests include the historical transformation and meaning of communities in urban areas. Master's thesis on the Armenian community in Saint-Etienne, published in 2006.

Christian Smigiel Dipl.-Geogr., studied Geography, Political Science, and Economics in Münster and Ljubljana. Research fellow at the Leibniz Institute for Regional Geography (IfL) in Leipzig since 2007. Currently working on urban development in Eastern and particularly South-Eastern Europe. His doctoral thesis investigates the proliferation of gated and guarded housing complexes ("gated communities") in Sofia.

Andreas Wesener Dipl.-Ing., MSc, registered architect in Germany (AKNW) and the UK (ARB), studied Architecture in Bochum and London, and is currently preparing a doctoral thesis in European Urban Studies at the Bauhaus University Weimar. Since 2007 research associate at Birmingham City University in a Knowledge Transfer Partnership (KTP) with D5 Architects LLP, Birmingham; visiting studio tutor at Birmingham School of Architecture. Previous work experience in architecture, urban design, and project management for architectural offices, and a building cooperative (Wohnungsbaugenossenschaft) in Germany.

IMAGE CREDITS

"Glückselige Städte": Johann Peter Willebrand's Conception of Urban Happiness

Mascha Bisping

▶ 1 and 2: Johann Peter Willebrand, *Grundriss einer schönen Stadt. Vols. 1-2* (Hamburg: Bohnsche Buchhandlung); (Leipzig: Hilschersche Buchhandlung, 1775-1776).

The Changing Pattern of Urban Form in Relation to the Perception of Happiness in Georgian Birmingham

Mohsen Aboutorabi, Andreas Wesener

▶ 1: William Westley, "The North Prospect of St Philip's Church, in Birmingham. (With The North Prospect of ye Square)," (Birmingham: 1732); Reproduced with the permission of Birmingham Libraries & Archives (permission No: 398).
▶ 2: "The Plan of Birmingham, survey'd in the year 1731," (Birmingham: T. Richards, 1789); Reproduced with the permission of Birmingham Libraries & Archives (permission No: 398).
▶ 3: Samuel Bradford and Thomas Jefferys, "A Plan of Birmingham: Surveyed in MDCCL," (London: Thomas Jefferys, 1751); Reproduced with the permission of Birmingham Libraries & Archives (permission No: 398).
▶ 4: Thomas Hanson, "Plan of Birmingham," (Birmingham: Pearson & Rollason, 1778); Reproduced with the permission of Birmingham Libraries & Archives (permission No: 398).
▶ 5: Photograph by Andreas Wesener, 2008.
▶ 6: John Cattell, Sheila Ely, and Barry Jones, The Birmingham Jewellery Quarter: An Architectural Survey (Swindon: English Heritage, 2002), 54; Crown copyright (AA99/06544). Reproduced with the permission of English Heritage (permission No: 1043).
▶ 7: John Cattell, Sheila Ely, and Barry Jones, The Birmingham Jewellery Quarter : An Architectural Survey (Swindon: English Heritage, 2002), 15; English Heritage. NMR (NMR 18493/24). Reproduced with the permission of English Heritage (permission No: 1043).
▶ 8: John Pigott Smith and W. R. Gardner, "To the Right Honourable William Earl of Dartmouth ... this Map of Birmingham engraved from a ... survey made in the years 1824 & 1825, is ... dedicated by ... Beilby, Knott & Beilby. J. Pigott Smith, Surveyor & Engineer. Engraved by W. R. Gardner. Scale of yards, 900[= 202 mm]," (Birmingham: Beilby, Knott & Beilby, 1828); Reproduced with the permission of Birmingham Libraries & Archives (permission No: 398).

The Attraction of Heimat. Homeland Protection in Vienna around 1900, or The Preservation and Reform of the City

Sándor Békési

▶ 1: R. Stepanek / Atelier Gerlach, Wien Museum.
▶ 2: *Hohe Warte*, 1906/07.
▶ 3: Die Zukunft des Karlsplatzes in Wien, 1911.
▶ 4: *Kunsthistorischer Atlas der k. k. Reichshaupt- und Residenzstadt Wien und Verzeichnis der erhaltenswerten historischen, Kunst- und Naturdenkmale des Wiener Stadtbildes* (Vienna: Schroll, 1916).
▶ 5: August Stauda, Wien Museum.

Happiness through Discipline. Soviet Cities in the Travelogues of Foreign Visitors in the Nineteen-twenties and Nineteen-thirties

Marina Dmitrieva

▶ 1: *Kunst und Macht im Europa der Diktatoren 1930 bis 1945,* ed. Dawn, Ades (Berlin: Octagon, 1996).
▶ 2: Julius Haydu, *Russland 1932* (Vienna-Leipzig: Phaidon-Verlag, 1932).
▶ 3: Herbert and Elisabeth Weichmann, *Alltag im Sowjetstaat. Macht und Mensch. Wollen und Wirklichkeit in Sowjet-Rußland* (Berlin: Brückenverlag, 1931).
▶ 4: Collection Centre Canadien d'Architecture/Canadian Centre for Architecture, Montreal.
▶ 5: Collection Centre Canadien d'Architecture/Canadian Centre for Architecture, Montreal.
▶ 6: Julius Haydu, *Russland 1932* (Vienna, Leipzig: Phaidon-Verlag, 1932).
▶ 7: *30 Jahre Sowjetische Architektur* (Leipzig: Bibliographisches Institut, 1950).
▶ 8: W.P. Coates and Zelda K. Coates, *Scenes from Soviet Life* (London: Lawrence and Wishart, 1936).
▶ 9: W.P. Coates and Zelda K. Coates, *Scenes from Soviet Life* (London: Lawrence and Wishart, 1936).
▶ 10: Collection Centre Canadien d'Architecture/Canadian Centre for Architecture, Montreal.

"… A Better, Happier World": Visions of a New Warsaw after World War Two

Jacek Friedrich

▶ 1: Bolesław Bierut, *Sześcioletni plan odbudowy Warszawy,* 1950.
▶ 2: Tadeusz Barucki, *Maciej Nowicki* (Warsaw: 1986).
▶ 3: Tadeusz Barucki, *Maciej Nowicki* (Warsaw: 1986).
▶ 4: Tadeusz Barucki, *Maciej Nowicki* (Warsaw: 1986).
▶ 5: Helena Syrkus, *Ku idei osiedla społecznego* (Warsaw: 1976).
▶ 6: Bolesław Bierut, *Sześcioletni plan odbudowy Warszawy,* 1950.
▶ 7: Zygmunt Skibniewski and Stanisław Dziewulski: General plan for rebuilding Warsaw, 1946.
▶ 8: Bolesław Bierut, *Sześcioletni plan odbudowy Warszawy,* 1950.
▶ 9: Bolesław Bierut, *Sześcioletni plan odbudowy Warszawy,* 1950.
▶ 10: Plan generalny Warszawy (Warsaw: 1965).

Happy Living in a New Socialist Town. The Construction, Distribution, Management, and Inhabitation of Apartments in Post-War Yugoslavia and Czechoslovakia

Ana Kladnik

▶ 1: Architectural Museum, Ljubljana (Velenje, urban plans 1956–1961).
▶ 2: Periodical *Dukla,* April 10, 1959.
▶ 3: Periodical *Rudar,* May 27, 1961, 4, and July 25, 1961, 5.
▶ 4: Velenje Museum.
▶ 5: Photograph by Ana Kladnik, 2005.

Does Urban Life Make Farmers Happy? The Central Settlements of Collective Farms in the Estonian SSR

Mart Kalm

▶ 1: Photograph by Mart Kalm, 2007.
▶ 2: *Ehitus ja Arhitektuur* (1967:4): 12.
▶ 3: Maaehituse küsimusi. Artiklite kogumik (Tallinn: Riiklik Ehituskomitee, 1964), 10.
▶ 4: Boris Mirov, *Saku, Vinni, Kurtna* (Moscow: Stroiizdat, 1977), 26.
▶ 5: Photograph Eesti Arhitektuurimuuseum.
▶ 6: Photograph by Mart Kalm, 2008.
▶ 7: *Eesti küla ehitab* (Tallinn: Eesti Raamat, 1983), 60.
▶ 8: Photograph by Mart Kalm.
▶ 9: Photograph by Mart Kalm.
▶ 10: *Eesti küla ehitab* (Tallinn: Eesti Raamat, 1983), 104.

New Horizons. The Representation of Ideal Practices in a Modern City: Firminy-Vert 1959

Clarisse Lauras

▶ 1: Mairie de Firminy.
▶ 2: Mairie de Firminy.
▶ 3: Mairie de Firminy.
▶ 4: Mairie de Firminy, Photograph by Georges Roux.
▶ 5: Mairie de Firminy.
▶ 6: Mairie de Firminy.

"On Holiday 365 Days a Year" on the Outskirts of Rome. Urban Form, Lifestyles, and the Pursuit of Happiness in the Suburb of Casalpalocco, ca. 1955–1980

Bruno Bonomo

▶ 1: Casalpalocco Società Generale Immobiliare, special issue of the *Quaderni della Società Generale Immobiliare,* 1973, 28–29.
▶ 2: Casalpalocco Società Generale Immobiliare, 51–52.
▶ 3: Realizzazioni e studi nel settore edilizio, 1962, 51.
▶ 4: Casalpalocco Società Generale Immobiliare, 45–46.
▶ 5: ACS, SGIS, Ufficio pubblicità, b. 3, *Un nuovo modo di abitare per i giovani di ieri, di oggi, di domani,* promotional booklet; concessione n. 748/08.
▶ 6: ACS, SGIS, Ufficio pubblicità, b. 1, f. Raccolta pubblicità 1969 quotidiani e periodici; concessione n. 748/08.
▶ 7: ACS, SGIS, Ufficio pubblicità, b. 1, f. Raccolta pubblicità 1969 quotidiani e periodici; concessione n. 748/08.
▶ 8: ACS, SGIS, Ufficio pubblicità, b. 1, f. Raccolta pubblicità 1969 quotidiani e periodici; concessione n. 748/08.

A Paradise behind Gates and Walls: Gated Communities in Eastern Europe and the Promise of Happiness

Jacek Gądecki, Christian Smigiel

▶ 1: Brochure, (Sofia sky, 2007).
▶ 2: Photograph by Christian Smigiel, 2007.
▶ 3: Photograph by Christian Smigiel, 2007.
▶ 4: Photograph by Christian Smigiel, 2008.
▶ 5: Advertisement, (Winslow Gardens, 2008).
▶ 6: Photograph by Christian Smigiel, 2009.

This publication was generously supported by

Geisteswissenschaftliches Zentrum
Geschichte und Kultur Ostmitteleuropas
an der Universität Leipzig

Bundesministerium
für Bildung
und Forschung